Social & Economic Studies within the Framework of Emerging Global Developments - Volume 4

Haşim Özüdoğru, Muhammed Veysel Kaya and
Ufuk Kaya (eds.)

Social & Economic Studies within the Framework of Emerging Global Developments - Volume 4

PETER LANG
Lausanne – Berlin – Bruxelles – Chennai – New York – Oxford

Bibliographic Information published by the Deutsche Nationalbibliothek
The Deutsche Nationalbibliothek lists this publication in the Deutsche Nationalbibliografie; detailed bibliographic data is available online at http://dnb.d-nb.de.

Library of Congress Cataloging-in-Publication Data
A CIP catalog record for this book has been applied for at the Library of Congress.

Cover illustration:
© gorodenkoff

ISBN 978-3-631-90842-6 (Print)
E-ISBN 978-3-631-90900-3 (E-PDF)
E-ISBN 978-3-631-91106-8 (E-PUB)
10.3726/b21202

Published by Peter Lang GmbH, Berlin, Deutschland

info@peterlang.com - www.peterlang.com

This publication has been peer reviewed.

Foreword

This book is the fourth in the series of "Social & Economic Studies within the Framework of Emerging Global Developments". The fourth volume includes empirical and theoretical original papers written by researchers from different countries and universities. The target audience of this book is researchers, students and academics interested in business, economics and social sciences.

Gunesch ("Art and Cultural Economics and Governmental Support for Creative Individuals and Industries from Economic, Political and Psychological Perspectives: For the Motion") combines historical, macroeconomic and sociopolitical perspectives in favor of government support and subsidies in cultural and creative industries. **Gunesch ("Rise of the Robots as Competitors in Human Healthcare, Compassion, and Emotion: An Interdisciplinary Literary Inquiry of Social, Cultural and Economic Implications")** contributes to the social awareness of implications of advanced artificial intelligence to all our lives in the area of healthcare. **Challoumis's** analysis is based on the money cycle, as well as the velocity of minimum escaped savings and the velocity of financial liquidity. **Oak** analyses the impact of the PAT scheme on the cement firms from cycles I to VI by estimating their energy efficiency scores using DEA models, for a sample period of 2010–2022. Results show that the firms that were not a part of the PAT cycles had higher efficiency scores in all years.

Misztal analyses the extent to which changes in the prices of imported goods are passed on to inflation in the European Union. The results of the conducted analysis indicate that changes in consumer prices in the EU were explained to the greatest extent by changes in the prices of imported consumer goods, and least by changes in the prices of imported capital goods. **Misztal and Kulakov** present the important and main factors determining the investment attractiveness of countries and to indicate various measures of this attractiveness on the examples. of Belarus and Poland. The research method is based on literature studies in the field of international economics, while statistical analysis and statistical inference were used in the work as well. The obtained research results show the main economic and non-economic determinants of the investment attractiveness of countries. **Savvopoulou** examines uncertainty and the belief process formation that leads to self-fulfilling sovereign debt crises to support forthcoming research. **Saseanu, Ghita and Gogonea** analyze the behavior of

European countries regarding the participation of Internet users in purchasing products and services through digital means, under the impact of social and economic factors. **Trifu** examines the importance and the impact of Generation Z on the operation of economic entities and on society in general. **Zhou, Chimucheka, Ayandibu, Masuku** review the literature on economic responses to the COVID-19 pandemic. They also compare responses from advanced economies with the South African case. **Enaifoghe** examines entrepreneurship and Small and Medium Enterprises in enhancing local economic development in South Africa. The study indicates that the promotion of LED is heavily dependent on small and medium-sized businesses. **Ahmadov, Gerstlberger and Bondegård** explore the motivators, enablers, and barriers to circular economy (CE) practices implementation in Swedish small and medium-sized enterprises (SMEs). Using a qualitative research approach, semi-structured interviews were conducted with managers and employees from twelve SMEs across different manufacturing companies.

Tanvir and Sarolta examine the impact of auctions on energy costs and their potential benefits to the local and national economy. The short study also examines the auction effect on the levelized cost of electricity (LCOE). Both qualitative and quantitative analyse-based research results suggest that a systematic auctioning scheme, coupled with socio-economic development instruments and a qualification requirement, can help emerging states with renewable energy resources to achieve various benefits in the society as well as the economy. **Siwek** aims to identify how pension adequacy is related to pensioners' subjective health assessment in Poland. **Knees** explores mutual expectations as to whether exchanges work or not, and what challenges professionals are confronted with in their everyday dealings with children. For this purpose, 20 future educators were interviewed at the end of their 3-year training. The interviewees all worked in different institutions, all of them in day care centers in rural areas in the western part of North Rhine-Westphalia near the Dutch border. The interviews were conducted in a qualitative design. **Peka** investigates the challenges in legal frameworks and the role that legislative measures play in promoting and protecting childern's rights from male abuse of children, and their rights, in any administration and public exercises of power. **Naletina, Stulec and Milkovic** analyse how companies that use maritime shipping services overcome the difficulties caused by the volatility of freight rates, as well as identify the most appropriate strategies for successfully overcoming disruptions in the market. **Luli** examines, through a brief general overview, the legal framework and the existing mechanisms and instruments applied in the pre-university educational environment (both elementary and secondary systems). **Yusof** and **Zolkaply**

investigate the learning outcomes and introduction of people to community relations, followed by discussions on relevant terms such as corporate and strategic philanthropy and community relations development in the USA and Malaysia.

Table of Contents

Konrad Gunesch

Art and Cultural Economics and Governmental Support for Creative Individuals and Industries from Economic, Political and Psychological Perspectives: For the Motion

1. Introduction and Overview

1.1. Recent Interest in, and Future Relevance of Cultural and Art Economics

The literature points out a recent "steady expansion in the […] interest in the economics of art and culture [with] suggestions for promising lines of future research [and] we are likely to see [its] expansion in the future" (Throsby, 2006, p. 21). At the same time, basic questions about art and cultural economics keep being asked for a long time now, exemplified by Blaug's 2019 book *The Economics of the Arts*: its sixteen chapters are all reprints of writings from between 1956 and 1974. Several of these are cited in detail in this research, revealing their thoughts still valid in today's globalized and complex economic, artistic and cultural landscape(s).

One challenge of analyzing "economics" together with "arts" and "culture" is the reputation of economics as "the dismal science" (see the book titles of Levy, 2002; Marglin 2008, and Rodrik, 2015), whereas art and culture, even when analyzed through an economic lens, are considered "sublime" human experiences (see the book and the chapter titles of Amariglio et al., 2009a, 2009b), characterized by "the creative genius in literature, music, and the visual arts" (see the chapter title of Simonton, 2014), in which the perceived value of the "aesthetic experience" (see the chapter headings of Locher, 2014) contribute to "art's economic exceptionalism" (see the book title of Beech, 2015).

Another challenge is the state of flux in the field's most basic elements – starting with its very name. As Ginsburgh and Throsby maintain in the second volume of their *Handbook of the Economics of Arts and Culture* (2016), the "historical evolution" within the decade since the publication of the first volume (2006) allowed for "the discipline known as cultural economics [to be] more appropriately referred to as the economics of art and culture" (2016, p. 1; similarly Frey, 2019, p. 3). I use the short terms "art economics" and "cultural economics" for euphony and concision.

The field is divided into numerous economic investigations of art aspects and products: from paintings (Throsby & Zednik, 2014, pp. 81–100) over music (Levinson, 2014, pp. 101–117) and concerts (Courty & Pagliero, 2014, pp. 299–356) to festivals and cultural awards (English, 2014, pp. 119–143; Frey, 2019, pp. 63–70), cultural heritage and museums (Frey, 2019; pp. 77–88, 97–114; Willis, 2014, pp. 145–182), up to movies and books (Walls, 2014, pp. 185–214), or from organizational and technical aspects such as new technologies (Potts, 2014, pp. 215–232) over labor, property and investment (Whitaker, 2021, pp. 177–243) to international transactions and trade (Bisin & Verdier, 2014, pp. 439–484; Mandel, 2014, pp. 233–260; Platteau & Wahhaj, 2014, pp. 633–678), up to cultural organizations (Castañer, 2014, pp. 263–276), or from legal aspects such as digitization and copyright (Waldfogel, 2014, pp. 277–298), over media ownership (Doyle, 2014, pp. 357–378) up to cultural trading systems (Iapadre, 2014, pp. 381–410; Macmillan, 2014, pp. 411–438), or finally from considerations of cultural values over diversity up to open conflict (Aldashev & Platteau, 2014, pp. 587–632; Ginsburgh & Weber, 2014, pp. 507–544; Montalvo & Reynal-Querol, 2014, pp. 485–506; Schwartz, 2014, pp. 547–586).

Against this plethora of viewpoints, and integrating the most relevant recent literature (see Whitaker 2021), we combine historical, macroeconomic and sociopolitical perspectives in favor of government support and subsidies in cultural and creative industries.

1.2. Origin, Terms and Relationship of Cultural and Art Economics

The birth of the field of Cultural Economics is acknowledged to be Baumol and Bowen's 1966 book *Performing Arts – The Economic Dilemma: A Study of Problems Common to Theater, Opera, Music and Dance*, in which the authors "demonstrate that straightforward economic analysis could illuminate [...] the role of the arts sector in the economy" (Throsby, 2006, p. 4). Yet only in the book's last part, "Sources of Financial Support", and in two of the last chapters do the authors deal with "Government Support in Practice" or the "Rationale of Public Support" (Baumol & Bowen, 1966, pp. 347 ff., 369 ff.).

The first journal in the field, *Journal of Cultural Economics*, was established in 1977, and only as of the end-1990s had the field gathered enough material to warrant an overview of it (Throsby, 2006, pp. 4–5). One of the first findings was that cultural economics was the wider area, embracing media, heritage and art studies, but also that it was not yet well defined, being concerned with multiple disciplines including art history, art philosophy, sociology, law, management and economics (Throsby, 2006, p. 5).

Only in the 21st century did scholarly confidence grow that "a sufficiently cohesive body of work has accumulated [...] to identify a field labeled "cultural economics" or "the economics of the arts and culture" [...] even though the outer boundaries [...] remain somewhat fuzzy", allowing the "assembling a purposeful collection of essays commissioned from researchers working at the theoretical and empirical frontiers of the field" (Throsby, 2006, p. 6).

I was immediately pointed out that "a basic issue [...] is that of defining whether and how cultural goods and services differ from other goods and services in the economy", and "whilst it is the mysterious and possible unfathomable nature of art in all its forms that ultimately must underlie much of the behavior of individuals, firms and markets in the arts, economics requires a more systematic basis on which its analysis can rest" (Throsby, 2006, p. 6).

1.3. Terminology and Differentiation

The terms "Cultural Economics" and "Art Economics" require definitions of "art" and "culture". For simplicity and inclusivity, I follow Throsby's broad definition of culture "comprising or being defined as a set of attitudes, beliefs or values common to a group that somehow identifies and binds the group together", which enables us "to speak of a national culture, a religious culture, a corporate culture and so on" (2006, p. 6).

Functionally, culture can also be defined as "the practices and products of cultural activity, including especially the arts", which are "sometimes divided into the performing arts (acting, dancing, singing, playing a musical instrument, etc.) and the initial creative arts (visual art, sculpture, craft, creative writing, musical composition, etc.) though there are obvious overlaps between these categories", all of which makes "the arts comprise a subset of culture more broadly defined" (Throsby, 2006, pp. 6–7).

Consequently, the concept of "cultural goods" includes overlapping elements of cultural, art and creative economics, in that "cultural goods have some public-good properties; in aggregate they yield positive externalities or diffused benefits that may be demanded in their own right" (Throsby, 2006, p. 7). On this basis, we follow the literature that defines "cultural industries" straightforward and "simply as those industries producing those good" (Throsby, 2006, p. 11).

2. Literature Review

2.1. Intersection of Cultural and Economic Policy

The literature reveals "four specific areas where cultural and economic policy intersect: support for the arts; trade in cultural goods, heritage; and urban and regional development issues" (Throsby, 2006, p. 19), and five areas of cultural policy that are especially well suited for economic analysis: "support for the creative arts; cultural goods in international trade; the management of cultural assets; industry and innovation; and foreign policy" (Throsby, 2012, p. 106). The first area, support for the (creative) arts, is the focus of this chapter.

This area is further defined in the literature as follows: "The intersections between cultural policy and economic policy are extensive, including […] the appropriate level for government support for the arts and culture, and the balance between direct (grant-related) and indirect (tax-related) means of support", as well as "the role of the arts and culture in employment creation and income generation in towns and cities; especially those affected by industrial decline" (Throsby, 2006, p. 18).

2.2. Discussion of State Support for the Arts

The originators of the field of Cultural Economics, Baumol and Bowen, expressed their insecurity about "the long-run prospect for government support in the arts", while for the United States they merely and generally stated that it "seems favorable" (1966, p. 405), or that "future professional performance may well survive and prosper" (1966, p. 407). One can see conceptual similarities to recent literature that highlights the relationship between the arts and state support, reasoning that there is a longstanding yet still conceptually and empirically unresolved practice, causing its proponents to call for more research (Throsby, 2006, p. 19):

> "The rationale for state support for the arts has been one of the longest-running issues […] in the literature of cultural economics over the last 40 years. […] The empirical evidence is by no means extensive, and positive theories of assistance may be more useful in explaining levels and patterns of support actually observed in various democratic countries around the world […] Why, at a time when the trend is towards privatization in many sectors of the economy, the provision of government grants, tax relief and regulatory protection continues in the arts and heritage industries. The answer […] lies in government skepticism that consumers know what is best for them; in these circumstances producer interests can exert a strong influence on government policy, with consequent effects on both allocative and productive efficiency".

This justification of governmental support and related regulations is apparently rooted in a liberal economic and political tradition.

2.3. Reaches of Cultural Policies

The literature differentiates between "the broad reach of cultural policy in general terms" and the fact that "its coverage and its level of importance in national policy agendas vary considerably between countries" (Throsby, 2006, p. 18). A comparison is made between Europe and the United States of America, yet only at an unspecified "central government level":

> In Europe [...] there are substantial differences between countries in the volume of public resources they devote to the arts and culture in the ways those resources are deployed. Administrative structures also vary [...] ranging from arm-lengths arts councils to full-scale Ministries of Culture. There are also sub-regional and supra-regional interests in cultural policy in Europe; on the one hand sub-national regions with distinctive cultural identities promote their own artistic and cultural endeavors; on the other hand the European Union and the Council of Europe have interests in developing pan-European cultural policies in various fields (Throsby, 2006, p. 18; similarly Baumol and Bowen, 1966, pp 360–365 for Western Europe before the establishment of the European Union).

Throsby (2006, pp. 18–19) contrasts this with America:

> In the United States [...] there has never been a great deal of interest in the formulation of specific cultural policies at the central government level; rather the major players in the formation and execution of direct public expenditure programs in the arts and culture are located at sub-national levels of government. [...] The largest share of support for the arts and culture is provided indirectly, via tax concessions for gifts to not-for-profit arts organizations and also via tax concessions to private owners of cultural heritage buildings and sites. The role of tax incentives in stimulating cultural donations and the significance of philanthropy as a characteristic of American life are [part of] the peculiarly American tradition of individual and corporate giving that has sustained the growth of the arts in the United States for more than a century. Despite the emergence of what many see as a distinctive and successful 'American model' for cultural support [...] it may be difficult to replicate it in other countries where institutional structures, income levels and tax-price responsiveness may differ markedly from the US situation.

We thus constate (as do Ekelund et al., 2017) a European preference for more centralized state subsidies for the arts, contrasting with a more individualistic, indirect and administrative hands-off American understanding of official artistic and cultural support.

3. Research Methodology: Transdisciplinary Framework of Analysis

The literature stresses the need to apply multidisciplinary frameworks for cultural economics: "if we were to adopt a broad definition of cultural goods that embraced popular cultural forms such as sports, television programs, magazines, etc., we would open up an enormous field of interest in mass cultural consumption and production, a field that has been extensively explored within sociology, contemporary cultural studies, and media economics" (Throsby, 2006, p. 7).

Support for such a multitude of disciplines for art, culture and economics is found in the field's recent publications that describe it as having turned "from a sub-discipline of economics into a sub-discipline of anthropology" (Ginsburgh & Throsby, 2014, p. 1).

Hence our multidisciplinary approach combines a sociopolitical and socioeconomic scope with a macroeconomic analytical focus. Going even further in disciplinary integration and related methodological benefits, and beyond the coexistence of approaches that could be described as multidisciplinary, I propose an explicitly "transdisciplinary enquiry" (see Martin, 2017, p. 130) as characterized by a mutual sharing and advancing of frameworks for fresh conceptual and/or methodological insights.

4. Analysis and Discussion: For Government Subsidies of the Arts and Culture

4.1. Inherent Value and Ineffable Contribution of Aesthetic Activity

Baumol and Bowen (1966, pp. 377–378) argue this point with parallels to defense spending, the courts system, and elementary education:

> The performing arts should be among those privileged activities which are granted exemption from the market test [...]. It must be phrased in terms of finer and less tangible concepts: the inherent value of beauty and the ineffable contribution of artistic activity [...]. One does not expect the defense establishment to show a profit, the courts to pay for themselves or the elementary schools to cover their costs out of their revenues. There are good grounds for these exemptions [...] fixed in economic analysis and [...] democratic ideals.

Further examples in support of this thought can be seen in environmental protection, health care, or wider social services alleviating poverty and improving well-being.

4.2. Inequality of Opportunity, and of Access

Baumol and Bowen (1966, pp. 378–379) invoke three further exemptions from the "market test" argument, in that "the economist recognizes three basic grounds which can legitimately be used to defend government subsidy of unprofitable activities", namely:

> "Inequality of opportunity. [...] No market test need support the flow of public funds devoted to the opening of opportunities to the impecunious. [...] The consumer decides what commodities shall be produced an in what quantities [...] not by casting votes, but by the way in which he spends his dollars. [However] under this system not all men have

> the same number of votes. The affluent consumer has a far greater influence on the course of events than does a purchaser whose funds are quite limited. Therefore, government funds intended to promote equality of opportunity directly or indirectly may be viewed as a means for improving the way in which the market election is conducted".

They add the thought of inequality of access (1966, p. 379):

> The extremely narrow audience is [because] a very large segment of the community has been denied the opportunity to learn to appreciate them. [...] Many persons cannot easily afford the admission charges [which] constitutes a denial of opportunity. How can people learn to enjoy the living arts if no plays, no concert performers and no dancers are available to them? People can be deprived of opportunities by phenomena other than poverty and ignorance, and if the government wishes to improve the situation as far as the arts are concerned, it may have to help in the provision of opportunities for attendance in many parts of the country.

One can see opportunity and access as two sides of the same coin of privilege, potential, personality development, and thus political justification for government support for the arts.

4.3. Education of Minors

Baumol and Bowen (1966, pp. 379–380) mention as "legitimate reason for government support" the beneficial effects of education at a young age:

> Minors [...] are not permitted to purchase alcoholic beverages, drive automobiles, or decide for themselves whether funds shall be devoted to their schooling. [...] If children and adolescents are not exposed to artistic performance [...] by the time they become adults it will be too late. The arts must be made available early, while tastes are still being formed and behavior patterns developed.

However, they also critically evaluate this argument (1966, p. 380):

> "No one seems to have any overpowering evidence that [...] taste for the arts is instilled by early experiences. No one has tracked down the children who attended the New York Philharmonic's young people's concerts [...] to see whether they subsequently showed greater interest in the arts than persons coming from otherwise similar backgrounds".

In the absence of research on the formation of artistic tastes of minors and later art-related actions as adults, the jury is still out on whether it serves as an argument for state subsidies.

4.4. Public Goods and Mixed Commodities

For Baumol and Bowen (1966, pp. 380–381) public goods, "the class of commodities, services or items which, when provided to one person, automatically and unavoidably become available to other members of the community" are another exception of the market test, exemplified with cleaning the air by removing pollution, or governmental defense for the benefit of all citizens:

> The profit motive and free enterprise, which work so effectively in bringing private goods to consumers when and as they want them, are subject to fatal limitations as regulators or the supply of public goods. The reason is that commodities of the latter type lack the basic requisite of the market – salability [Hence] a government's decision to supply a public good [...] may be the only way in which the wishes of the body of consumers can be put into effect.

Baumol and Bowen refine the public goods argument with the notion of "mixed commodities" or "quasi-public goods" (1966, pp. 381–382), with examples of education, medical services, and public hygiene:

> The situation is slightly more complicated in the case of mixed commodities – goods and services whose characteristics are partly private, partly public [...] Education is a private good – it can be sold to an individual purchaser because it yields benefits specifically to him. But [it] is also a public service because it enriches society a whole [...] Unlike pure public goods, mixed commodities can be expected to cover part of their cost by sale to the public. One can charge a price for the direct benefits which flow from the provision of facilities for higher education, for inoculations against contagious diseases, slum clearance projects, etc. [...] The consumer cannot, however, be excluded from the indirect benefits associated with mixed commodities, since these are unavoidably made available to all members of the community. Therefore, the price tag which can be put on quasi-public goods may be insufficient to cover their cost of production [Hence] public support may be entirely justified as the only available means to make demand effective.

Baumol and Bowen (1966, pp. 382–383) consider the performing arts to be such mixed services:

> If the performing arts are mixed commodities which confer direct benefits on those who attend a performance but which also offer benefits to the community as a whole, government support of the arts might well be completely consistent with the desires of the entire community. To determine whether the arts do or do not fall into this category it is necessary to look closely at the advantages they offer to the public at large.

4.5. General and Indirect Benefits from State Support

Finally, Baumol and Bowen lay out "four types of general benefit which may flow from the arts" (1966, p. 382):

> "[First,] the prestige conferred on a nation by its performing arts [such as] an opera or a program of contemporary dance [giving] pride in the international recognition conferred on our singers and the creativity of our choreographers" (1966, pp. 382–383).

"[Second,] the availability of cultural activity confers [advantages] on business in its vicinity [...] it brings customers to shops, hotels, restaurants and bars. On a national level, distinguished performing arts organizations may serve, analogously, as a significant tourist attraction" (1966, p. 383).

"[Third,] the performing arts involves future generations. [The] ability to appreciate the arts cannot always be achieved without a suitable period of training and acquaintance [with] a significant extension to the posterity of the community as a whole. We support programs for the conservation of natural resources and for improvement of architecture in part because few of us are willing to take the responsibility of passing on to future generations a country whose beauty has been destroyed. [...] Funds must be provided today if the arts are to be kept alive for tomorrow [...] These benefits [cannot] be priced and their cost covered by an admission charge" (1966, pp. 384–385).

"[A fourth] indirect benefit provided by the arts is their educational contribution. If [...] a liberal education confers indirect and non-priceable benefits upon the community, the same must be true of the arts. If the teaching of the humanities makes for a finer civilization, for a richer community, for a better life for everyone, this is necessarily so with the arts as well; for without the arts a vital element is taken from the humanities. How can drama be taught if there is no drama available for the student to experience? What can the teaching of music mean if no one can hear performances of professional quality?" (1966, p. 385).

Baumol and Bowen (1966, pp. 385–386) conclude that the state is ultimately responsible for the funding of the arts, in the general interest of the community and its citizens:

> If [...] arts confer general benefits on the community [...], arts are public goods whose benefits demonstrably exceed [...] the box office. [...] If the wishes and interests of the public are to be followed in the allocation of the nation's resources [then] governmental expenditures [will] find their justification. Government must provide funds only where the market has no way to charge for all the benefits offered by an activity. [...] In such circumstances government outlays are [...] a response to [...] the needs of the society.

5. Macroeconomic Solution Suggestions

5.1. National Tax Exemptions

For the United States, Baumol and Bowen (1966, p. 353) propose tax exemptions for the performing arts:

> The main federal contribution to the performing arts comes indirectly, through various tax exemption provisions. The most obvious of these is the basic exemption of non-profit organizations from the corporate income tax. Since so many performing organizations operate at a deficit, savings as a result of this exemption probably do not amount to very much, but at least the exemption simplifies their existence.

5.2. National Tax Credits

Also for the United States context, Baumol and Bowen (1966, p. 356) point out:

> Under [the tax credit] a person is permitted simply to reduce his tax payment by the same specified proportion of his contribution regardless of his income level. On grounds of equity, the tax credit is widely preferable to the deduction. However [...] since the tax credit in effect increases the giving power of the less affluent at the expense of the wealthy, such a change might very well cause a decrease in the amount of support that is channeled into the arts.

6. Conclusions

There seems much conceptual and practical potential for public and private support for art and culture, on macroeconomic, social and political levels. To borrow an analogies from the so-called "resource blessing", one could further think of subsidies for artistic and creative industries and individuals in these forms: cash transfers to artists and institutions; good cultural governance and fair and equitable artistic allocation and revenue distribution; careful nationwide artistic and cultural management; enhanced public cultural investment for encouraging private artistic growth; foreign artistic aid for global cultural trade liberalization.

Applying the literature's comparison of European and American artistic and cultural policies, many examples of financial, technical or popular support on city, county, country or continental levels for artistic productions come to mind, and only for visual and moving media range from Hollywood to Bollywood, and from Arte to National Geographic.

With increasing globalization and intensifying artistic and cultural relationships, art and cultural economics seem well positioned for governmental support for creative individuals and industries from economic, political and psychological perspectives, and thus for the motion.

References

Aldashev, G., & Platteau, J. P. (2014). Religion, Culture, and Development. In V. A. Ginsburgh & D. Throsby (Eds.), *Handbook of the Economics of Art and Culture, Volume 2* (pp. 587–632). Amsterdam, Boston, New York and Oxford: Elsevier.

Amariglio, J., Childers, J. W., & Cullenberg, S. E. (Eds.) (2009a). *Sublime Economy: On the Intersection of Art and Economics*. London and New York: Routledge.

Amariglio, J., Childers, J. W., & Cullenberg, S. E. (2009b). Introduction: Sublime Economy: On the Intersection of Art and Economics. In J. Amariglio, J. W. Childers & S. E. Cullenberg (Eds.), *Sublime Economy: On the Intersection of Art and Economics* (pp. 1–26). London and New York: Routledge.

Baumol, W. J., & Bowen, W. G. (1966). *Performing Arts – The Economic Dilemma: A Study of Problems Common to Theater, Opera, Music and Dance*. New York: Kraus Reprint.

Beech, D. (2015). *Art and Value: Art's Economic Exceptionalism in Classical, Neoclassical and Marxist Economies*. Leiden and Boston: Brill.

Bisin, A., & Verdier, T. (2014). Trade and Cultural Diversity. In V. A. Ginsburgh & D. Throsby (Eds.), *Handbook of the Economics of Art and Culture, Volume 2* (pp. 439–484). Amsterdam, Boston, New York and Oxford: Elsevier.

Blaug, M. (2019). *The Economics of the Arts*. New York and Oxon: Routledge.

Castañer, X. (2014). Cultural Innovation by Cultural Organizations. In V. A. Ginsburgh & D. Throsby (Eds.), *Handbook of the Economics of Art and Culture, Volume 2* (pp. 263–276). Amsterdam, Boston, New York and Oxford: Elsevier.

Courty, P., & Pagliero, M. (2014). The Pricing of Art and the Art of Pricing: Pricing Styles in the Concert Industry. In V. A. Ginsburgh & D. Throsby (Eds.), *Handbook of the Economics of Art and Culture, Volume 2* (pp. 299–356). Amsterdam, Boston, New York and Oxford: Elsevier.

Doyle, G. (2014). Media Ownership: Diversity Versus Efficiency in a Changing Technological Environment. In V. A. Ginsburgh & D. Throsby (Eds.), *Handbook of the Economics of Art and Culture, Volume 2* (pp. 357–378). Amsterdam, Boston, New York and Oxford: Elsevier.

Ekelund, R. B., Jackson, J. D., & Tollison, R. D. (2017). *The Economics of American Art: Issues, Artists and Market Institutions*. Oxford and New York: Oxford University Press.

English, J. F. (2014). The Economics of Cultural Awards. In V. A. Ginsburgh & D. Throsby (Eds.), *Handbook of the Economics of Art and Culture, Volume 2* (pp. 119–143). Amsterdam, Boston, New York and Oxford: Elsevier.

Frey, B. S. (2019). *Economics of Art and Culture*. Cham: Springer.

Ginsburgh, V., & Throsby, D. (2014). Introduction and Overview. In V. A. Ginsburgh & D. Throsby (Eds.), *Handbook of the Economics of Art and Culture, Volume 2* (pp. 1–12). Amsterdam, Boston, New York and Oxford: Elsevier.

Ginsburgh, V., & Weber, S. (2014). Culture, Linguistic Diversity, and Economics. In V. A. Ginsburgh, & D. Throsby (Eds.), *Handbook of the Economics of Art and Culture, Volume 2* (pp. 507–544). Amsterdam, Boston, New York and Oxford: Elsevier.

Iapadre, P. L. (2014). Cultural Products in the International Trading System. In V. A. Ginsburgh, & D. Throsby (Eds.), *Handbook of the Economics of Art and Culture, Volume 2* (pp. 381–410). Amsterdam, Boston, New York and Oxford: Elsevier.

Levinson, J. (2014). Values of Music. In V. A. Ginsburgh, & D. Throsby (Eds.), *Handbook of the Economics of Art and Culture, Volume 2* (pp. 101–117). Amsterdam, Boston, New York and Oxford: Elsevier.

Levy, D. M. (2002). *How the Dismal Science Got Its Name: Classical Economics and the Ur-Text of Racial Politics.* Ann Arbor: The University of Michigan Press.

Locher, P. J. (2014). Contemporary Experimental Aesthetics: Procedures and Findings. In V. A. Ginsburgh, & D. Throsby (Eds.), *Handbook of the Economics of Art and Culture, Volume 2* (pp. 49–80). Amsterdam, Boston, New York and Oxford: Elsevier.

Macmillan, F. (2014). Cultural Diversity, Copyright, and International Trade. In V. A. Ginsburgh, & D. Throsby (Eds.), *Handbook of the Economics of Art and Culture, Volume 2* (pp. 411–438). Amsterdam, Boston, New York and Oxford: Elsevier.

Mandel, B. R. (2014). Investment in Visual Art: Evidence from International Transactions. In V. A. Ginsburgh, & D. Throsby (Eds.), *Handbook of the Economics of Art and Culture, Volume 2* (pp. 233–260). Amsterdam, Boston, New York and Oxford: Elsevier.

Marglin, S. A. (2008). *The Dismal Science: How Thinking Like an Economist Undermines Community.* Cambridge, Massachusetts and London, England: Harvard University Press.

Martin, V. (2017) *Transdisciplinarity Revealed: What Librarians Need to Know.* Santa Barbara and Denver: Libraries Unlimited and ABC-CLIO.

Montalvo, J. G., & Reynal-Querol, M. (2014). Cultural Diversity, Conflict, and Economic Development. In V. A. Ginsburgh, & D. Throsby (Eds.), *Handbook of the Economics of Art and Culture, Volume 2* (pp. 485–506). Amsterdam, Boston, New York and Oxford: Elsevier.

Platteau, J. P., & Wahhaj, Z. (2014). Strategic Interactions Between Modern Law and Custom. In V. A. Ginsburgh, & D. Throsby (Eds.), *Handbook of the Economics of Art and Culture, Volume 2* (pp. 633–678). Amsterdam, Boston, New York and Oxford: Elsevier.

Potts, J. (2014). New Technologies and Cultural Consumption. In V. A. Ginsburgh, & D. Throsby (Eds.), *Handbook of the Economics of Art and Culture, Volume 2* (pp. 215–232). Amsterdam, Boston, New York and Oxford: Elsevier.

Rodrik, D. (2015). *Economics Rules: The Rights and Wrongs of the Dismal Science.* New York and London: W. W. Norton.

Schwartz, S. H. (2014). National Culture as Value Orientations: Consequences of Value Differences and Cultural Distance. In V. A. Ginsburgh, & D. Throsby (Eds.), *Handbook of the Economics of Art and Culture, Volume 2* (pp. 547–586). Amsterdam, Boston, New York and Oxford: Elsevier.

Simonton, D. K. (2014). Creative Genius in Literature, Music, and the Visual Arts. In V. A. Ginsburgh, & D. Throsby (Eds.), *Handbook of the Economics of Art and Culture, Volume 2* (pp. 15–48). Amsterdam, Boston, New York and Oxford: Elsevier.

Throsby, D. (2006). Introduction and Overview. In V. A. Ginsburgh, & D. Throsby (Eds.), *Handbook of the Economics of Art and Culture, Volume 1* (pp. 3–22). Amsterdam, Boston, New York and Oxford: Elsevier.

Throsby, D. (2012). Why Should Economists Be Interested in Cultural Policy? *Economic Record, 88*(1), 106–109.

Throsby, D. & Zednik, A. (2014). The Economic and Cultural Value of Paintings: Some Empirical Evidence. In V. A. Ginsburgh & D. Throsby (Eds.), *Handbook of the Economics of Art and Culture, Volume 2* (pp. 81–100). Amsterdam, Boston, New York and Oxford: Elsevier.

Waldfogel, J. (2014). Digitization, Copyright, and the Flow of New Music Products. In V. A. Ginsburgh, & D. Throsby (Eds.), *Handbook of the Economics of Art and Culture, Volume 2* (pp. 277–298). Amsterdam, Boston, New York and Oxford: Elsevier.

Walls, W. D. (2014). Bestsellers and Blockbusters: Movies, Music, and Books. In V. A. Ginsburgh, & D. Throsby (Eds.), *Handbook of the Economics of Art and Culture, Volume 2* (pp. 185–214). Amsterdam, Boston, New York and Oxford: Elsevier.

Whitaker, A. (2021). *Economics of Visual Art: Market Practice and Market Resistance.* Cambridge and New York: Cambridge University Press.

Willis, K. G. (2014). The Use of Stated Preference Methods to Value Cultural Heritage. In V. A. Ginsburgh, & D. Throsby (Eds.), *Handbook of the Economics of Art and Culture, Volume 2* (pp. 145–182). Amsterdam, Boston, New York and Oxford: Elsevier.

Konrad Gunesch

Rise of the Robots as Competitors in Human Healthcare, Compassion, and Emotion: An Interdisciplinary Literary Inquiry of Social, Cultural and Economic Implications

1. Introduction and Overview

1.1. AI and Healthcare in Recent Literature

Recent literature depicts humanity at medical, social, technical and philosophical crossroads, leading either to extraordinary technological developments of artificial intelligence (AI), or to threats for the human condition. One explanation for this paradigm shift in the understanding of human life is the algorithmic power of computer applications in the human healthcare sector. Exponential quantitative improvements are predicted to lead to qualitative repercussions of machines outperforming humans even for qualities traditionally considered exclusively human, such as emotions, creativity, or social interactions.

Recent popular literary and science bestsellers have advanced these thoughts, convincingly analyzing related historical, philosophical, political, social and cultural contexts. These writings apply social and computer science, historical documentation and popular prose to recent technological developments in artificial intelligence and the automation economy. We will analyze their writings as to whether they predict the developments in automation and algorithms to be potential threat or opportunity for humanity, and will look in depth at the fear of human obsolescence, or losing work and meaning to machines in human healthcare.

We acknowledge that many people in the world might struggle to ensure adequate healthcare, regardless of AI or machine influences. We simply wish to contribute to the social awareness of implications of advanced artificial intelligence to all our lives in the area of healthcare. We thus limit this research to an investigation of specific yet widely accessible literary sources, from specific cultural and methodological yet easily generalizable perspectives, by examining selected popular and expert writings, with social science and comparative literature methods.

1.2. Literary Investigation of Socio-Economic Implications

We investigate human-machine relationships and implications in human healthcare so as to best serve human healthcare providers (doctors, nurses, analysts, or prognosis professionals such as radiologists, among others) and their users (patients and other healthcare beneficiaries). This research is relevant since we are all, at some time or other, healthcare providers or seekers, caretakers or caregivers, providers or patients, and sometimes many of these together.

We examine writings of these three literary types and levels: (1) specialized literature in medical healthcare discussing AI; (2) academic literature by authors of popular science not specialized in medical fields, such as in history, politics, or philosophy, or anthropology; (3) popular prose, such as recent literary bestsellers addressing the relationship between humans and computers, which we then apply to artificial intelligence and healthcare. The investigated voices all share concerns about the potential and the prospects of artificial intelligence for human life, work and welfare. We particularly discuss how they address human redundancy in healthcare.

Multidisciplinary investigation usually merely allows the involved fields to coexist, while transdisciplinary enquiry strives to share and advancing of frameworks and insights (Martin 2017, p. 130). Our research is a transdisciplinary content analysis, comparing literary voices at the intersections of medicine, healthcare, anthropology, artificial intelligence, the automation economy, social and political sciences, as well as history and philosophy. This variety of fields and concerns will often require series of quotations to reflect the involved complexities.

Corresponding to our growing and refining insights, our analysis will move from general and popular literary sources to specialized medical ones. Hence, popular positions on AI that reflect widespread concerns of human redundancy are followed by specific medical literature on technologies and machines prognosticated to replace healthcare workers and services. But we will also step back to broader macroeconomic levels, such as when reframing those discussions against recent developments in abundance or automation economics.

2. Literature Review

2.1. Popular Literature Predicting the AI-Human Relationship

Dan Brown's 2017 novel *Origin* combines scientific data and entertaining dramatization on the topic of conviviality of human and artificial life forms. Brown introduces a new life form, the "technium", in a final scene, the protagonists conveying a range of intellectual and emotional reactions and attitudes, from technological shock over social pessimism to cultural optimism up to technological utopia. We fade in at the moment of a global online transmission of famous futurologist Edmond Kirsch, witnessed by Harvard Professor Robert Langdon and Spanish arts personality Ambra Vidal (Brown, 2017, pp. 405–412, original emphases):

> The diagram expanded again, now displaying the timeline up until 2050. Langdon jumped to his feet, staring in disbelief. […] The diagram clearly showed the menacing black bubble expanding at a staggering rate, and then, by the year 2050, entirely swallowing up the light blue bubble of humanity.
> Edmond said […] "The human species evolved to our current point in history, and then, very abruptly, a new species materialized, and erased us from the earth. […] This new species does not entirely erase us. More accurately…it absorbs us." […] Langdon had recently heard about in a TED talk by digital-culture writer Kevin Kelly. Prophesied by some of the earliest science-fiction writers, this new kingdom of life came with a twist. It was a kingdom of *nonliving* species. It was called: *Technium*. […]
> "If you don't believe that humans and technology will fuse," Edmond said, "take a look around you. Human beings are evolving into something *different*," he declared. "We are becoming a hybrid species – a fusion of biology and technology. The same tools that today live *outside* our bodies – smartphones, hearing aids, reading glasses, most pharmaceuticals – in fifty years will be incorporated into our bodies to such an extent that we will no longer be able to consider ourselves *Homo sapiens*." […]
> Edmond persuasively described a future where technology […] erased the gap between the haves and the have-nots provided billions of people with drinking water, nutritious food, and access to clean energy […] diseases like Edmond's cancer were eradicated, thanks to genomic medicine […] the awesome power of the Internet was finally harnessed for education, even in the most remote corners of the world [and] robotics would free workers from mind-numbing jobs so they could pursue more rewarding fields that would open up in areas not yet imagined [with] an abundance of humankind's critical resources.

2.2. Automation and Abundance Economics: Paradigm Shift of Life Quality

We can further analyze Brown's last lines of an "abundance of humankind's critical resources" with macroeconomic literature on "automation economy" and "abundance economics": these voices maintain that "technology has supplemented or replaced non-elective human labor" (Swan, 2017, p. 27) and predict "an automation economy that focuses on reduced requirements for human labor" (Swan, 2016, p. 903) via "social robotics connecting with both the mechanical labor-saving and the emotional side of human needs [for an] improved human quality of life" (Swan 2016, p. 907). Specifically, "advances in nanotechnology [include] self-replicating automated mining of asteroids, energy from nuclear fusion or solar-powered satellites, and products from personal nanofactories or fabrication laboratories automated through artificial intelligence" (Jennings, 2015, p. 6) lets them "emphasize the benefits of nanotechnology with an abundance of raw material and self-replicating technologies" (Peters, 2009, p. 11).

These voices even call for a whole new understanding of economics, naming it "abundance economics" (Swan 2016, 907), "economics of abundance" (Jennings, 2015, p. 6; Shi, 2018, p. 432), "post-scarcity economics" (Pressman, 2011, p. 3), or "post-scarcity" (Peters 2009, p. 11). Other economics literature holds this to be a genuine "paradigm shift" (Saunders, 2015, pp. 22–23; Swan, 2017, p. 25, 2016, p. 905; Weller, 2011, p. 85; Yamash'ta et al., 2018, pp. 4–5).

Similar opinions express optimism about artificial intelligence replacing human labor within an automation economy across national and industry borders: "Why not [use] AI personal robots, creating a digital utopia that everyone can enjoy? [An] AI-drive economy would not only eliminate stress and drudgery and produce and abundance of everything we want today, but would also supply a bounty of wonderful products and services" (Tegmark, 2017, p. 119). "The drudge work, the repetitive, dangerous, menial, labor-intensive tasks will first go to robots [...] This is when automation will see an explosion of possibilities" (Verma, 2019, p. 9).

These socio-economic perspectives paint a mostly uplifting picture of working and living with artificial intelligence. By contrast, the below positions express more pessimistic or even dystopian views on man, machine, and professional future, especially in human healthcare.

2.3. AI Tools and Applications: Paradigm Shift of Healthcare Diagnosis

Voices at the intersection of AI and human healthcare consider AI's integration as a paradigm shift in human healthcare, even still cautious about possible human professional redundancy:

> AI [is] upsetting [the] healthcare domain. [It] improves the quality of services and allows better coordination of care (Bouchemal, 2019, p. xiv).
>
> AI is bringing about a paradigm shift in behavioral and mental health care [by] improving public health by assisting with the detection of health risks and information interventions. [...] AI can assist healthcare professionals with clinical decision-making, testing, diagnostics, and care management [with] tools to improve the lives of people, such as [...] mobile health [...] apps that learn the patterns and preferences of users.

> [...] No longer will knowledge and skills of the medical profession be limited to the physician, psychologist, counselor, social worker or other professionals (Luxton, 2016, pp. 1–2, 20).

Journalistic examples of technological progresses in AI dramatically increasing popular access to medical quality diagnoses are Google services predicting concrete ailments. Implying that healthcare services with such wide access to diagnostic facilities would reduce the need for specialized personal services just as for competent personal providers:

> Google has developed a system for grading prostate cancer that does it more accurately than US pathologists [...] AI can help humans make better decisions [...] Attention to AI has become too sustained and the financial and intellectual resources [...] enormous [so that] competing in AI is a matter of prestige for major nations (Bershidsky, 2018, p. 9). Google Flue Trends [...] tracks flu outbreaks [...] ringing the flue alarm bells ten days before traditional health services [via] a mammoth database on human health, establishing the 'perfect health' profile. Identifying even the smallest deviations from the baseline will hopefully make it possible to alert people to burgeoning health problems [...] If we give Google and its competitors free access to our biometric devices [...] we will get an all-knowing medical health service, that will not only fight epidemics, but will also shield us from cancer, heart attacks and Alzheimer's (Harari, 2017, pp. 391–392).

While some of these voices start raising concern of human redundancy, they do not yet take decisive positions in the rising stakes of automation of healthcare provisions:

> The advent of many technologies applied to health care, such as [...] eHealth and mobile devices [...] mHealth, has been creating economic opportunities for mental healthcare professionals, rather than eliminating their jobs. [...] What may be the most worrisome thought for healthcare professionals, however, is whether continued technological advances will make it possible to build and deploy intelligent machine systems that equal or exceed the social and intellectual capabilities or human care providers (Luxton, 2016, pp. 17–18).

3. Research Methodology: Transdisciplinary Framework of Analysis

The below definitions of "medical anthropology" reveal this field to be a suitable framework for investigating complex issues across medicine, the social sciences, economics, politics, and culture, and hence for our literary inquiry of implications of artificial intelligence in healthcare:

> Anthropologists have always been interested in health. This interest has recently been systematized and synthesized into the area of specialization called 'medical anthropology' (Sobo, 2004, p. 10).

> Medical anthropology has been an eclectic field with roots in many disciplines and methodologies [that] thrives in interdisciplinary stimulation (McElroy & Townsend, 2018, p. xv).
>
> The extremely wide variety of topics included within medical anthropology […] is based on the broad, holistic approach that anthropology takes to the study of human biology and cultures. […] Most medical anthropologists […] concentrate on the cultural end of the field (Brown & Closser, 2016, p. 9).
>
> Medical anthropology [integrates] biological and cultural views of humankind. [It] has already made significant theoretical and empirical contributions to our understanding of […] the impact of general political and economic forces on the health of individuals and communities, and […] political and economic arrangements (Joralemon, 2017, p. ix).
>
> Medical [covers] insights about economic precarity, powerlessness, workplace exploitation, inequality […] to locate medical anthropology within the larger social science literature (Manderson et al., 2016, pp. 6–10).

To maximize disciplinary integration, beyond to go beyond merely coexisting approaches often labeled "multidisciplinary", I propose a "transdisciplinary enquiry" as characterized by mutual sharing and advancing of frameworks between disciplines, aiming at fresh conceptual and/or methodological insights (see Martin, 2017, p. 130). Hence the cultural framework of "medical anthropology" supports our transdisciplinary literary analysis of the relationship between healthcare providers, artificial intelligence, and the automation economy, as well as between human-machine interaction and human professional redundancy in human healthcare.

4. Analysis and Discussion: AI and Human Redundancy

4.1. AI Diagnosis Competence

Authors of popular science, whose work encompasses fields such as history and philosophy, take more decisive stances on the issue of artificial intelligence and human redundancy. Yuval Noah Harari's books *A Brief History of* Tomorrow (2017) and *Lessons for the 21st Century* (2018) predict the redundancy of human healthcare professionals due to unmatched algorithmic powers, as no human organization or capacity can compete with an the near unlimited processing power of an interconnected system of computers:

> It is […] wrong to compare the abilities of […] a single human doctor to that of a single AI doctor. Rather, we should compare the abilities of a collection of human individuals to the abilities of an integrated network. […] It is almost impossible to update all the human doctors in the world about [all diseases or developments]. In contrast […] you can still update all [the computers] within a split second [to] communicate to each other their feedback on the new disease or medicine. These personal advantages of

connectivity and updateability are so huge that [one could] replace all humans with computers, even if individually some humans still do a better job than the machines (Harari, 2018, pp. 22–23).

Harari details how humans would stand little chance in diagnostic depth or quality against networks' technological connectively and informational quantity. Other authors invoke machines' superiority in terms of innate human limitations such as working time or energy:

AI [...] has enormous [diagnostic] advantages over human doctors. Firstly, [it] can hold in its databanks information about every known illness and medicine in history. It can then update these databanks daily, not only with the findings of new researches, but also with medical statistics gathered from every linked-in clinic and hospital in the world. Secondly, [it] will be intimately familiar not only with my entire genome and my day-to-day medical history, but also with the genomes and medical histories of my parents, siblings, cousins, neighbours and friends. Thirdly, [it] will never be tired, hungry or sic (Harari, 2017, pp. 366–367; similarly Keni, 2019, p. 6; Sadaqat, 2019, p. 14).

Specialized medical literature reiterates the advantages of artificial intelligence for behavioral and mental healthcare, especially machines' immunity to human routine shortcomings, in strikingly similar terms and examples. Hence we notice a literary agreement about machine superiority in human healthcare across levels of literary genre and medical expertise:

Machines have [...] greater efficiency, accuracy, and reliability than humans [as not] susceptible to fatigue, boredom, burnout, or forgetfulness [and] immune to personal biases that human therapists may have. Some patients may prefer encounters with intelligent machines [and] experience less anxiety when discussing intimate, private issues with a machine [because] virtual humans are able to spend more time with patients, are always friendly, and do not make users feel rushed or judged (Luxton, 2016, p. 15).

4.2. AI Superiority Even in Traditional Human Domains

Luxton (2016, p. 16) provides examples of AI superiority even in traditional human domains:

Machines [...] could [...] deliver the most appropriate therapy or integrate different approaches based on a patient's diagnostic profile, preferences, or treatment progress [and] be capable of sensitivity and adaptation to specific aspects of a patient's culture such as race/ethnicity or socioeconomic status [and] develop and enhance rapport with a patient and improve overall communication. By integrating data from other intelligent services such as environmental sensors, wearables, and biofeedback devices, intelligent systems can further customize services [and improve capabilities] as technology continues to become smaller in size, more integrated with other technologies, and more ubiquitous in everyday life.

Specialized scientific literature thus agrees on certain categories of healthcare redundancies, while Harari (2017, p. 268) stresses that such redundancies would not just afflict medical generalists, but even more strongly, healthcare specialists:

> It might prove easier to replace doctors specialising in relatively narrow fields such as cancer diagnosis. In recent experiments a computer correctly diagnosed 90 per cent of lung cancer cases presented to it, while human doctors had a success rate of only 50 per cent.

For such displacements of humans by AI, Harari (2017, p. 368) differentiates: short-term, AI might still be prohibitively expensive, while long-term, even immense initial investments can be recovered via economies of scale:

> After a decade or so of studies and internships, all you get is one doctor. If you want two doctors, you have to repeat the entire process from scratch. In contrast, if and when you solve the technical problems hampering Watson, you will get not one, but an infinite number of doctors, available 24/7 in every corner of the world. So even if its costs $100 billion to make it work, in the long run it would be much cheaper than training human doctors.

This economies-of-scale-argument is echoed in the specialized healthcare and AI literature (Luxton, 2016, p. 17):

> [AI] can [...] bring an economy of scale to care delivery. The increased accessibility and lower cost of intelligent machines [...] provide opportunities for longer-term treatments that are currently restricted by managed-care costs. [...] Patients will have the opportunity to participate in longer-term therapies and also receive periodic check-ups at greatly reduced costs.

4.3. Machine Superiority as Medical Advantage

Harari (2017, p. 268, 2018, p. 23) exacerbates the objection of AI's lack of human qualities with the image of horrific amplified system errors. Yet he still arrives at human redundancy:

> You might object that by switching from individual humans to a computer network we will lose the advantages of individuality. For example, if one human doctor makes a wrong judgement, he does not kill all the patients in the world, and he does not block the development of all new medications. In contrast, if all doctors are really just a single system, and that system makes a mistake, the results might be catastrophic [...] However, just as armies no longer need millions of GI's, so future healthcare services will not need millions of GPs.

Harari even turns that popular objection around: it is precisely the lack of human individuality that lets AI outdo human doctors or diagnosticians – at least on average, long-term, and for ever-growing patient numbers, as these are propitious conditions for algorithmic power, which would be all the stronger in be absence of human elements and weaknesses:

> An integrated computer system can maximise the advantages of connectivity without losing the benefits of individuality [...] so that a patient in a remote jungle village can access through her smartphone not just a single authoritative doctor, but [...] a hundred different AI doctors, whose relative performance is constantly being compared (2018, p. 23).
>
> A human doctor [is] analysing external signals such as your facial expressions and your tone of voice. Watson could [...] analyse such external signals more accurately [by] monitoring your blood pressure, brain activities and countless other biometric data [and with] statistics garnered from millions of previous social encounters, Watson would then tell you precisely what you need to hear in just the right tone of voice [and] would always offer the most appropriate response to your emotional state (2017, pp. 369–370).

Specifically, Big Data would enable algorithms to analyze and advise humans better than humans themselves, based on in-built biometric sensors feeding constant live data streams from bodies to computers. Other writers similarly highlight the chasm between human and machine information processing:

> Big data [are] the 'three V's' of volume (large quantities) [and] variety (heterogeneity) [and] velocity (fast access) [...] from many sources: electronic health records, medical literature, clinical trials, insurance claims data, pharmacy records, and even information entered by patients into their smartphones or recorded on fitness trackers (Price, 2017, p. 10).
>
> Biometric data could monitor our health 24/7 [to] detect the very beginnings of influenza, cancer or Alzheimer's disease, long before we feel anything is wrong with us [and] recommend appropriate treatments, diets and daily regimens, custom-built for our unique physique, DNA and personality. [...] The key invention is the biometric sensor, which people can wear on or inside their bodies, and which converts biological processes into electronic information that computers can store and analyze (Harari, 2018, pp. 48–50).

4.4. Machine Superiority as Healthcare Democratization

Harari concludes that the machines' non-humanness is not just superior but ultimately advantageous for humanity. It could even completely democratize human healthcare:

> A poor villager in an underdeveloped country might come to enjoy far better healthcare via her smartphone than the richest person in the world gets today from the most advanced urban hospital. [...] In Toronto, Tokyo, Tehran or Tel Aviv, you will [...] meet doctors [...] who learned the same scientific theories in the same medical colleges [and] follow identical protocols [...] to reach very similar diagnoses [and] then dispense the same medicines produced by the same international drug companies (Harari, 2018, pp. 23, 106–107).

The specialized literature at the intersection of human healthcare and AI concurs that wider geographical and egalitarian distribution would benefit patients and providers:

> Telehealth services [would be] providing services [...] in remote geographical areas and provide access to specialty care services that may not be available in the patient's area [...] accessible anywhere and at any time on mobile devices to [...] conduct question-and-answer assessments, provide self-care counseling, and deliver therapeutic interventions. [...] Wearable devices can increase the amount of data that are [...] to assess health and monitor progress toward individualized health goals (Luxton, 2016, pp. 15–16).

Harari concludes that full healthcare automation would benefit humanity, and should thus be rationally pursued. Redundant doctors might still have perspectives, voluntary rather than obligatory qualifications, and even raised status, demand, and remuneration:

> It would be madness to block automation [...] to protect human jobs. After all, what we ultimately ought to protect is humans – not jobs. [...] GPs who focus on diagnosing known diseases and administering familiar treatments will probably be replaced by AI doctors. But [...] there will be much more money to pay human doctors and lab assistants to do groundbreaking research and develop new medicines or surgical procedures. [...] Instead of humans competing with AI, they could focus on servicing and leveraging AI (2018, pp. 24, 28–29).

4.5. Super Clinicians and Ethical Concerns

While some of the literature specializing on AI and healthcare forwards the hypothesis of an ideal caregiver, the "super clinician", it also highlights conceptual and practical weaknesses. These point towards future research, taken up in our conclusions:

> The super clinician [unites] technologies [such as] facial recognition technology [with] advanced sensory technologies to observe and analyze nonverbal behavior such as facial expressions, eye blinking, vocal characteristics, and other patterns of behavior [including] internal states that are not detectable by the human eye, such as by observing changes in body temperature with infrared cameras or blood flow in the face with high-resolution digital video processing techniques. The system could be capable of accessing and analyzing all data available about patients from electronic medical records, previous testing results, and real-time assessments collected via mobile health devices. [It could also] learn every therapeutic approach, and [...] apply the best treatment or intervention. [...] Technological barriers [include the] reliable integration of the component technologies and the ability to process complex and ambiguous meaning from conversations in order to function autonomously [besides] the loss of something inherent to the helping professions: human-to-human expression of empathy, care, and compassion [and] basic human physical presence and contact, such as shaking hands before and after a session

with a patient, placing a hand on the shoulder of a person who is overcome with grief, or handing a patient a tissue to dry their tears (Luxton, 2016, 18–19).

4.6. Delegation of Morality to Machines

As for the relationship between power and responsibility, Steve Jobs was cited in a 1994 interview thus:

> Technology is nothing. What's important is that you have faith in people, that they're basically good and smart, and if you give them tools, they'll do wonderful things with them. It's not the tools that you have faith in […] It's people that you have faith in (Belle, 2018, p. 5).

By contrast, Harari highlights the de-personalization of delegating human processes, including their decision-making, to AI, if based only on algorithmic parameters:

> If the algorithms indeed understand what's happening within you better than you understand it, authority will shift to them. […] If, however, you want to retain some control of your personal existence […] you have to run faster than the algorithms […] to know yourself before they do (2018, pp. 48, 56, 268).

Recent popular science writings connect AI with even larger ethical concerns, such as monitoring people's lives from shopping decisions to the most private and incisive matters, with authors asking for wider ethical frameworks and standards:

> Data science teams have access to […] patient data [in addition to] explicit clinical and operational domain knowledge […] The overall solution (in which AI may play only a small part) is often required to undergo strict regulatory approval before becoming part of a healthcare product (Vdoviak, 2019, p. 6).

3. Conclusions and Recommendations

We have seen how some consider artificial intelligence mostly in a black-and-white fashion, in future scenarios divided into personal and social winners and losers in a zero-sum-game. The humans in those scenario are largely pitted on the losing, and the machines and their algorithms on the winning side. Even writers who are successfully straddling the scientific and the popular realms occasionally give in to technological pessimism and to social determinism.

Such technological pessimism even seems reflected in popular entertainment, as in films about machines taking control of the world and its human inhabitants. The 2004 action movie *I, Robot* depicts a dystopian man-machine relationship via a one-sided superiority of machines over people including their creators and against best social intentions and technological safeguards.

Other popular entertainment forms, such as Dan Brown's novels, take us through rollercoaster rides of technologically-induced end-of-earth scenarios, but conclude with optimistic scenes, such as in the cited passage where Professor Langdon comes to terms with the "technium" and finds inner peace in the embrace of humanity's inevitable technological fusion with machines.

The literature at the intersection of medical healthcare and anthropology seems more at ease with all forms of AI, welcoming man-machine interactions as technologically efficient and humanly beneficial. This position is literally spelled out in the signature phrase of the main protagonist in the 1999 sci-fi comedy drama *Bicentennial Man*: "One is happy to serve".

The socio-economic literature on the automation economy and on abundance or post-scarcity economics seems theoretically and practically most at ease with all artificial intelligence in human, social, scientific and academic life, from social robotics to nanotechnology, advocating for facilitating of human labor via omnipresent suitable technology.

The literature at the interface of human healthcare and artificial intelligence has suggested future research areas such as the interaction between people and machines, or persons' reactions to medical caregiving delivered automatedly but perceived as personally efficiently.

If notions such as the relationship between power and responsibility, based on timeless human wisdom, prevail, then epiphanies about the coexistence of man and machine like Professor Langdon's at the end of Dan Brown's novel *Origin* might bless doctors and patients alike.

References

Belle, N. (2018). Seismic Changes in Modern Times: Emerging Technology Can Be Harnessed and Implemented for Its Potential in Broader Domains of Industry, Commerce and Civil Life. *Tech & Transformation*, Khaleej Times Supplement, 2 October, pp. 4–5.

Bershidsky, L. (2018). AI Wars Are Breaking Out, the Winners Will Rule the World: The US Is Emerging as a Leader in Patents But China and Europe Are Not Far. *Khaleej Times*, 30 December, p. 9.

Bouchemal, N. (2019). Preface. In N. Bouchemal (Ed.), *Intelligent Systems for Healthcare Management and Delivery* (pp. xiv–xxv). IGI Global.

Brown, D. (2017). *Origin*. Penguin.

Brown, P. J. & Closser, S. (2016). To the Student. In P. Brown & S. Closser (Eds.), *Understanding and Applying Medical Anthropology* (3rd ed., pp. 9–10). Routledge.

Harari, Y. N. (2017). *Homo Deus: A Brief History of Tomorrow*. Penguin.

Harari, Y. N. (2018). *21 Lessons for the 21st Century*. Penguin.

Jennings, F. B. (2015). Abundance and Scarcity. In F. F. Wherry, & J. B. Schor (Eds.), *The Sage Encyclopedia of Economics and Society* (pp. 5–7). Sage Publications.

Joralemon, D. (2017). *Exploring Medical Anthropology* (4th ed.). Routledge.

Keni, R. (2019). Why Humans Should Not Be Replaced by Machines with AI. *Khaleej Times*, 12 January, p. 6.

Luxton, D. D. (2016). An Introduction to Artificial Intelligence in Behavioral and Mental Health Care. In D. D. Luxton (Ed.), *Artificial Intelligence in Behavioral and Mental Health Care* (pp. 1–26). Elsevier.

Manderson, L., Cartwright, E., & Hardon, A. (2016). Introduction: Sign Posts. In L. Manderson, E. Cartwright, & A. Hardon (Eds.), *The Routledge Handbook of Medical Anthropology* (pp. 2–14). Routledge.

Martin, V. (2017). *Transdisciplinarity Revealed: What Librarians Need to Know*. ABC-CLIO.

McElroy, A. & Townsend, P. K. (2018). *Medical Anthropology in Ecological Perspective* (6th ed.). Routledge.

Peters, M. A. (2009). Introduction: Knowledge Goods, the Primacy of Ideas and the Economics of Abundance. In M. A. Peters, S. Marginson & P. Murphy (Eds.), *Creativity and the Global Knowledge Economy* (pp. 1–22). Peter Lang.

Pressman, S. (2011). John Kenneth Galbraith and the Post Keynesian Tradition in Economics. In S. Pressman (Ed.), *The Legacy of John Kenneth Galbraith* (pp. 1–15). Routledge.

Price, W. N. (2017). Artificial Intelligence in Health Care: Applications and Legal Implications. *The SciTech Lawyer, 14*(1), 10–13

Sadaqat, R. (2019). Robotics Future of Construction. *Khaleej Times*, 19 January, p. 14.

Saunders, O. (2015). *Tomato Economics: Shifting Economics from Scarcity to Abundance*. Xlibris.

Shi, J. (2018). Buddhist Economics: A Cultural Alternative. In S. Yamash'ta, T. Yagi, & S. Hill (Eds.), *The Kyoto Manifesto for Global Economics: The Platform of Community, Humanity, and Spirituality* (pp. 417–435). Springer.

Sobo, E. J. (2004). Theoretical and Applied Issues in Cross-Cultural and Applied Health Research: Key Concepts and Controversies. In C. R. Ember, & M. Ember (Eds.), *Encyclopedia of Medical Anthropology: Health and Illness in the World's Cultures*, Volume 1 (pp. 3–11). Springer.

Swan, M. (2016). Philosophy of Social Robotics: Abundance Economics. In A. Agah, J. J. Cabibihan, A. M. Howard, M. A. Salichs, & H. He (Eds.), *Social Robotics: 8th International Conference*. Springer.

Swan, M. (2017). Is Technological Unemployment Real? An Assessment and a Plea for Abundance Economics. In K. LaGrandeur, & J. J. Hughes (Eds.), *Surviving the Machine Age: Intelligent Technology and the Transformation of Human Work* (pp. 19–34). Springer.

Tegmark, M. (2017). *Life 3.0: Being Human in the Age of Artificial Intelligence*. Penguin.

Vdoviak, R. (2019). Smart Healthcare Is Here to Help. The Future of AI: Personifying Machines and Transforming Businesses. *Khaleej Times Special Report*, August, p. 6.

Verma, S. (2019). Hello, Super Intelligence. Will Robots Get Along with Mortals? A New Breed of Humans and Machines Will form the Coming Plutocracy. *Khaleej Times*, 31 December, p. 9.

Weller, M. (2011). *The Digital Scholar: How Technology Is Transforming Scholarly Practice*. Bloomsbury.

Yamash'ta, S., Yagi, T., & Hill, S. (2018). The Path: From the Sacred Harmony of Humanity to a New Economics. In S. Yamash'ta, T. Yagi, & S. Hill (Eds.), *The Kyoto Manifesto for Global Economics: The Platform of Community, Humanity, and Spirituality* (pp. 3–11). Springer.

Constantinos Challoumis

A Comparison of the Velocities of Minimum Escaped Savings and Financial Liquidity

1. Introduction

Banking is a network of commercial savings, as well as other specialized banks that provide financial services, including the acceptance of deposits, the provision of loans and credits, transferring money and the provision of investment facilities. Today we all know what banks are, since we will surely have made a transaction with one of them. Formally, a bank is defined as an institution whose business is to raise money by accepting deposits from the public and then using that money to make loans to individuals and companies (AL-Ubaydli et al., 2021; Bento, 2009; Biernaski & Silva, 2018; Chubarova et al., 2020; Jensen, 2020; Kreft & Sobel, 2005; Lal et al., 2018; Marques, 2019; Porter, 2007; Scholvin & Malamud, 2020; Urwannachotima et al., 2020; Wright et al., 2017). In an economy there are usually many and various types of banks, such as commercial, cooperative, investment, the central bank etc. All these banks of an economy constitute its Banking System (Camous & Gimber, 2018; "Changing the Narrative: Economics After Covid-19," 2020; Fernandez & Raine, 2019; Giglio et al., 2021; Maestre-Andrés et al., 2019; Marume, 2016; Montenegro Martínez et al., 2020; OECD, 2017; Prestianawati et al., 2020; Rasmussen & Callan, 2016; Saleem et al., 2017; Sultana et al., 2020; Zayats O.I., 2019). This chapter examines the money cycle with the velocity of financial liquidity and the velocity of minimum escaped savings. The basic principles of the money cycle are then applied in this examination, some of which are included in the next two sections of this chapter (Challoumis, 2018b, 2018a, 2019b, 2019c, 2019e, 2019 f, 2019g, 2020a, 2020d, 2021a, 2021c, 2021e, 2021h). Then, using the Q.E. method, conclusions were drawn about the significance of these velocities in the economy. Furthermore, the relationship between the velocity of minimum escaped savings and the velocity of financial liquidity is defined based on this analysis. Contracts and agreements between participants in control transactions determine the allocation of profits and losses. The changes in the contracts should be mentioned in the agreements. This is the reason the tax authorities should make periodic inspections. The periodic specification of contracts is important for the comparability analysis. The arm's length principle requires periodic inspections of companies that participate in controlled transactions (AL-UBAYDLI et al., 2021; Bento, 2009; Biernaski & Silva, 2018; Chubarova et al., 2020; Jensen, 2020; Kreft & Sobel, 2005; Lal et al., 2018; Marques, 2019; Porter, 2007; Scholvin & Malamud, 2020; Urwannachotima et al., 2020; Wright et al., 2017). The cost-sharing is then determined based on a periodic review of companies that have been tested as parties. The scope of controlled transaction companies is to face issues related to the taxation of their activities. As a result, the requirements for companies conducting controlled transactions with tax authorities should fall within the scope of the arm's length principle (Andriansyah et al., 2019; Arabyan, 2016; Carfora et al., 2021; Castro & Scartascini, 2019; Kalambokidis, 2014; Khadzhyradieva et al., 2019; Kreft & Sobel, 2005; Maier, 2012; Martinez & Rodríguez, 2020; Nowlin et al., 2020; OECD, 2020; Oueslati, 2015; Ruiz et al., 2017; Snow, 1988). As a result, the agreement for controlled transaction companies is one that allows them to maximize profits in tax environments with low tax rates while minimizing costs in tax environments with high tax rates.

The companies of controlled transactions should be notified that tax authorities' inspections are conducted under the condition of proportional adjustments. Interpreting the proportional adjustments condition is that companies that take part in controlled transactions frequently lack the appropriate data and uncontrolled transactions of similar circumstances to compare, so they proportionally adjust their data (Challoumis, 2019b, 2022a, 2023c, 2023b). This means that if the tested parties conclude that the profits and losses of companies from uncontrolled transactions are significantly higher or significantly lower, they use a proportional analogy to compare them with their data. The production of goods or services generates profits and costs for businesses:

$$u = s\left(zf + \tilde{z}d\right) \tag{1}$$

$$z = \left|\tilde{z} - 1\right| \tag{2}$$

The symbol u is about the impact factor of the comparability analysis which has any method to the s. The symbol z is a coefficient that takes values between 0 and 1. What value could receive is determined by the influence of the method (using the best method rule) to the s. The symbol of f is about the cost which comes up from the production of goods, and the symbol of d is about the cost which comes from the distribution of the goods.

According to Eqs. (1) to (6) is plausible to determine the following equations:

$$u_c = zf + \tilde{z}d \tag{3}$$

$$b = (p - u_c)^* j_1 \tag{4}$$

The symbol b in the preceding equation refers to the amount of taxes that should be paid by companies involved in controlled transactions under the arm's length principle. The u_c is the amount of tax obligations that can avoid through the allocations of profits and losses. Moreover, j_1 is a coefficient for the rate of taxes (Challoumis, 2018c, 2019d, 2020b, 2021 f, 2021h, 2021i, 2022b). Then, Eq. (8) shows the case of the arm's length principle. Furthermore, there is the case of the fixed length principle.:

$$v = p^* j_2 \tag{5}$$

The symbol of v in the previous equation shows the taxes that should pay the enterprises of controlled transactions in the application of the fixed length principle. Then, j_2 is a coefficient for the rate of taxes in the case of the fixed length principle:

$$v \geq b \tag{6}$$

The tax on companies that participate in controlled transactions of transfer pricing under the fixed length principle is higher or at least equal to the tax on companies that participate under the arm's length principle. As a result, using the fixed length principle, enterprises of controlled transactions can address issues arising from profit and loss allocation. The tax authorities will then have to deal with the effects of transfer pricing on global tax revenue. The fixed length principle allows for the recovery of global tax revenue losses from transfer pricing controlled transactions. The following scheme illustrates the procedure that controlled transaction companies use for profit and loss allocations, data proportional adjustments, and the fixed length principle:

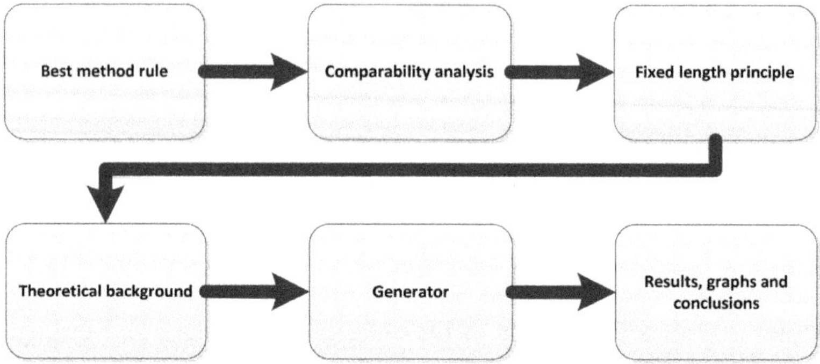

Figure 1: Cost sharing and application of fixed length principle.

The procedure of the fixed length principle and its quantity analysis for determining the model's behavior is determined in Figure 1. The theory of the money cycle is presented in the following section. Furthermore, the methodology that followed is based on the Q.E. method.

2. The Ideal Case of the Cycle of Money

The tax revenues correspond to the savings that businesses could realize if taxes were avoided. The manner in which these savings are administered varies from case to case. The benefits of the companies could then be managed in a completely different way, as they could be saved or taxed. The theory of the money cycle shows when savings strengthen the economy and when taxes strengthen the economy. It is crucial for this determination to be a separation of savings into non-returned savings (or escaped savings) and the returned savings (or enforcement savings). For the scope of this analysis below are demonstrated the equations which are:

$$\alpha = \alpha_s + \alpha_t, or, \frac{1}{v} + \alpha_t \tag{7}$$

$$x_m = m - a \tag{8}$$

$$m = \mu + \alpha_p \tag{9}$$

$$\mu = \sum_{\iota=0}^{n} \mu_\iota \tag{10}$$

$$\alpha_p = \sum_{j=0}^{m} \alpha_{pj} \tag{11}$$

$$c_m = \frac{dx_m}{dm} \tag{12}$$

$$c_\alpha = \frac{dx_m}{da} \tag{13}$$

$$c_y = c_m - c_\alpha \tag{14}$$

The variable of α has symbolized the case of the escaped savings. This means that there are savings that are not returning to the economy, or come back after a long-term period. The variable of α_s symbolizes the case that there have escaped savings that come from transfer pricing activities. The variable of α_t it symbolizes the case that there have escaped savings not from transfer pricing activities but from any other commercial activity. For instance α_t could refer to the commercial activities which come from uncontrolled transactions. The variable of m symbolizes the financial liquidity in an economy. The variable of μ symbolizes the consumption in an economy. The variable of α_p symbolizes the enforcement savings, which come from the citizens and small and medium-sized enterprises. The variable of x_m symbolizes the condition of financial liquidity in an economy. The variable of c_m symbolizes the velocity of financial liquidity increases or decreases. The variable of c_α symbolizes the velocity of escaped savings. Therefore, the variable of c_y symbolizes the term of the cycle of money (Challoumis, 2019a, 2019e, 2020c, 2021d, 2021e, 2021b, 2021f, 2021h, 2021g, 2021c, 2022c, 2023a, 2023c). Thereupon, the cycle of money shows the level of the dynamic of an economy and its robustness.

The citizens, the small and the middle-sized enterprises substitute the services and the property of the companies which save their money and not invest them or consume it proportionally in the economy. Thereupon, the companies of the controlled transactions are the main cause of the escape savings. The escaped savings are responsible for the decline of the economic dynamic of the economy. The key point of escape savings is that the companies of controlled transactions of transfer pricing are responsible for not reenter of this amount of money in the market. This situation causes a lack of financial liquidity in an economy (Acs et al., 2016; Arai et al., 2018; Bernasconi & Espinosa-Cristia, 2020; Bourdin & Nadou, 2018; Camous & Gimber, 2018; de Mello-Théry et al., 2020; Engström et al., 2020; Fernandez & Raine, 2019; Giglio et al., 2021; Haigh, 2020; Laplane & Mazzucato, 2020; Levi, 2021; Maestre-Andrés et al., 2019; Marume, 2016; Montenegro Martínez et al., 2020; Nash et al., 2017; Naudé & Dimitri, 2020; Paes-Sousa et al., 2019; Peres et al., 2020; Prestianawati et al., 2020; Rasmussen & Callan, 2016; Saleem et al., 2017; Schwartz, 2019). The substitution of controlled transactions is not substituted from the citizens and the small and middle size companies when there is not plausible to offer the same added value to the products and the services. This case happens especially in the instance of factories, and research centers. Therefrom, these cases in the appropriate tax policy should be taxed as uncontrolled transactions independently if they participate in controlled transactions (using the fixed length principle). The enforcement savings are responsible for the high economic dynamic of the economy. Therefore, investments and consumption are these elements that come from the savings of the citizens and the small and middle size companies.

The velocity of financial liquidity shows how rapidly the economy's robustness grows or declines accordingly. Then is an index for how well structured is any economy. The velocity of escaped savings shows how rapidly the non-return savings are lost from the market, or by the lack of investments, or by the lack of consumption. The cycle of money represents the condition of the economy. The level of a well-structured tax system, and in general the dynamic of the economy. If this indicator is high then the economy could have high robustness otherwise has low financial liquidity. As controlled transactions in the theory of the cycle of money are considered not only the cases of transfer pricing, but any kind of administration of profits and losses to avoid taxation. Uncontrolled transactions in the theory of the cycle of money are the case of the commercial activity of citizens, small and medium-sized enterprises, factories, research centers, and any kind of commercial activity that cannot substitute for the companies of controlled transactions.

The fixed length principle tackles issues subjects like the case cycle of money. But, this doesn't mean that restriction must apply the fixed length principle as the cycle of money is more widely a theory which exceeds the transfer pricing scope. Therefrom, obtained that the cycle of money grows when there is a tax system like the case of the fixed length principle, which permits the low taxation of uncontrolled transactions and the higher taxation of controlled transactions. Should be mentioned that as uncontrolled transactions are considered, the same happens with the cases of the financial liquidity of citizens and small and middle-size companies. Moreover, there are three basic impact factors of rewarding taxes.

The rewarding taxes are the only taxes that have an immediate and important role in the market of any economy. These factors are affiliated with education, with the health system of each society, and with the rest relevant structural economic factors of the prior two impact factors. This issue is illustrated in the next scheme:

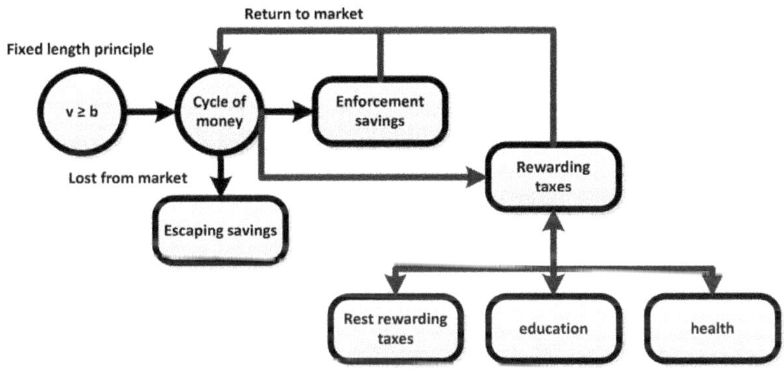

Figure 2: The cycle of money with rewarding taxes.

In the previous figure, presented that the tax system includes all the tax factors and all the rewarding tax factors.

3. Results

For the mathematical approach to the cycle of money, used the prior equations subject to the next condition:

$$\mu > \alpha_p > \alpha_t > \alpha_s \tag{15}$$

Therefore, used the Eqs. (1) to (15) and the next table for the coefficients of the values of the cycle of money:

Table 1. Compiling coefficients

Factors	Values
α_s	–
α_t	–
μ	0.9
α_p	0.8

The generator of this procedure used the coefficients, which appeared in the previous table. Therefrom, the factors have an upper limit of 1, and a lower limit of 0, but s and $\tilde{s}$ are plausible to receive values greater than one as their mathematical structure allows this. After 461 iterations extracted the following diagram:

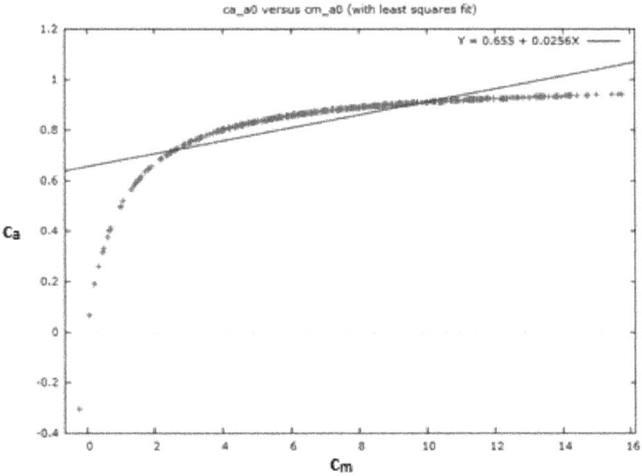

Figure 3: Velocities of minimum escaped savings and financial liquidity.

Based on Figure 3 presented that the values of the velocity financial liquidity are higher than the values of the minimum escaped savings. This shows that under these conditions the dynamic of any economy is positive, and the velocity of financial liquidity takes very high values, as the cycle of money in this economy is without the escaped savings.

4. Conclusions

This chapter shows that the general behavior of the velocity of financial liquidity is very high when there the velocity of escaped savings is approximately equal to zero. This means that the economy has a positive orientation, and therefore the economy in this case is growing rapidly. Thence, the consumption, and investments in this economy will be at a very high level.

Appendix

The source code is the following one:

```
% (c)(r) 2017 All rights reserved Q.E. mwthod Constantinos Challoumis
    as=0.05;
    at=0.05;
    xm=0;
    m=0;
    m1=0;
    ap=0;
    cm=0;
    ca=0;
    cy−0;
    t=0;
    while t<10
    t=t+1;
    if rand()<9
    m1=0.9*rand();
    end
    if rand()<9
    ap=0.8*rand();
    end
    a=as+at;
    m=m1+ap;
    xm=m-a;
    cm=xm/a;
    ca=xm/m;
    cy=cm-ca;
    tab=[a,xm,m,cm,ca,cy;tab];
    end
```

References

Acs, Z., Åstebro, T., Audretsch, D., & Robinson, D. T. (2016). Public Policy to Promote Entrepreneurship: A Call to Arms. *Small Business Economics*, *47*(1). https://doi.org/10.1007/s11187-016-9712-2

Al-Ubaydli, O., Lee, M. S., List, J. A., Mackevicius, C. L., & Suskind, D. (2021). How Can Experiments Play a Greater Role in Public Policy? Twelve Proposals from an Economic Model of Scaling. *Behavioural Public Policy*, *5*(1). https://doi.org/10.1017/bpp.2020.17

Andriansyah, A., Taufiqurokhman, T., & Wekke, I. S. (2019). Responsiveness of Public Policy and Its Impact on Education Management: An Empirical Assessment from Indonesia. *Management Science Letters*, *9*(3). https://doi.org/10.5267/j.msl.2018.12.008

Arabyan, O. (2016). Public Infrastructure Policies and Economic Geography. *Glasnik Srpskog Geografskog DrustvaBulletin of the Serbian Geographical Society*, *96*(1). https://doi.org/10.2298/gsgd1601093a

Arai, R., Naito, K., & Ono, T. (2018). Intergenerational Policies, Public Debt, and Economic Growth: A Politico-Economic Analysis. *Journal of Public Economics*, *166*. https://doi.org/10.1016/j.jpubeco.2018.08.006

Bento, A. (2009). Biofuels: Economic and Public Policy Considerations. In R.W. Howarth, & S. Bringezu (Eds.), *Biofuels: Environmental Consequences and Implications of Changing Land Use*, September 2008.

Bernasconi, O., & Espinosa-Cristia, J. F. (2020). No Politics, No Society: Questioning the Justification of Entrepreneurship in Chilean Public Policies. *RAE Revista de Administracao de Empresas*, *60*(2). https://doi.org/10.1590/S0034-759020200206

Biernaski, I., & Silva, C. L. (2018). Main Variables of Brazilian Public Policies on Biomass USE and Energy. *Brazilian Archives of Biology and Technology*, *61*(Special issue). https://doi.org/10.1590/1678-4324-smart-2018000310

Bourdin, S., & Nadou, F. (2018). French Tech: A New form of Territorial Mobilization to Face Up to Global Competition? *Annales de Geographie*, *2018*(723–724). https://doi.org/10.3917/ag.723.0612

Camous, A., & Gimber, A. R. (2018). Public Debt and Fiscal Policy Traps. *Journal of Economic Dynamics and Control*, *93*. https://doi.org/10.1016/j.jedc.2018.02.009

Carfora, A., Pansini, R. V., & Scandurra, G. (2021). The Role of Environmental Taxes and Public Policies in Supporting RES Investments in EU Countries: Barriers and Mimicking Effects. *Energy Policy*, *149*. https://doi.org/10.1016/j.enpol.2020.112044

Castro, E., & Scartascini, C. (2019). Imperfect Attention in Public Policy: A Field Experiment During a Tax Amnesty in Argentina. *IDB Discussion Paper*, April.

Challoumis, C. (2018a). Analysis of the Velocities of Escaped Savings with That of Financial Liquidity. *Ekonomski Signali*, *13*(2), 1–14. https://doi.org/10.5937/ekonsig1802001c

Challoumis, C. (2018b). Methods of Controlled Transactions and the Behavior of Companies According to the Public and Tax Policy. In *Economics* (Vol. 6, Issue 1). https://doi.org/10.2478/eoik-2018-0003

Challoumis, C. (2018c). The Impact Factor of Health on the Economy Using the Cycle of Money. *Bulletin of the Transilvania University of Brașov*, *11*(60), 125–136. http://rs.unitbv.ro/Bulletin/SeriesV/2018/BULETINI/15_Challoumis.pdf

Challoumis, C. (2019a). Journal Association "SEPIKE" Edition 25, October, 2019. *Journal Association SEPIKE*, *2019*(25), 12–21. https://5b925ea6-3d4e-400b-b5f3-32dc681218ff.filesusr.com/ugd/b199e2_dd29716b8bec48ca8fe7fbcfd47cdd2e.pdf

Challoumis, C. (2019b). The Arm's Length Principle and the Fixed Length Principle Economic Analysis. *World Scientific News*, *115*(2019), 207–217. http://www.worldscientificnews.com/wp-content/uploads/2018/11/WSN-115-2019-207-217.pdf

Challoumis, C. (2019c). The Cycle of Money With and Without the Escaped Savings. *Ekonomski Signali*, *14*(1), 89–99. https://doi.org/336.76336.741.236.5

Challoumis, C. (2019d). The Impact Factor of Education on the Public Sector and International Controlled Transactions. *Complex System Research Centre*, *2019*, 151–160. https://www.researchgate.net/publication/350453451_The_Impact_Factor_of_Education_on_the_Public_Sector_and_International_Controlled_Transactions

Challoumis, C. (2019e). The R.B.Q. (Rational, Behavioral and Quantified) Model. *Ekonomika*, *98*(1). https://doi.org/10.15388/ekon.2019.1.1

Challoumis, C. (2019f). Theoretical Analysis of Fuzzy Logic and Q. E. Method in Economics. *IKBFU's Vestnik*, *2019*(01), 59–68. https://doi.org/330.42

Challoumis, C. (2019g). Transfer Pricing Methods for Services and the Policy of Fixed Length Principle. *Economics and Business*, *33*(1), 222–232. https://doi.org/https://doi.org/10.2478/eb-2019-0016

Challoumis, C. (2020a). Analysis of the Theory of Cycle of Money. *Acta Universitatis Bohemiae Meridionalis*, *23*(2), 13–29. https://doi.org/https://doi.org/10.2478/acta-2020-0004

Challoumis, C. (2020b). Impact Factor of Capital to the Economy and Tax System. *Complex System Research Centre*, *2020*, 195–200. https://www.researchgate.net/publication/350385990_Impact_Factor_of_Capital_to_the_Economy_and_Tax_System

Challoumis, C. (2020c). The Impact Factor of Costs to the Tax System. *Journal of Entrepreneurship, Business and Economics*, *8*(1), 1–14. http://scientificia.com/index.php/JEBE/article/view/126

Challoumis, C. (2020d). The Impact Factor of Education on the Public Sector – The Case of the U.S. *International Journal of Business and Economic Sciences Applied Research*, *13*(1), 69–78. https://doi.org/10.25103/ijbesar.131.07

Challoumis, C. (2021a). Index of the Cycle of Money – The Case of Belarus. *Economy and Banks, 2.*

Challoumis, C. (2021b). Index of the Cycle of Money – – The Case of Greece. *International Journal of Business and Economic Sciences Applied Research (IJBESAR), 14*(2).

Challoumis, C. (2021c). Index of the Cycle of Money – The Case of Latvia. *Economics and Culture, 17*(2), 5–12. https://doi.org/10.2478/jec-2020-0015

Challoumis, C. (2021d). Index of the Cycle of Money – – The Case of Serbia. *Open Journal for Research In Economics (OJRE), 4*(1). https://centerprode.com/ojre.html

Challoumis, C. (2021e). Index of the Cycle of Money – The Case of Slovakia. *Studiacommercia liabratislavensia Ekonomická Univerzita v Bratislave, 14*(49), 176–188.

Challoumis, C. (2021f). Index of the Cycle of Money – The Case of Thailand. *Chiang Mai University Journal of Economics, 25*(2).

Challoumis, C. (2021g). Index of the Cycle of Money – The Case of Ukraine. *Actual Problems of Economics, 243*(9).

Challoumis, C. (2021h). Index of the Cycle of Money – The Case of Bulgaria. *Economic Alternatives, 27*(2). https://www.unwe.bg/eajournal/en

Challoumis, C. (2021i). *The Cycle of Money With and Without the Enforcement Savings*. Complex System Research Centre.

Challoumis, C. (2022a). Conditions of the CM (Cycle of Money). In V. Kaya (Ed.), *Social and Economic Studies Within the Framework of Emerging Global Developments, Volume -1,* (pp. 13–24).

Challoumis, C. (2022b). Impact Factor of the Rest Rewarding Taxes. *Complex System Research Centre*. https://doi.org/10.2139/ssrn.3154753

Challoumis, C. (2022c). Index of the Cycle of Money – The Case of Poland. *Research Papers in Economics and Finance, 6*(1).

Challoumis, C. (2023a). Index of the Cycle of Money – The Case of Canada. *Journal of Entrepreneurship, Business and Economics.*

Challoumis, C. (2023b). Liability of Tax Revenue According to the Theory of Cycle of Money. In V. Kaya (Ed.), *Social and Economic Studies within the Framework of Emerging Global Developments, Volume -1.*

Challoumis, C. (2023c). Utility of Cycle of Money Without the Escaping Savings (Protection of the Economy). In V. Kaya (Ed.), *Social and Economic Studies within the Framework of Emerging Global Developments Volume 2,.*

Changing the Narrative: Economics after Covid-19. (2020). *Journal, 10*(1).

Chubarova, T., Maly, I., & Nemec, J. (2020). Public Policy Responses to the Spread of COVID-19 as a Potential Factor Determining Health Results: A

Comparative Study of the Czech Republic, the Russian Federation, and the Slovak Republic. *Central European Journal of Public Policy*, *14*(2). https://doi.org/10.2478/cejpp-2020-0008

de Mello-Théry, N. A., de Lima Caldas, E., Funatsu, B. M., Arvor, D., & Dubreuil, V. (2020). Climate Change and Public Policies in the Brazilian Amazon State of Mato Grosso: Perceptions and Challenges. *Sustainability (Switzerland)*, *12*(12). https://doi.org/10.3390/su12125093

Engström, G., Gars, J., Jaakkola, N., Lindahl, T., Spiro, D., & van Benthem, A. A. (2020). What Policies Address Both the Coronavirus Crisis and the Climate Crisis? *Environmental and Resource Economics*, *76*(4). https://doi.org/10.1007/s10640-020-00451-y

Fernandez, M. A., & Raine, K. D. (2019). Insights on the Influence of Sugar Taxes on Obesity Prevention Efforts. In *Current Nutrition Reports* (Vol. 8, Issue 4). https://doi.org/10.1007/s13668-019-00282-4

Giglio, C., Musmanno, R., & Palmieri, R. (2021). Cycle Logistics Projects in Europe: Intertwining Bike-Related Success Factors and Region-Specific Public Policies with Economic Results. *Applied Sciences (Switzerland)*, *11*(4). https://doi.org/10.3390/app11041578

Haigh, Y. (2020). Increasing Complexities: Teaching Public Policy in the Age of Discontent. *Teaching Public Administration*, *38*(1). https://doi.org/10.1177/0144739419879483

Jensen, P. H. (2020). Experiments and Evaluation of Public Policies: Methods, Implementation, and Challenges. *Australian Journal of Public Administration*, *79*(2). https://doi.org/10.1111/1467-8500.12406

Kalambokidis, L. (2014). Creating Public Value with Tax and Spending Policies: The View from Public Economics. *Public Administration Review*, *74*(4). https://doi.org/10.1111/puar.12162

Khadzhyradieva, S., Hrechko, T., & Smalskys, V. (2019). Institutionalisation of Behavioural Insights in Public Policy. In *Public Policy and Administration* (Vol. 18, Issue 3). https://doi.org/10.5755/J01.PPAA.18.3.24726

Kreft, S. F., & Sobel, R. S. (2005). Public Policy, Entrepreneurship, and Economic Freedom. In *Cato Journal* (Vol. 25, Issue 3).

Lal, A., Moodie, M., Peeters, A., & Carter, R. (2018). Inclusion of Equity in Economic Analyses of Public Health Policies: Systematic Review and Future Directions. In *Australian and New Zealand Journal of Public Health* (Vol. 42, Issue 2). https://doi.org/10.1111/1753-6405.12709

Laplane, A., & Mazzucato, M. (2020). Socializing the Risks and Rewards of Public Investments: Economic, Policy, and Legal Issues. *Research Policy: X, 2*. https://doi.org/10.1016/j.repolx.2020.100008

Levi, S. (2021). Why Hate Carbon Taxes? Machine Learning Evidence on the Roles of Personal Responsibility, Trust, Revenue Recycling, and Other Factors across 23 European Countries. *Energy Research and Social Science*, *73*. https://doi.org/10.1016/j.erss.2020.101883

Maestre-Andrés, S., Drews, S., & van den Bergh, J. (2019). Perceived Fairness and Public Acceptability of Carbon Pricing: A Review of the Literature. *Climate Policy*, *19*(9). https://doi.org/10.1080/14693062.2019.1639490

Maier, E. (2012). Smart Mobility – Encouraging Sustainable Mobility Behaviour by Designing and Implementing Policies with Citizen Involvement. *JeDEM – EJournal of EDemocracy and Open Government*, *4*(1). https://doi.org/10.29379/jedem.v4i1.110

Marques, E. C. L. (2019). Notes on Networks, the State, and Public Policies. *Cadernos de Saude Publica*, *35*. https://doi.org/10.1590/0102-311x00002318

Martinez, M. C. V., & Rodríguez, M. C. M. (2020). Public Policies of Electronic Governance and Corruption in Mexico. *Public Policy and Administration*, *19*(3). https://doi.org/10.5755/J01.PPAA.19.3.27769

Marume, S. B. M. (2016). Public Policy and Factors Influencing Public Policy. *International Journal of Engineering Science Invention*, *5*(6).

Montenegro Martínez, G., Carmona Montoya, A., & Franco Giraldo, Á. (2020). Models for Public Health Policy Analysis Reported in Scientific Publications. In *Gaceta Sanitaria*. https://doi.org/10.1016/j.gaceta.2019.11.007

Nash, V., Bright, J., Margetts, H., & Lehdonvirta, V. (2017). Public Policy in the Platform Society. In *Policy and Internet* (Vol. 9, Issue 4). https://doi.org/10.1002/poi3.165

Naudé, W., & Dimitri, N. (2020). The Race for an Artificial General Intelligence: Implications for Public Policy. *AI and Society*, *35*(2). https://doi.org/10.1007/s00146-019-00887-x

Nowlin, M. C., Gupta, K., & Ripberger, J. T. (2020). Revenue Use and Public Support for a Carbon Tax. *Environmental Research Letters*, *15*(8). https://doi.org/10.1088/1748-9326/ab92c3

OECD. (2017). *OECD Transfer Pricing Guidelines for Multinational Enterprises and Tax Administrations 2017*. OECD Publications.

OECD. (2020). Foreign Direct Investment Flows in the Time of COVID-19. *Oecd.Org*, May 2020.

Oueslati, W. (2015). Growth and Welfare Effects of Environmental Tax Reform and Public Spending Policy. *Economic Modelling*, *45*. https://doi.org/10.1016/j.econmod.2014.10.040

Paes-Sousa, R., De Andrade Schramm, J. M., & Pereira Mendes, L. V. (2019). Fiscal Austerity and the Health Sector: The Cost of Adjustments. *Ciencia e Saude Coletiva*, *24*(12). https://doi.org/10.1590/1413-812320182412.23232019

Peres, M. F. P., Oliveira, A. B., Sarmento, E. M., Rocha-Filho, P. S., Peixoto, P. M., Kowacs, F., Goulart, A. C., & Benseñor, I. M. (2020). Public Policies in Headache Disorders: Needs and Possibilities. *Arquivos de Neuro-Psiquiatria*, *78*(1). https://doi.org/10.1590/0004-282X20190144

Porter, M. E. (2007). Clusters and Economic Policy: Aligning Public Policy with the New Economics of Competition. *Business*, November.

Prestianawati, S. A., Mulyaningsih, S., Manzilati, A., & Ashar, K. (2020). *Rethinking Tax Leakage: Is It the Impact of Public Policy Failure?* https://doi.org/10.2991/aebmr.k.200606.024

Rasmussen, K., & Callan, D. (2016). Schools of Public Policy and Executive Education: An Opportunity Missed? *Policy and Society*, *35*(4). https://doi.org/10.1016/j.polsoc.2016.12.002

Ruiz, J. C., Jurado, E. B., Moral, A. M., Uclés, D. F., & Viruel, M. J. M. (2017). Measuring the Social and Economic Impact of Public Policies on Entrepreneurship in Andalusia. *CIRIEC-Espana Revista de Economia Publica, Social y Cooperativa*, *1*(90).

Saleem, M., Prot, S., Anderson, C. A., & Lemieux, A. F. (2017). Exposure to Muslims in Media and Support for Public Policies Harming Muslims. *Communication Research*, *44*(6). https://doi.org/10.1177/0093650215619214

Scholvin, S., & Malamud, A. (2020). Is Brazil a Geoeconomic Node? Geography, Public Policy, and the Failure of Economic Integration in South America. *Brazilian Political Science Review*, *14*(2). https://doi.org/10.1590/1981-3821202000020004

Schwartz, M. (2019). Social and Economic Public Policy Goals and Their Impact on Defense Acquisition – A 2019 Update. *Defense Acquisition Research Journal*, *26*(3). https://doi.org/10.22594/dau.19-827.26.03

Snow, M. S. (1988). Telecommunications Literature. A Critical Review of the Economic, Technological and Public Policy Issues. *Telecommunications Policy*, *12*(2). https://doi.org/10.1016/0308-5961(88)90007-9

Sultana, A., Or Rashid, M. H., Akter Eva, S., & Sultana, A. (2020). Assessment of Relationship Among Regional Economic Development Policy, Urban Development Policy and Public Policy. *Sumerianz Journal of Economics and Finance*, *310*. https://doi.org/10.47752/sjef.310.171.177

Urwannachotima, N., Hanvoravongchai, P., Ansah, J. P., Prasertsom, P., & Koh, V. R. Y. (2020). Impact of Sugar-Sweetened Beverage Tax on Dental Caries: A

Simulation Analysis. *BMC Oral Health*, *20*(1). https://doi.org/10.1186/s12903-020-1061-5

Wright, A., Smith, K. E., & Hellowell, M. (2017). Policy Lessons from Health Taxes: A Systematic Review of Empirical Studies. In *BMC Public Health* (Vol. 17, Issue 1). https://doi.org/10.1186/s12889-017-4497-z

Zayats O.I. (2019). Category the Competitive Force of the Country. *Actual Problems of Economics*, *12*(222).

Hena Oak

Impact of Policy on Energy Efficiency: Case of the Indian Cement Industry

1. Introduction

In India, the industrial sector has been the largest consumer of energy, particularly primary energy. In 2019 this sector accounted for about 56 % of total energy consumption (Energy Statistics, 2019). A big part of this is non-renewable energy, because fossil fuel energy consumption as a percentage of total primary energy consumption has been rising steadily (Indicators, World Bank). The decadal average rose from 59 % in 1990–99 to 66 % in 2000–09 to 72 % in 2010–14. Of course, the figures are much smaller when compared to countries like Russian Federation, China and USA where the average for the period 2010–14 was 91 %, 88 % and 83 % respectively. Clearly, this is in contradiction with the goal of sustainable economic development. Therefore, a policy measure that can target to reduce energy intensity of the industrial sector will go a long way in helping the sector become more environment friendly.

There are some examples of initiatives taken for the industrial sector globally. Doris et al. (2009) highlights various federal, state, and local level initiatives taken in USA, like Green Energy Fund R&D Program, Pennsylvania Energy Development Authority Grants, Energy Improvement Loan Program, etc. Department of Energy Industrial Assessment Centers help industrial plants accomplish large-scale energy efficiency improvements. ASEAN Plan of Action for Energy Cooperation aims to increase the share of renewables to 23 % in total primary energy supply by 2025, and promote clean coal technologies (ASEAN Centre for Energy, 2015). Numerous energy efficiency action plans, minimum energy performance requirements for buildings, energy performance certificates, etc. have contributed substantially to save energy from buildings in the EU (Economidou et al., 2020). Some other examples include Italy's tradable White Certificate obligation scheme for the industry, Britain's Energy Company Obligation, etc. (Malinauskaite et al., 2019).

In the Indian case, Perform-Achieve-Trade or the PAT scheme was introduced in 2012 with the objective of reducing energy intensity of high energy consuming industries. This is because in India a bulk of the growth in fossil fuel consumption can be attributed to the industrial sector. Plants, also called designated consumers, with an annual energy consumption above a certain threshold from the industries identified under PAT cycle I, were given energy intensity reduction targets to be achieved within a specified time period. Failure to achieve the targets required the plant to buy tradable energy saving certificates to undertake production. Currently PAT is in its sixth cycle. It was introduced on a rolling basis from PAT cycle III onwards. New industries have been added and from the existing industries, along with the old plants, new ones have been included in the successive cycles.

One of the industries that has been a part of all the PAT cycles is the cement industry, with different number of designated consumers. The scheme has helped the industry become more energy proficient. If coal is taken as the representative fossil fuel, then data shows that since 2011–12 when PAT-I was introduced, year wise consumption of coal by the cement industry has been declining. The average energy intensity target has also declined in the successive PAT cycles I to IV from 0.088 toe per tonne[1] of cement to 0.072 toe per tonne of cement. It increased briefly under PAT-V to 0.096 toe per tonne of cement, but fell substantially under PAT-VI to 0.021 toe per tonne of cement. Within a given cycle, there exists inter-firm differences. There are also differences in the energy efficiency performance among the PAT identified firms and the rest of the firms from the cement industry.

The objective of the chapter is to calculate energy efficiency scores using data envelopment analysis (DEA). The two basic DEA models used in the study are radial models given by Charnes Cooper and Rhodes (CCR model) and Banker Charnes and Cooper (BCC model). Efficiency scores calculated from the two models are then used to estimate scale efficiency of the firms. Results show that firms common to PAT-I, II and VI are large sized firms, majorly established before 1980 with low capacity utilization. The energy efficiency scores do not show any consistent trend over the thirteen year period. But on an average, firms not identified under any of the PAT cycles show higher efficiency scores, before PAT-I was implemented, and also during the course of the various PAT cycles. In general, for all the cement firms, pure technical inefficiency was the main cause behind overall technical inefficiency. In particular, within the designated consumers, both managerial and scale inefficiency were equally responsible for low scores.

---

1 Author's calculations are based on official figures published in Gazette of India, various years.

2. Econometric Methodology

Energy efficiency scores are calculated using two input-oriented DEA models, viz., CCR and BCC models for 47 cement firms for the sample period 2010 to 2022. DEA is a non-parametric method that is used to gauge the efficiency of homogeneous units by placing them on a frontier, as they convert one or more inputs into the final output. The homogeneous units are called decision making units or DMUs. The input-oriented model minimizes the inputs used to produce the final output, while keeping the output constant. Here, a single input is considered, viz., power and fuel expenditure in millions of rupees incurred by the cement firms because the objective is to analyse the energy efficiency of firms. The output is given by sale of goods in millions of rupees, where goods refers to cement. The following equations describe the CCR model for the jth cement firm, for j=1,….,47 (Cooper et. al., 2007):.

$$Minimize\ \theta_{CCR}$$

$$subject\ to\ \theta_{CCR} x_j - X\lambda \geq 0, Y\lambda \geq y_j, \lambda \geq 0$$

where X and Y are input and output data matrices respectively, and λ is the non-negativity vector. The solution to the above equations gives the optimal value θ^*_{CCR}. This value is used to maximize the sum of input and output slacks. If the optimal solution obtained as $\left(\theta^*_{CCR}, \lambda^*, s^{-*}, s^{+*}\right)$ satisfies the conditions $\theta^*_{CCR} = 1$ and $\left(s^{-*} = 0, s^{+*} = 0\right)$ where s^{-*} and s^{+*} are the input and output slack values, then the jth DMU is said to be CCR efficient. If only the first condition is met, i.e., $\theta^*_{CCR} = 1$ then the DMU is said to meet the weak efficiency condition. If both the conditions are satisfied, then the jth DMU satisfies the Pareto-Koopmans strong efficiency condition, which implies that it is not possible to improve any input or output without worsening some other input or output. The BCC model follows the same steps with the added constraint of $\lambda_j = 1$. The CCR and BCC models make the assumption of constant and variable returns to scale respectively. Results from the CCR model gives the overall technical efficiency and the BCC model gives the pure technical efficiency of the firm. Scale efficiency is calculated as the ratio of overall technical efficiency and pure technical efficiency, to check if the jth firm is operating at the optimal size.

Data on all the variables has been collected from the ProwessIQ database provided by Centre for Monitoring Indian Economy Private Limited (CMIE).

3. Results and Discussion

An efficiency score gives the location of the jth DMU on the efficiency frontier. If $\theta^{*}_{CCR} = 1$ then the jth DMU will be located on the frontier and will exhibit overall technical efficiency with respect to energy consumption. If $\theta^{*}_{CCR} < 1$ then the jth DMU will be located inside the frontier, and will be technically inefficient. This inefficiency can arise due to managerial inefficacy that is shown by the values of the BCC model, and inappropriate size of operation that is indicated by scale efficiency. Table 1 gives the descriptive statistics for the three types of inefficiencies w.r.t. energy use.

Table 1. Descriptive statistics

	Industry average					PAT firms					Remaining firms				
Variable	**Obs**	**Mean**	**Std. Dev.**	**Min**	**Max**	**Obs**	**Mean**	**Std. Dev.**	**Min**	**Max**	**Obs**	**Mean**	**Std. Dev.**	**Min**	**Max**
Overall technical efficiency	525	0.186	0.189	0.001	1	322	0.170	0.154	0.001	1	203	0.212	0.232	0.001	1
Pure technical efficiency	525	0.392	0.320	0.001	1	322	0.440	0.323	0.001	1	203	0.315	0.299	0.002	1
Scale efficiency	525	0.592	0.314	0.002	1	322	0.521	0.326	0.002	1	203	0.706	0.258	0.048	1

Table 1 shows that the average overall technical efficiency for 47 firms w.r.t energy use is 0.186, which implies an overall technical inefficiency of 81.4 %. 61 % of this inefficiency is due to managerial incompetence, while the remaining is due to inappropriate scale of operation. Since the average value of pure technical efficiency is smaller than scale efficiency, it implies that a greater part of the overall technical inefficiency can be explained by managerial inefficiency. Categorizing the industry into PAT identified firms and remaining firms shows the average technical efficiency to be lower for the former. Overall technical inefficiency of 83 % in the PAT firms and 78.8 % in the remaining firms is mainly attributable to pure technical inefficiency. Table 2 below gives a more detailed analysis of the energy efficiency scores based on the CCR model for 47 cement firms for the period 2010 to 2022.

Table 2. Overall technical efficiency of cement firms as per CCR model

DMU	2010	2011	2012	2013	2014	2015	2016	2017	2018	2019	2020	2021	2022
Firms identified under PAT Cycles I and II													
ACC Ltd.	0.088	0.245	0.156	0.111	0.262	0.002	0.131	0.290	0.198	0.227	0.062	0.197	0.156
Ambuja Cements	0.086	0.226	0.157	0.101	0.259	0.002	0.128	0.289	0.191	0.204	0.056	0.193	0.137
Anjani Portland	0.062	0.156	0.116	0.067	0.147	0.001	0.103	0.193	0.126	0.136	0.041	0.148	0.097
Birla Corporation	0.098	0.244	0.158	0.103	0.231	0.002	0.118	0.265	0.171	0.225	0.068	0.230	0.164
Chettinad Cement	0.078	0.188	0.134	0.091	0.211	0.001	0.126	0.274	0.146	0.154	0.053	0.178	0.116
Deccan Cements	0.049	0.176	0.130	0.076	0.179	0.002	0.124	0.208	0.134	0.134	0.035	0.141	0.124
Gujarat Sidhee	0.047	0.110	0.075	0.058	0.134	0.001	0.070	0.135	0.105	0.114	0.041	0.126	0.080
Heidelberg Cement	0.092	0.231	0.141	0.089	0.209	0.001	0.103	0.234	0.168	0.211	0.063	0.171	0.124
India Cements	0.064	0.176	0.137	0.086	0.194	0.001	0.123	0.274	0.158	0.151	0.045	0.157	0.102
JK Cement	0.087	0.200	0.146	0.101	0.246	0.002	0.136	0.353	0.205	0.249	0.079	0.223	0.167
JK Lakshmi	0.089	0.176	0.152	0.121	0.279	0.002	0.131	0.289	0.169	0.198	0.062	0.222	0.167
JSW Cement	0.187	0.588	0.428	0.073	0.184	0.002	0.163	0.326	0.217	0.281	0.090	0.338	0.232
KCP	0.102	0.223	0.136	0.083	0.220	0.002	0.166	0.251	0.151	0.175	0.047	0.183	0.120
Kesoram Industries	0.127	0.388	0.270	0.151	0.350	0.029	1.000	0.339	1.000	1.000	1.000	0.159	0.110
Malabar Cements	0.064	0.478	0.383	0.174	0.393	1.000	0.281	0.400	0.103	0.336	0.086	0.315	0.281
Mangalam Cement	0.054	0.176	0.147	0.086	0.233	0.001	0.133	0.266	0.145	0.148	0.047	0.175	0.129
Meghalaya Cements	0.074	0.194	0.141	0.072	0.201	0.002	0.102	0.238	0.177	0.229	0.044	0.149	0.143
My Home Inds. Pvt.	0.075	0.232	0.171	1.000	0.204	0.001	0.095	0.199	0.154	0.171	0.053	0.227	0.160
Penna Cement	0.228	0.581	0.188	0.088	NA	NA	NA	NA	NA	0.182	0.052	0.160	0.107
Prism Johnson	0.116	0.388	0.220	0.147	NA	NA	NA	NA	NA	0.305	0.088	0.283	0.230

(Continued)

Table 2. Continued

DMU	2010	2011	2012	2013	2014	2015	2016	2017	2018	2019	2020	2021	2022
Rain Cements	1.000	0.277	0.148	0.074	NA	NA	NA	NA	NA	0.163	0.054	0.173	0.152
Ramco Cements	0.078	0.199	0.168	0.113	NA	NA	NA	NA	NA	0.227	0.096	0.373	0.229
Sagar Cements	0.052	0.158	0.134	0.074	NA	NA	NA	NA	NA	0.166	0.050	0.206	0.115
Sanghi Industries	0.058	0.154	0.120	0.097	NA	NA	NA	NA	NA	0.168	0.053	0.164	0.098
Saurashtra Cement	0.065	0.130	0.095	0.080	NA	NA	NA	NA	NA	0.137	0.048	0.167	0.098
Shree Cement	0.100	0.187	0.130	0.074	NA	NA	NA	NA	NA	0.193	0.066	0.249	0.159
Shree Digvijay	0.050	0.116	0.091	0.063	NA	NA	NA	NA	NA	0.133	0.043	0.148	0.106
Ultratech Cement	0.086	0.225	0.159	0.116	NA	NA	NA	NA	NA	0.200	0.062	0.211	0.150
Average of PAT firms	**0.120**	**0.244**	**0.165**	**0.127**	**0.230**	**0.059**	**0.180**	**0.268**	**0.207**	**0.222**	**0.092**	**0.202**	**0.145**
Remaining firms													
Barak Valley	0.075	0.203	0.116	0.073	0.203	0.001	0.070	0.214	0.139	0.145	0.050	0.144	0.130
Bhilai Jaypee	0.034	0.104	0.131	0.096	0.199	0.001	0.081	0.078	0.068	0.078	0.021	0.074	0.048
Burnpur Cement	0.153	0.405	0.394	0.230	0.476	0.003	0.268	0.399	0.499	0.751	0.215	0.788	0.725
Calcom Cement	0.346	0.591	0.481	0.393	1.000	0.007	0.282	0.270	0.176	0.212	0.055	0.225	0.221
Cement Corpn. Of India	0.054	0.141	0.086	0.053	0.125	0.001	0.064	0.112	0.080	0.089	0.024	0.091	0.071
Cochin Cements	0.335	1.000	1.000	0.545	0.970	0.005	0.423	1.000	0.645	0.544	0.120	0.917	0.861
Greygold Cements	0.152	0.408	0.377	0.132	0.313	0.003	0.197	0.368	0.278	0.349	0.098	0.378	0.328
Hemadri Cements	0.038	0.121	0.086	0.044	0.269	0.002	0.145	0.118	0.076	0.089	0.028	0.092	0.071
Hills Cement Co.	0.094	0.122	0.134	0.093	0.130	0.001	0.085	0.165	0.141	0.230	0.099	0.252	0.194
Kakatiya Cement	0.061	0.090	0.088	0.055	0.098	0.001	0.106	0.293	0.241	0.161	0.038	0.131	0.117
Keerthi Industries	0.045	0.159	0.120	0.058	0.130	0.001	0.087	0.154	0.102	0.115	0.032	0.117	0.104
NCL Industries	0.087	0.220	0.146	0.080	0.169	0.001	0.115	0.220	0.159	0.141	0.056	0.180	0.134
Parasakti Cement	0.056	0.175	0.133	0.072	NA	NA	NA	NA	NA	NA	0.038	0.138	0.101

Shiva Cement	0.120	0.349	0.191	0.246	NA	NA	NA	NA	NA	0.097	0.025	0.071	0.061
Shri Keshav Cements & Infra	0.033	0.247	0.210	0.118	NA	NA	NA	NA	NA	0.858	0.326	1.000	1.000
Shristi Cement	0.108	0.326	0.147	0.071	NA	NA	NA	NA	NA	0.925	0.101	0.270	0.142
Sri Chakra Cement	0.074	0.174	0.140	0.067	NA	NA	NA	NA	NA	0.123	0.036	0.108	0.090
Star Cement	0.071	0.175	0.144	0.071	NA	NA	NA	NA	NA	0.576	0.149	0.537	0.450
Average of non-PAT firms	**0.108**	**0.278**	**0.229**	**0.139**	**0.340**	**0.002**	**0.160**	**0.282**	**0.217**	**0.322**	**0.084**	**0.306**	**0.269**
Overall average	**0.114**	**0.255**	**0.189**	**0.130**	**0.274**	**0.036**	**0.172**	**0.274**	**0.211**	**0.257**	**0.088**	**0.241**	**0.192**

Source: Author's own calculations using deaR: Data Envelopment Analysis in R

Note: NA refers to data not available on power & fuel expenditure and/or sales to calculate efficiency scores.

For all the years, most firms lie below the energy efficiency frontier, thus indicating technical inefficiency. When PAT identified firms are considered separately, their average scores are found to be less than that of the non-PAT identified firms, as seen in Figure 1 below, thereby explaining their inclusion in the scheme. But the average energy efficiency scores of the firms identified under the PAT scheme did not show any consistent trend over the thirteen-year period.

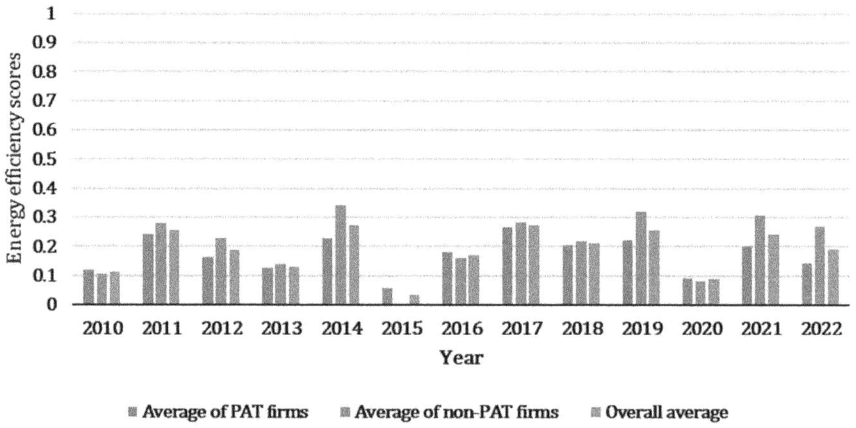

Figure 1. Average overall technical efficiency scores for PAT and non-PAT firms
Source: Author's own calculations.

The non-PAT firms have consistently reported higher scores than the PAT firms, both when cycles I and II were in progress and even after the cycles ended. The only exceptional years were 2016 and 2020 when PAT-I and II had just ended respectively. In fact the data on power and fuel expenditure shows that for the PAT firms there was a decline in 2016 and 2020 as compared to the previous years, that can explain the slightly improved efficiency scores (Figure 2 below).

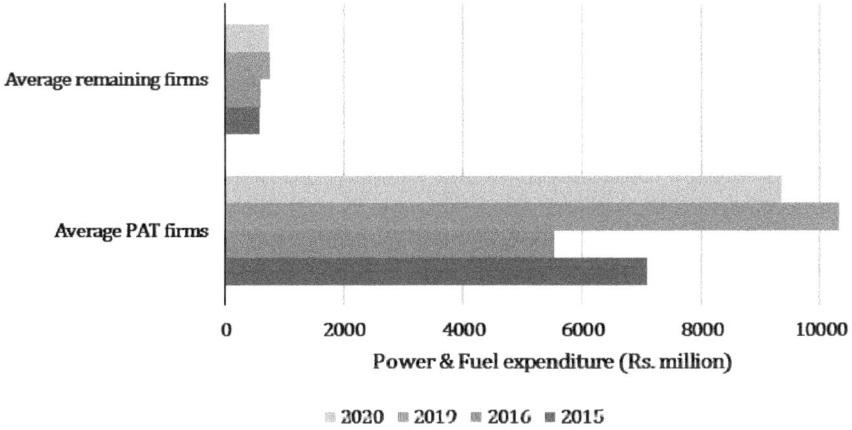

Figure 2. Average power and fuel expenditure for PAT and non-PAT firms.
Source: Author's own calculations using data from ProwessIQ database.

As per Figure 2 above, the PAT identified firms recorded a fall in the power and fuel expenditure for two specific years after cycles I and II ended. The remaining firms did not show any change between the subsequent years. PAT scheme involves a penalty that comes in the form of mandatory purchase of energy saving certificates by the defaulting firms in order to continue with production. That can be one of the possible reasons for a dip in expenditure related to energy consumption at the end of the target period. Trends in compound annual growth rate shows that the power and fuel expenditure of the PAT identified firms was 19 % and the other firms was 23 % before the implementation of PAT-I. During the period 2013–2019 when both the PAT cycles were in operation, the CAGR was 5.7 % and 5.2 % respectively. After PAT Cycle II ended, CAGR for the PAT firms became 12 % between 2020–2022 and it was 8.8 % for the remaining firms. The CAGR in sales for the PAT identified firms during these sub-periods was 14 %, 4 % and 7.1 %, while for the remaining firms it was 25 %, 8 %, and 10 % respectively. The higher CAGR for power and fuel expenditure as compared to sales for the PAT firms shows that in general these firms remained more inefficient than the non-PAT identified firms.

PAT cycles I and II mostly identified large sized firms for implementation of the scheme. The Prowess IQ database arranges firms in different decile groups based on their total income and total assets. Out of the 29 firms identified under the two PAT cycles in this sample, 38 % are from deciles 1 and 2 together. Decile 1 comprises of the largest 10 % of the firms, and decile 2 has the next largest 10 % of the firms, while decile 10 has the smallest 10 % of the firms. Firms that have higher income and assets are also likely to have high capacity. For the period 2016–2017 to 2019–2020, most of the firms that belong to deciles 1 and 2 have high capacity, except for Barak Valley Cement, Hemadri Cement Limited, Kakatiya Cement & Sugar Industries Limited, and Sri Chakra Cements who have a capacity of less than one million tonne of production annually. But high production capacity does not necessarily translate into high-capacity utilization. Capacity utilization by firms with a capacity of less than 9 million tonnes[2] per annum is much higher than the firms with capacity of more than 9 million tonnes. This implies that the relatively small firms in terms of capacity use their resources more efficiently than the large firms. For example, UltraTech Cement Limited has the highest capacity in the sample, and it is also one of the top cement producers in the country. But the capacity utilization is approximately 41 % in the sample period. In the sample, all the firms that have an average capacity of more than 9 million tonnes, are also PAT identified firms for cycles I and II.

The CCR model captures the overall technical efficiency of the cement firms, which can be further divided into pure technical efficiency and scale efficiency. Pure technical efficiency given by the BCC model, can be regarded as an index to capture managerial efficiency in organizing inputs in the production process. Scale efficiency indicates if the firms are operating at their optimal size. Table 3 gives the results from the BCC model.

2 The average capacity of the cement firms for the period 2016–17 to 2019–20 is between 8.26 and 9.70 million tonnes, as per calculations. Therefore 9 million tonnes is taken as the benchmark capacity.

Table 3. Pure technical efficiency of cement firms as per BCC model

DMU	2010	2011	2012	2013	2014	2015	2016	2017	2018	2019	2020	2021	2022
Firms identified under PAT Cycles I and II													
ACC	1.000	0.869	0.805	0.890	1.000	1.000	1.000	1.000	1.000	1.000	0.854	0.733	0.853
Ambuja Cements	0.931	0.791	0.788	0.795	0.953	0.882	0.889	0.978	0.896	0.846	0.710	0.673	0.727
Anjani Portland	0.063	0.256	0.323	0.072	0.247	0.001	0.110	0.507	0.130	0.137	0.048	0.241	0.180
Birla Corporation	0.608	0.516	0.574	0.459	0.651	0.051	0.113	0.752	0.200	0.617	0.553	0.580	0.618
Chettinad Cement	0.342	0.340	0.484	0.390	0.587	0.047	0.126	0.775	0.146	0.223	0.204	0.428	0.401
Deccan Cements	0.050	0.297	0.426	0.078	0.390	0.026	0.128	0.564	0.137	0.135	0.038	0.251	0.257
Gujarat Sidhee	0.047	0.185	0.236	0.060	0.284	0.015	0.073	0.362	0.107	0.114	0.044	0.218	0.164
Heidelberg Cement	0.237	0.396	0.492	0.089	0.563	0.048	0.104	0.659	0.169	0.211	0.063	0.343	0.274
India Cements	0.482	0.424	0.505	0.534	0.552	0.052	0.197	0.838	0.392	0.451	0.354	0.389	0.366
JK Cement	0.522	0.422	0.531	0.503	0.693	0.060	0.136	1.000	0.450	0.771	0.732	0.586	0.703
JK Lakshmi	0.426	0.302	0.545	0.395	0.771	0.060	0.131	0.818	0.169	0.458	0.411	0.554	0.628
JSW Cement	0.191	0.941	1.000	0.075	0.454	0.042	0.165	0.913	0.218	0.287	0.254	0.793	0.783
KCP	0.102	0.373	0.450	0.084	0.529	0.034	0.171	0.694	0.152	0.175	0.049	0.337	0.261
Kesoram Industries	1.000	1.000	1.000	1.000	1.000	1.000	1.000	0.962	1.000	1.000	1.000	0.338	0.350
Malabar Cements	0.064	0.790	0.999	0.190	0.545	1.000	0.298	1.000	0.108	0.338	0.109	0.486	0.462
Mangalam Cement	0.054	0.299	0.490	0.087	0.574	0.039	0.136	0.739	0.146	0.148	0.048	0.322	0.281
Meghalaya Cements	0.074	0.322	0.375	0.076	0.371	0.009	0.109	0.620	0.181	0.230	0.048	0.255	0.281
My Home Inds. Pvt.	0.143	0.398	0.601	1.000	0.548	0.039	0.096	0.558	0.154	0.171	0.054	0.421	0.352
Penna Cement	1.000	1.000	0.675	0.273	NA	NA	NA	NA	NA	0.182	0.053	0.341	0.311
Prism Johnson	0.696	0.921	0.811	0.918	NA	NA	NA	NA	NA	1.000	0.799	0.729	0.907

(Continued)

Table 3. Continued

DMU	2010	2011	2012	2013	2014	2015	2016	2017	2018	2019	2020	2021	2022
Rain Cements	1.000	0.475	0.512	0.075	NA	NA	NA	NA	NA	0.164	0.056	0.314	0.330
Ramco Cements	0.536	0.445	0.617	0.653	NA	NA	NA	NA	NA	0.661	1.000	1.000	1.000
Sagar Cements	0.052	0.268	0.449	0.075	NA	NA	NA	NA	NA	0.166	0.052	0.381	0.250
Sanghi Industries	0.058	0.264	0.418	0.098	NA	NA	NA	NA	NA	0.168	0.056	0.297	0.209
Saurashtra Cement	0.065	0.220	0.294	0.083	NA	NA	NA	NA	NA	0.137	0.052	0.295	0.202
Shree Cement	0.741	0.446	0.481	0.467	NA	NA	NA	NA	NA	0.805	0.850	0.939	0.862
Shree Digvijay	0.051	0.193	0.267	0.066	NA	NA	NA	NA	NA	0.133	0.048	0.254	0.214
Ultratech Cement	0.932	1.000	1.000	1.000	NA	NA	NA	NA	NA	1.000	1.000	1.000	1.000
Average of PAT firms	**0.410**	**0.505**	**0.577**	**0.374**	**0.595**	**0.245**	**0.277**	**0.763**	**0.320**	**0.419**	**0.341**	**0.482**	**0.472**
Remaining firms													
Barak Valley	0.076	0.309	0.234	0.090	0.204	0.003	0.086	0.502	0.149	0.146	0.069	0.177	0.173
Bhilai Jaypee	0.035	0.175	0.458	0.101	0.490	0.025	0.085	0.167	0.072	0.078	0.026	0.117	0.071
Burnpur Cement	0.163	0.442	0.571	0.295	0.478	0.020	0.336	0.866	0.608	0.762	0.351	1.000	1.000
Calcom Cement	1.000	0.759	0.740	0.494	1.000	0.008	0.301	0.736	0.179	0.212	0.058	0.405	0.469
Cement Corpn. Of India Ltd.	0.054	0.237	0.252	0.057	0.239	0.011	0.067	0.295	0.083	0.090	0.030	0.152	0.133
Cochin Cements	0.364	1.000	1.000	1.000	1.000	0.085	1.000	1.000	1.000	1.000	1.000	1.000	1.000
Greygold Cements	0.166	0.500	0.407	0.307	0.321	0.022	0.314	0.595	0.375	0.375	0.425	0.792	0.702
Hemadri Cements	0.039	0.169	0.170	0.058	0.271	0.006	0.180	0.267	0.086	0.090	0.053	0.105	0.072
Hills Cement	0.113	0.161	0.271	0.131	0.254	0.006	0.108	0.374	0.156	0.232	0.122	0.391	0.325
Kakatiya Cement	0.062	0.138	0.198	0.062	0.098	0.002	0.118	0.735	0.258	0.163	0.053	0.158	0.150
Keerthi Industries	0.047	0.241	0.277	0.070	0.131	0.002	0.097	0.379	0.108	0.116	0.043	0.172	0.164
NCL Industries	0.088	0.371	0.479	0.083	0.375	0.029	0.118	0.610	0.160	0.142	0.057	0.332	0.294
Parasakti Cement	0.057	0.295	0.425	0.075	NA	NA	NA	NA	NA	NA	0.045	0.230	0.195

DMU	2010	2011	2012	2013	2014	2015	2016	2017	2018	2019	2020	2021	2022
Shiva Cement	0.126	0.444	0.208	0.347	NA	NA	NA	NA	NA	0.103	0.075	0.141	0.634
Shri Keshav Cements & Infra	0.038	0.286	0.238	0.180	NA	NA	NA	NA	NA	0.889	0.728	1.000	1.000
Shristi Cement	0.120	0.670	0.456	0.261	NA	NA	NA	NA	NA	1.000	0.264	0.680	0.757
Sri Chakra Cement	0.075	0.266	0.308	0.079	NA	NA	NA	NA	NA	0.124	0.051	0.148	0.133
Star Cement	0.071	0.294	0.416	0.075	NA	NA	NA	NA	NA	0.576	0.149	1.000	1.000
Average of non-PAT firms	**0.150**	**0.375**	**0.395**	**0.209**	**0.405**	**0.018**	**0.234**	**0.544**	**0.269**	**0.359**	**0.200**	**0.444**	**0.460**
Overall average	**0.307**	**0.451**	**0.505**	**0.306**	**0.519**	**0.154**	**0.260**	**0.676**	**0.300**	**0.391**	**0.281**	**0.464**	**0.463**

The energy efficiency scores as per the BCC model shows that the pure technical efficiency of the PAT firms is higher than the non-PAT firms for all the years. But within the PAT firms, for most of the years, there are higher number of firms with an efficiency score of less than the average for that year. Table 4 reports the scale efficiency of the 47 cement firms.

Table 4. Scale efficiency of cement firms

DMU	2010	2011	2012	2013	2014	2015	2016	2017	2018	2019	2020	2021	2022
Firms identified under PAT Cycles I and II													
ACC	0.088	0.282	0.193	0.125	0.262	0.002	0.131	0.290	0.198	0.227	0.072	0.268	0.182
Ambuja Cements	0.092	0.286	0.200	0.127	0.271	0.002	0.144	0.295	0.214	0.241	0.079	0.287	0.189
Anjani Portland	0.989	0.610	0.359	0.931	0.596	0.897	0.931	0.380	0.972	0.996	0.852	0.616	0.537
Birla Corporation	0.162	0.472	0.275	0.224	0.355	0.030	0.999	0.353	0.856	0.364	0.122	0.396	0.265
Chettinad Cement	0.227	0.553	0.276	0.234	0.360	0.030	0.997	0.354	0.999	0.691	0.263	0.417	0.289
Deccan Cements	0.997	0.593	0.305	0.975	0.460	0.058	0.972	0.368	0.983	0.998	0.916	0.561	0.484
Gujarat Sidhee	1.000	0.594	0.319	0.962	0.471	0.060	0.959	0.372	0.982	0.998	0.922	0.577	0.490
Heidelberg Cement	0.390	0.584	0.287	0.995	0.371	0.031	0.992	0.355	0.997	1.000	1.000	0.498	0.451
India Cements	0.133	0.414	0.271	0.161	0.351	0.029	0.624	0.327	0.403	0.335	0.128	0.404	0.280
JK Cement	0.166	0.474	0.274	0.201	0.356	0.029	1.000	0.353	0.456	0.323	0.108	0.381	0.238
JK Lakshmi	0.210	0.581	0.278	0.306	0.362	0.031	0.997	0.353	1.000	0.432	0.150	0.401	0.265
JSW Cement	0.979	0.624	0.428	0.978	0.404	0.038	0.988	0.357	0.996	0.981	0.354	0.426	0.297
KCP	0.997	0.596	0.303	0.983	0.415	0.048	0.975	0.361	0.992	0.999	0.958	0.544	0.459
Kesoram Industries	0.127	0.388	0.270	0.151	0.350	0.029	1.000	0.353	1.000	1.000	1.000	0.469	0.315
Malabar Cements	0.992	0.605	0.383	0.916	0.720	1.000	0.944	0.400	0.953	0.994	0.787	0.648	0.607
Mangalam Cement	0.999	0.589	0.300	0.983	0.405	0.038	0.980	0.360	0.993	0.999	0.975	0.544	0.458
Meghalaya Cements	0.996	0.600	0.375	0.939	0.541	0.176	0.937	0.383	0.976	0.997	0.907	0.584	0.509
My Home Inds. Pvt.	0.525	0.583	0.285	1.000	0.372	0.034	0.988	0.357	0.996	1.000	0.986	0.539	0.454
Penna Cement	0.228	0.581	0.278	0.323	NA	NA	NA	NA	NA	1.000	0.997	0.470	0.344
Prism Johnson	0.166	0.421	0.271	0.160	NA	NA	NA	NA	NA	0.305	0.110	0.389	0.254
Rain Cements	1.000	0.584	0.290	0.991	NA	NA	NA	NA	NA	0.999	0.966	0.550	0.462

(*Continued*)

Table 4. Continued

DMU	2010	2011	2012	2013	2014	2015	2016	2017	2018	2019	2020	2021	2022
Ramco Cements	0.146	0.447	0.273	0.173	NA	NA	NA	NA	NA	0.343	0.096	0.373	0.229
Sagar Cements	0.998	0.589	0.298	0.979	NA	NA	NA	NA	NA	0.999	0.952	0.543	0.459
Sanghi Industries	1.000	0.584	0.288	0.993	NA	NA	NA	NA	NA	0.999	0.956	0.553	0.468
Saurashtra Cement	0.999	0.593	0.323	0.968	NA	NA	NA	NA	NA	0.998	0.928	0.565	0.484
Shree Cement	0.135	0.419	0.270	0.159	NA	NA	NA	NA	NA	0.240	0.078	0.266	0.185
Shree Digvijay	0.995	0.598	0.341	0.954	NA	NA	NA	NA	NA	0.997	0.899	0.584	0.498
Ultratech Cement	0.092	0.225	0.159	0.116	NA	NA	NA	NA	NA	0.200	0.062	0.211	0.150
Average of PAT firms	**0.565**	**0.517**	**0.292**	**0.607**	**0.412**	**0.142**	**0.864**	**0.354**	**0.831**	**0.738**	**0.594**	**0.466**	**0.368**
Remaining firms													
Barak Valley	0.985	0.659	0.498	0.808	0.996	0.427	0.816	0.427	0.930	0.989	0.718	0.812	0.749
Bhilai Jaypee	0.971	0.594	0.287	0.957	0.406	0.048	0.951	0.465	0.947	0.995	0.800	0.631	0.682
Burnpur Cement	0.938	0.918	0.691	0.779	0.996	0.161	0.799	0.460	0.821	0.986	0.614	0.788	0.725
Calcom Cement	0.346	0.779	0.650	0.794	1.000	0.864	0.940	0.367	0.986	0.998	0.946	0.555	0.470
Cement Corpn. Of India Ltd.	0.997	0.597	0.341	0.933	0.521	0.080	0.950	0.379	0.968	0.995	0.809	0.600	0.536
Cochin Cements	0.921	1.000	1.000	0.545	0.970	0.059	0.423	1.000	0.645	0.544	0.120	0.917	0.861
Greygold Cements	0.916	0.815	0.926	0.432	0.974	0.127	0.628	0.619	0.742	0.929	0.230	0.477	0.467
Hemadri Cements	0.963	0.716	0.506	0.755	0.993	0.316	0.808	0.444	0.879	0.979	0.525	0.874	0.982
Hills Cement	0.830	0.757	0.494	0.706	0.513	0.193	0.791	0.440	0.902	0.992	0.812	0.645	0.596
Kakatiya Cement	0.986	0.655	0.441	0.882	0.999	0.486	0.898	0.398	0.934	0.986	0.715	0.827	0.779
Keerthi Industries	0.976	0.658	0.432	0.826	0.998	0.569	0.896	0.405	0.944	0.992	0.738	0.680	0.635
NCL Industries	0.995	0.592	0.306	0.965	0.451	0.049	0.976	0.360	0.993	0.999	0.974	0.542	0.457
Parasakti Cement	0.997	0.595	0.314	0.960	NA	NA	NA	NA	NA	NA	0.848	0.601	0.517
Shiva Cement	0.952	0.786	0.916	0.710	NA	NA	NA	NA	NA	0.937	0.335	0.505	0.095

Shri Keshav Cements & Infra	0.891	0.865	0.882	0.654	NA	NA	NA	NA	NA	0.965	0.447	1.000	1.000
Shristi Cement	0.902	0.486	0.323	0.271	NA	NA	NA	NA	NA	0.925	0.383	0.397	0.187
Sri Chakra Cement	0.987	0.653	0.454	0.855	NA	NA	NA	NA	NA	0.992	0.696	0.733	0.679
Star Cement	0.996	0.597	0.347	0.945	NA	NA	NA	NA	NA	1.000	0.994	0.537	0.450
Average of non-PAT firms	**0.919**	**0.707**	**0.545**	**0.765**	**0.818**	**0.282**	**0.823**	**0.480**	**0.891**	**0.953**	**0.650**	**0.673**	**0.604**
Overall average	**0.695**	**0.591**	**0.389**	**0.667**	**0.575**	**0.198**	**0.848**	**0.404**	**0.855**	**0.823**	**0.624**	**0.546**	**0.460**

Results from Tables 2, 3 and 4 are analyzed for years 2010 which is the beginning of the sample period, 2013 which is the first year of implementation of PAT-I, 2019 which is the last year of PAT-II and 2022 which is the year when PAT-VI is ongoing. In 2010 the overall technical efficiency ranged from 0.03341 to 1. Pure technical efficiency for 32 firms was lower than scale efficiency, implying that managerial inefficiency in organizing energy input in the best possible way was the dominant reason for explain inefficiency. 15 out of the 32 firms were PAT firms and 75 % to 95 % of technical inefficiency for these firms can be explained due to pure technical inefficiency. For 14 firms, out of which 13 were PAT firms, inappropriate scale of operation was the primary reason behind technical inefficiency. Scale efficiency is less than 1 for all the firms, indicating a need to increase capacity utilization in order to benefit from economies of large-scale production. In 2013, the results did not change much. In 2019, out of 33 firms, 18 were PAT firms where pure technical efficiency was less than scale efficiency. 66 % to 89 % of the technical inefficiency for these firms can be explained due to pure technical inefficiency. Finally, in 2022, out of a total of 27 firms where managerial inefficiency was mainly responsible for technical inefficiency, 16 were PAT firms. 54 % to 84 % of the inefficiency in energy use can be explained by inability to organize inputs efficiently. While there does not exist any clear trend in the share of pure technical and scale inefficiency in explaining overall inefficiency, the minimum value for overall inefficiency increased from 0.033 in 2010 to 0.044 in 2013 to 0.078 in 2019, before dropping to 0.048 in 2022. The upward trend in the three years prior to 2022 can be attributed to the PAT cycles.

The impact of PAT can also differ based on firm size. The two reference years are 2012 and 2020 as they are the years immediately preceding PAT-I and succeeding PAT-II. Figure 3 below gives the energy efficiency scores for the two years as per the CCR model.

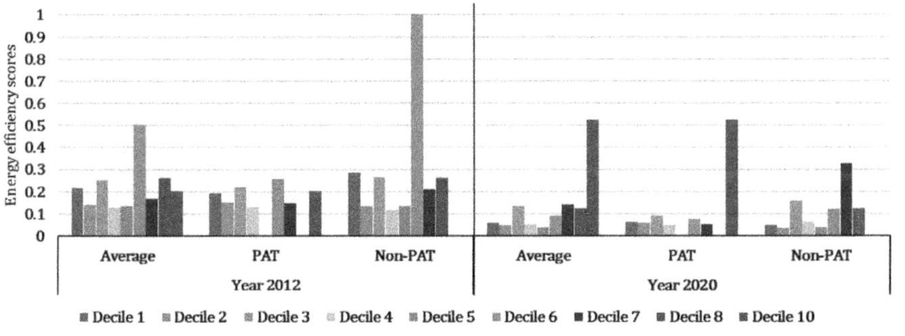

Figure 3. Overall technical efficiency scores as per size for PAT & non-PAT firms.
Note: Some deciles may not have both categories of firms.

In 2012, firms that lie in decile 6 recorded the highest energy efficiency score, followed by firms in decile 8. Year 2020 recorded a fall in the energy efficiency scores for all deciles. But here too the small sized firms had higher scores than the large sized firms. Firms in decile 10 had the highest efficiency scores on an average, followed by decile 7. This shows that the small sized firms had a higher overall technical efficiency than the large sized firms in both years. While comparing between the firms identified by the PAT scheme in cycles I and II, and the remaining firms, the results show that for every decile in the year 2012, firms that later became a part of PAT cycles I and II had lower energy efficiency scores than the other firms. This explains why these firms became a part of the PAT scheme. By the time the second cycle ended in 2020, large sized PAT identified cement firms that were a part of deciles 1 and 2, had higher energy efficiency scores than the non-PAT identified firms from the same size group. But for the small sized firms from deciles 6 and 7, the non-PAT firms recorded higher scores than the PAT firms. Figure 4 below breaks down the average into pure technical efficiency and scale efficiency.

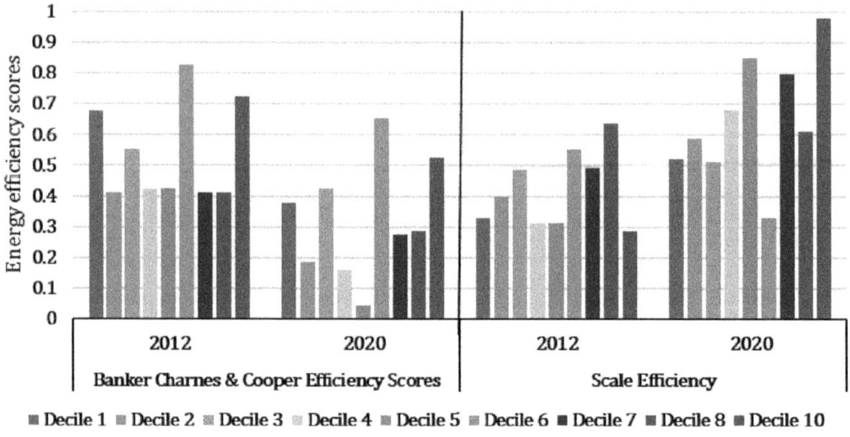

Figure 4. Average BCC efficiency scores and scale efficiency scores.
Note: Some deciles may not have both categories of firms.

Figure 4 shows that in 2012 all the firms recorded higher pure technical efficiency scores than scale efficiency, except for firms in deciles 7 and 8. A greater proportion of overall technical inefficiency arose because these firms were not fully utilizing their capacity. Scale inefficiency was higher for firms in deciles 1 and 2, than the smaller deciles, implying greater untapped potential in the large sized firms. But in 2020, for all the firms except decile 6, managerial inefficiency contributes more towards overall technical inefficiency. Pure technical inefficiency explains approximately 72 % of overall technical inefficiency on an average for firms from deciles 1 and 2, while the figure is 64 % for firms from deciles 7, 8 and 10.

For a closer analysis of the trends in overall technical efficiency, the firms that were a part of PAT cycles I, II and VI are considered. PAT cycles III and IV were introduced while PAT-II was still in operation, because the implementation had started on a rolling basis since PAT-III. PAT-V had 5 new firms, and it was only with PAT-VI that some of the previous firms were brought back for implementation of the scheme. 21 firms were common to PAT-I and II and within them six were further a part of PAT-VI. Figure 5 shows the changing baseline and target energy intensity values for the twenty-one firms. The values have been taken from Gazette notification of Government of India for various years (Department of Publication, Ministry of Housing and Urban Affairs, The Gazette of India, 2016, 2017, 2018, 2020).

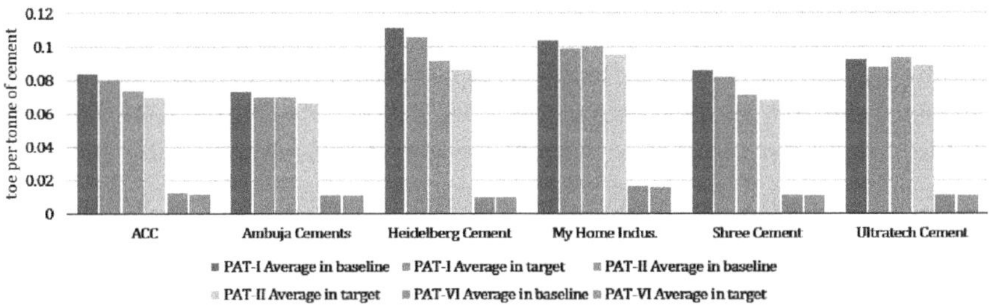

Figure 5. Average baseline and target energy intensity values for 6 firms common to PAT-I, II and VI.

Source: Baseline and target energy intensity values taken from Gazette of India.

One trend common to all the firms is that the average baseline energy intensity value falls considerably under PAT-VI, due to which the target values are also extremely low. This indicates a marked improvement in the general energy intensity levels for these six firms. Between PAT-I and II also there is a fall in the baseline values, resulting in lower targets, except for Ultratech Cement Limited that did not see much deviation. All the six firms belong to decile 1 or 2, implying that they are large sized firms. They are also relatively old firms, with the year of establishment being before 1980, except Ultratech Cement Limited. Four out of the six firms have an average production capacity of more than 9 million tonnes per annum, except Heidelberg Cement India Limited and My Home Industries Private Limited with a capacity of 5.21 and 6.8 million tonnes respectively for the period 2016–17 to 2019–20. Their capacity utilization is also less than 100 %. For example, in 2020 all the firms used less than 60 % of their production capacity. Both in 2019 when PAT-II ended and in 2020 before these firms were incorporated into PAT-VI, pure technical efficiency was greater than scale efficiency, implying that inappropriate scale of operation played a dominant role in explaining technical inefficiency than managerial inefficiency. This is true for the four firms with high production capacity. But for the remaining 15 firms that were a part of PAT-I and II only, 11 firms had pure technical inefficiency as the main cause of technical inefficiency. These firms have to invest more in improving managerial efficiency in organizing energy inputs than size of production. This group mainly comprises of firms that have a production capacity of less than 9 million tonnes, except for Kesoram Industries Limited, JK Lakshmi Cement Limited, Chettinad Cement, and India Cement Limited.

4. Conclusion

Legally binding policies specifically designed for the industrial sector energy efficiency can provide incentives in the form of designated targets to be achieved within a time span. Failure to achieve the same can lead to penalty. This will motivate the firms to take up technological improvements to raise process productivity to beat the cost of non-compliance. PAT scheme is one such effort in this direction. The success of the PAT scheme can be gauged by the fact that the average energy intensity targets given to the designated consumers from the cement industry declined continuously till PAT-IV. It rose under PAT-V, which could be due to the introduction of completely new set of plants in this cycle. But the target dropped considerably under PAT-VI.

However, firms belonging to both the PAT and non-PAT categories need to move up to be on the efficiency frontier. For the non-PAT firms, overall technical inefficiency is mainly explained by pure technical inefficiency and a relatively small portion is due to scale of operation. This implies that these firms need to focus more on improving managerial ability to arrange energy inputs more productively. For the PAT identified firms, there is no such clear trend. But the energy efficiency scores have remained above the score at the beginning of the sample period, except in 2020 which can be explained by the COVID-19 pandemic and its repercussions on industry.

Cement industry has taken constructive steps towards sustainable production. Out of industry's consumption of raw coal, 2.88 % went to the cement industry in 2010–11, which fell to less than 1 % in 2020–21. Some of the PAT identified firms like Chettinad Cement, J K Lakshmi Cement Limited, Kesoram Industries Limited, Shree Cement Limited, etc. have also increased their research and development expenditure. More incentives can be given to the old firms to upgrade their technology. Finally, demand for cement is a derived demand, linked with the general growth of the economy. The large unutilized capacity can be put to use only if there is demand for the product. A robust economic growth can propel this industry forward and help it to benefit from economies of large-scale production. Along with this, more stringent targets and lowering of the threshold energy consumption can bring more number of firms under the PAT scheme, and help achieve the dual objective of growth with energy conservation.

References

ASEAN Plan of Action for Energy Cooperation. (2015). *ASEAN Centre for Energy*.

Cooper, W., Seiford. L., & Tone, K. (2007). Data Envelopment Analysis: A Comprehensive Text with Models, Applications, References and DEA-Solver Software. 2nd edition, Springer.

Department of Publication, Ministry of Housing and Urban Affairs. (2016). *The Gazette of India*.

Department of Publication, Ministry of Housing and Urban Affairs. (2017). *The Gazette of India*

Department of Publication, Ministry of Housing and Urban Affairs. (2018). *The Gazette of India*

Department of Publication, Ministry of Housing and Urban Affairs. (2020). *The Gazette of India*.

Doris, E., Cochran, J., & Vorum, M. (2009). Energy Efficiency Policy in the United States: Overview of Trends at Different Levels of Government. *Technical Report National Renewable Energy Laboratory*, TP-6A2-46532.

Economidou, M., Todeschi, V., Bertoldi, P., D'Agostino, D., Zangheri, P., and Castellazzi, L. (2020). Review of 50 Years of EU Energy Efficiency Policies for Buildings. *Energy & Buildings*, *225* (1).

Energy Statistics. (2019). *Ministry of Statistics and Programme Implementation*, Government of India, 26th issue .

Malinauskaite, J., Jouhara, H., Ahmad, L., Milani, M., Montorsi, M., & Venturelli, M. (2019). Energy Efficiency in İndustry: EU and National Policies in Italy and the UK. *Energy*, *172*, 255–269.

ProwessIQ database. *Centre for Monitoring Indian Economy*, https://prowessiq.cmie.com/.

The World Bank Data. https://data.worldbank.org/indicator.

Piotr Misztal

Transmission Mechanism of Import Prices to Inflation in the European Union

1. Impact of Import Prices on Inflation in the Light of Economic Theory

When analyzing the issue of the impact of import prices on inflation (transfer of import prices to inflation), one can distinguish the so-called two transfer phases, i.e. first and second. The first transfer phase is defined as the elasticity of domestic prices of imported goods to changes in the exchange rate (Öğünç et.al., 2018). In contrast, the second phase of pass-through is defined as the elasticity of consumer prices to changes in domestic prices of imported goods. The second phase of the transfer is complete when changes in the prices of imported goods do not cause changes in the importers' margins.

From the point of view of the impact of changes in the price of imported goods on inflation, two channels of transmission of price impulses (imported prices) are distinguished, i.e. direct and indirect (Arsova, 2021). The direct impact of changes in the prices of imported goods on inflation is related to the import to the country of final (end) goods, i.e. goods purchased by the end user. These are consumer goods purchased by households or investment (capital) goods purchased by enterprises.

Changes in the prices of imported goods also indirectly affect changes in inflation in the country. This situation is related to the import of the so-called intermediate goods, that is partially processed goods, which are an input in the production process in those enterprises where they are consumed (raw materials, materials, energy).

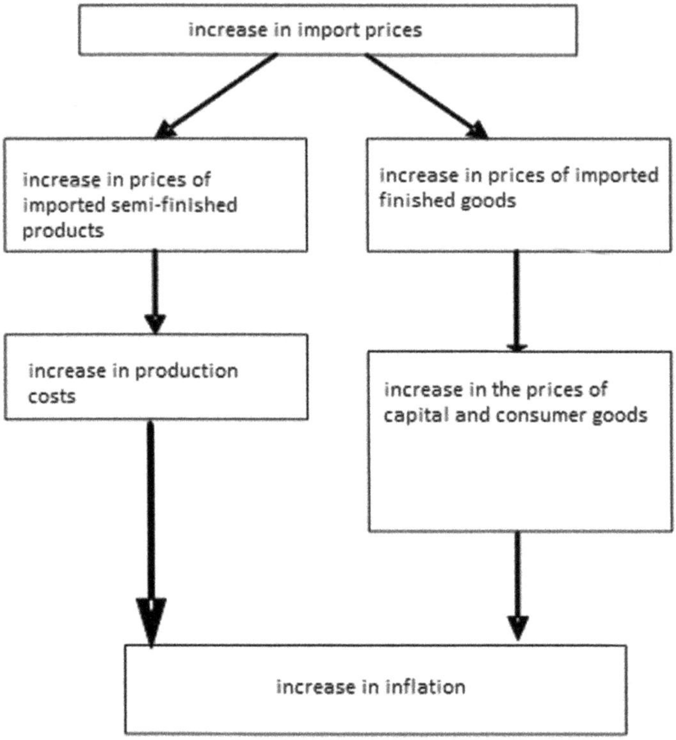

Figure 1. Direct and indirect impact of changes in the price of imported goods on inflation.

Source: Own study.

In the literature on the subject, there are many factors determining the extent to which changes in import prices are passed on to inflation. The first is the size of the economy of the importing country. Well, according to the classical approach, the larger the country's economy, the smaller the inflationary effects of changes in import prices. The explanation for this type of relationship is the fact that the increase in import prices in a large country will be counteracted by a decrease in world prices as a result of a decrease in global demand for a given commodity, which in turn will lead to a decrease in the degree of transfer of changes in import prices to inflation. On the other hand, in a small country, the import price will not affect world commodity prices, which will lead to an increase in the pass-through of changes in import prices to inflation (McCarthy, 1999).

Another factor determining the extent to which import prices are passed on to inflation is the nature of changes in import prices. Well, the lower the volatility of import prices and the greater the durability of these changes, the greater the tendency on the part of enterprises to transfer the changes of import prices to inflation. If, on the other hand, the change in import prices is temporary and there is less volatility of these prices, then enterprises are more willing to adjust their margins than to pass on changes in import prices to consumer prices. Thus, the greater the persistence of changes in import prices and the lower the volatility of import prices, the greater the degree of inflation pass-through of import prices (Taylor, 2000).

At the same time, it should be noted that the degree of pass-through of changes in import prices to the prices of final consumer goods is generally lower than to the prices of semi-finished products. This situation results from the fact that in the first case imported goods are delivered to final consumers through the distribution sector. If tradable goods sold to consumers contain a significant proportion of local added value, consumer prices are not as sensitive to changes in import prices. In the second case, the imported goods are semi-finished products, often combined with domestic semi-finished products to produce a finished product and then sell it to consumers. Thus, pricing decisions are made on two different levels, i.e. at the level of intermediate goods and final goods (Türkcan, 2005).

2. Impact of Import Prices on Inflation in the Light of the Results of Empirical Analyses

Kamin, Marazzi, and Schindler (2004) based on the analysis of data from 1992–2002 and using autoregressive models, estimated that growing imports from China contributed to the decrease in the price of imported goods in the United States by an average of 0.8% per year, which meant a relatively small decrease inflation, which is about 0.1% a year.

Similar research results were revealed by the IMF (2006) suggesting that a 1% decrease in import prices in the world's largest developed economies contributed to a reduction in inflation of less than 0.1% after one year of the price change, and after three years the impact of import prices on inflation expired completely. Moreover, the authors of the report also estimated that the drop in import prices in 1998–1999 contributed to a decrease in inflation in developed countries by about half a percentage point, in 2002 by about a quarter of a percentage point, and the total impact of import prices on inflation was completely neutral in the period 2003–2005. Thus, the results of these studies indicated a small and short-term impact of import prices on inflation in economically developed countries.

Interesting results of the analysis were also obtained by Çağlar (2009), who examined the degree of transmission of changes in exchange rates and import prices to consumer prices in Turkey in the period 2002–2009 using a vector autoregression (VAR) model. The results of the conducted research indicated that the cumulative degree of transfer of exchange rate changes and import prices to consumer prices was similar, although changes in import prices were transferred faster than changes in the exchange rate. Moreover, compared to previous studies, the degree of pass-through of import prices to consumer prices in Turkey has significantly decreased. The reduction in the degree of pass-through of import prices to consumer prices can be explained by a decrease in the volatility and persistence of external shocks and a decrease in inflation as a result of Turkey's direct inflation targeting strategy.

Mortaza and Rahman (2008) studied the impact of imported commodity prices on the consumer price index in Bangladesh over the period 2000–2008 using the Vector Error Correction Model (VECM). The results of the analysis confirmed the phenomenon of incomplete pass-through of changes in the prices of imported goods to inflation in this country . Moreover, according to the results of the conducted research, in the case of goods with a greater share in the domestic supply, there was a lower degree of transfer of changes in import prices to domestic consumer prices.

Syed and Sahminan (2020) empirically investigated whether the change in international prices has an effect on inflation in the BRIICS between 2006 and 2020. They found that for Indonesia and India, imported energy and equipment prices have a positive effect on inflation. Thus, rising commodity prices create inflationary pressures in these economies. In the case of Brazil, China and South Africa, energy prices and food prices have positive impact on domestic inflation. In contrast, the impact of energy and oil prices on domestic inflation in Russia is the opposite, as the Russian Ruble tends to appreciate in response to an increase in energy prices because energy commodities heavily dominate the country's exports.

3. Impact of Import Prices on Inflation in the EU

The imports of the EU in the period 2002–2022 were dominated by intermediate goods, whose share oscillated around 60 %, while the smallest share in imports was characterized by capital goods, and their share was close to 15 %. On the other hand, the share of consumer goods in the total import of the EU was in the range of 16–23 % throughout the analyzed period.

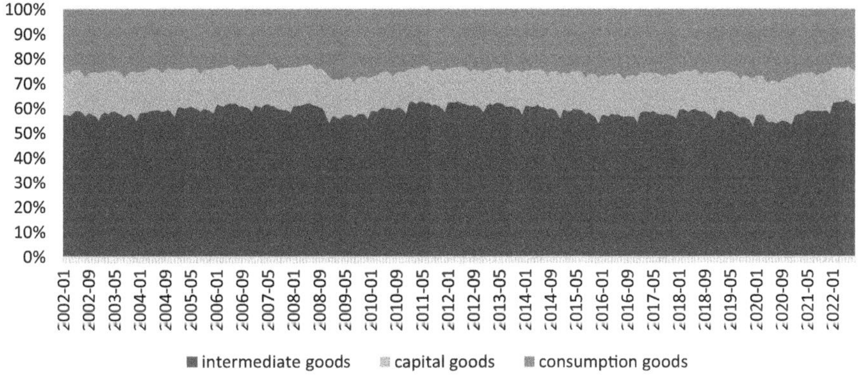

Figure 2. The structure of imports of the European Union in the period 2002–2022 [in %].

Source: Eurostat.

Taking into account the changes in inflation in the EU member states in the period 2002–2022, it can be seen that the highest dynamics was observed in the so-called new EU member states, where the inflation rate significantly exceeded the average inflation rate in all member states. Thus, the so-called the old EU member states were characterized by much greater price stability compared to the new member states. This situation is obviously related to the higher level of economic development of the old EU member countries.

Table 1. Harmonized index of consumer prices in the European Union in the period 2002–2022 [in %, 2015=100]

Time	2002	2004	2006	2008	2010	2012	2014	2016	2018	2020	2022
European Union	77,9	81,0	84,6	89,7	92,5	97,9	99,9	100,3	103,9	106,2	119,3
Belgium	78,0	80,6	84,6	90,0	92,1	97,7	99,4	101,8	106,4	108,2	123,3
Bulgaria	61,4	66,8	76,0	91,6	96,7	102,3	101,1	98,7	102,5	106,3	123,5
Czechia	78,2	80,2	83,2	91,0	92,6	98,0	99,8	100,7	105,1	111,4	132,1
Denmark	81,2	83,5	86,5	91,2	94,1	98,9	99,8	100,0	101,8	102,9	113,8
Germany	81,5	83,8	87,0	91,4	92,7	97,0	99,3	100,4	104,0	105,8	118,7
Estonia	63,7	66,6	72,4	85,5	88,0	96,3	99,9	100,8	108,1	109,8	137,0
Ireland	84,0	89,3	93,7	99,5	96,2	99,2	100,0	99,8	100,8	101,2	112,0
Greece	76,5	81,5	87,1	93,6	99,3	103,4	101,1	100,0	101,9	101,2	111,2
Spain	75,9	80,6	86,3	92,4	94,1	99,3	100,6	99,7	103,5	103,9	116,0
France	81,2	84,9	88,1	92,3	94,1	98,3	99,9	100,3	103,6	105,5	114,0
Croatia	74,1	77,5	82,5	89,6	92,6	97,8	100,3	99,4	102,2	103,1	117,1
Italy	77,9	81,9	85,6	90,4	92,6	98,4	99,9	99,9	102,5	103,0	114,2
Cyprus	78,5	83,2	86,8	92,6	95,1	101,5	101,6	98,8	100,2	99,7	110,2
Latvia	57,7	63,1	71,8	91,1	93,0	99,1	99,8	100,1	105,6	108,6	131,5
Lithuania	70,0	70,0	74,6	87,7	92,4	99,3	100,7	100,7	107,1	110,6	137,6
Luxembourg	73,6	77,9	83,2	88,9	91,4	97,6	99,9	100,0	104,2	105,9	118,6
Hungary	59,6	66,7	71,8	82,1	89,5	98,2	99,9	100,5	105,8	113,2	137,2
Malta	76,1	79,7	83,8	88,3	91,8	97,1	98,8	100,9	104,0	106,4	113,7
Netherlands	81,4	84,3	87,0	90,3	92,1	97,0	99,8	100,1	103,0	107,0	122,8
Austria	78,0	80,6	83,7	88,3	90,1	95,8	99,2	101,0	105,4	108,5	121,1
Poland	75,2	78,5	81,2	86,8	92,7	99,8	100,7	99,8	102,6	108,6	129,4
Portugal	79,2	83,9	88,3	92,8	93,2	99,2	99,5	100,6	103,4	103,6	113,0
Romania	46,1	59,5	69,2	78,3	87,7	96,0	100,4	98,9	104,1	110,7	129,1
Slovenia	72,4	79,3	83,3	91,2	93,9	98,5	100,8	99,9	103,4	104,8	116,9
Slovakia	68,2	79,5	85,2	90,2	91,7	99,0	100,4	99,5	103,5	108,5	125,1
Finland	80,4	81,6	83,3	87,9	90,8	96,8	100,2	100,4	102,4	104,0	113,7
Sweden	83,5	86,3	88,3	92,8	96,4	98,7	99,3	101,1	105,1	107,6	119,4

Source: Eurostat.

In general, a price shock transmitted from enterprises to consumers can lead to an increase in the overall costs of producers and consumers, thus reducing real consumption and real production in the country. In response to the increase in production costs, domestic producers may reduce their profit margins, which in turn will lead to a decrease in investment by these enterprises. In order to analyze the relationship between the dynamics of prices of imported goods and inflation in the EU in the period 2002–2022, the following econometric model was used:

CPI = f (IMP_interm, PPI_interm, IMP_capital, PPI_capital, IMP_consumer, PPI_consumer) (1)

where:

CPI – consumer price index (inflation rate) in the EU;
IMP_interm – import prices of intermediate goods in the EU;
PPI_ interm – production prices of intermediate goods in the EU;
IMP_capital – import prices of capital goods in the EU;
PPI_capital – production prices of capital goods in the EU;
IMP_consumer – import prices of consumer goods in the EU;
PPI_consumer – production prices of consumer goods in the EU.

All the time series mentioned above had a monthly frequency and covered the period from January 2002 to July 2022. From the time series a seasonal factor was also distinguished, as the occurrence of a seasonal factor could lead to problems in interpreting changes in a given phenomenon in the period under study. For this purpose, the X12-ARIMA procedure was used. Finally, changes in the indicators used in the model were presented in the period 2002–2022 as shown in the Figure 3 below.

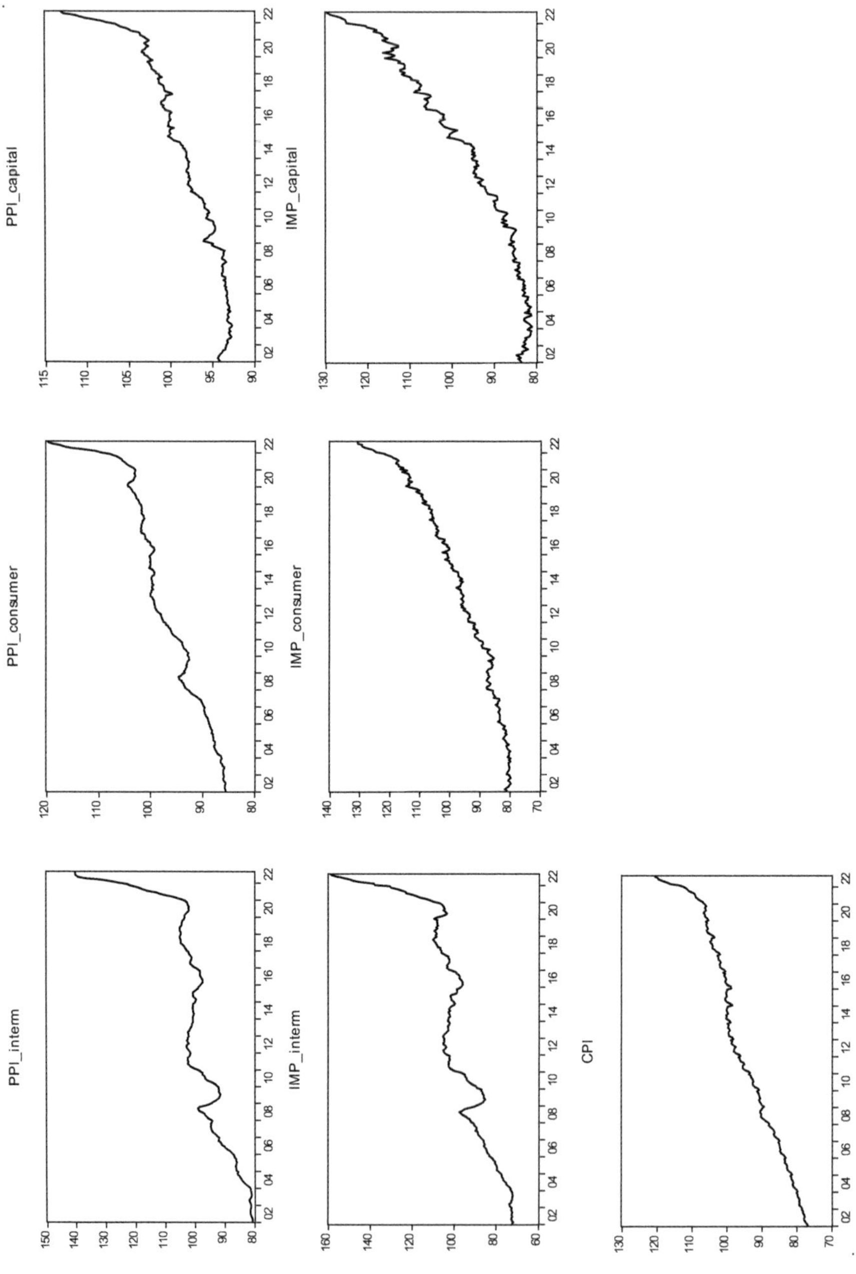

Figure 3. Dynamics of import, production and consumer prices in the EU in 2002–2022.

Source: Own elaboration based on Eurostat data.

The next step of the analysis was to determine the stationarity of the analyzed time series. For this purpose, the extended Dickey -Fuller test – ADF. The data included in the model included time series with the order of integration 0, 1 and 2. In the case of two analyzed variables there was no stationarity of the time series, and in the case of five variables the order of integration was 0. The lack of stationarity of the time series forced the modification of the functional form of the model, in to bring the variables to stationarity. This modification, in the case of first-level integrated variables, consisted in replacing the size of the analyzed variables by their first differences, and in replacing the size of the analyzed variables by their second differences in the case of second-level integrated variables.

Then, the model was estimated using the vector autoregression model proposed by Sims (1980). This approach was first used by McCarthy (1999) when he studied various macroeconomic interdependencies in member countries of the Organization for Economic Co-operation and Development (OECD).

The analysis assumed two periods of time lag between the explanatory variables and the dependent variable (two months). The choice of the lag order was made according to the results of the information criteria of the Akaike, Schwartz – Bayesian and Hannan-Quinn models . According to these criteria, the model with two lags had the greatest information capacity.

Table 2. Results of the estimation of structural parameters of the VAR model for the EU

Variables	CPI
CPI(-1)	1.043304
	(0.06589)
	[15.8347]
CPI(-2)	−0.115706
	(0.06444)
	[−1.79552]
IMP_CAPITAL(−1)	−0.205480
	(0.03221)
	[−6.37868]
IMP_CAPITAL(−2)	0.171970
	(0.03330)
	[5.16393]
IMP_CONSUMER(−1)	0.050749
	(0.03559)
	[1.42608]
IMP_CONSUMER(−2)	0.005408
	(0.03587)
	[0.15073]
IMP_INTERM(−1)	0.051512
	(0.03451)
	[1.49269]
IMP_INTERM(−2)	−0.030210
	(0.03469)
	[−0.87076]
PPI_CAPITAL(−1)	0.208833
	(0.11420)
	[1.82862]
PPI_CAPITAL(−2)	−0.192216
	(0.11754)
	[−1.63533]
PPI_CONSUMER(−1)	−0.133681
	(0.13120)
	[−1.01890]
PPI_CONSUMER(−2)	0.163433
	(0.13686)
	[1.19420]

Table 2. Continued

Variables	CPI
PPI_INTERM(−1)	0.094375
	(0.06400)
	[1.47463]
PPI_INTERM(−2)	−0.103047
	(0.06444)
	[−1.59901]
R-squared	0.998974
F-statistic	16058.10
Akaike information criterion	6.178712
Schwarz criterion	7.674890

Standard errors in () & t-statistics in []
Source: Own study.

Based on the results of estimations, it can be seen that one of the factors that significantly determined the inflation dynamics in the EU in the period 2002–2022 were import prices of capital goods and production prices of capital goods. It should be noted that the negative impact of one-month lag prices of imported capital goods on inflation was revealed. The negative impact of the prices of imported capital goods (machinery, buildings, etc.) on inflation may have resulted from the fact that the rising prices of machinery and real estate caused a decrease in the purchasing power of enterprises, which resulted in a decline in consumer demand and a decline in inflation. The results of the research also confirmed the existence of a positive impact of import prices of consumer goods on inflation in the EU. Moreover, the impact of imported consumer goods on inflation was smaller than the share of consumer goods in the EU imports.

On the other hand, the impact of the prices of imported intermediate goods on inflation in the EU turned out to be statistically significant only in the case of one-month lag prices. This situation may have resulted from a high degree of substitutability of imported intermediate goods by intermediate goods manufactured in the EU. Namely, in the situation of an increase in the prices of imported intermediate goods, there were appropriate adjustments on the side of demand for these goods, resulting in a decrease in the share of imported intermediate goods in the total demand of enterprises. In this situation, the degree of pass-through of import prices of intermediate goods to inflation was smaller.

Taking into account the impact factors of import prices of both intermediate, capital and consumer goods on inflation, it can be concluded that the overall increase in the prices of imported goods led to an increase in inflation in the EU. On the other hand, taking into account the factors of the impact of production prices of intermediate, capital and consumer goods on inflation, it can be noticed that the general increase in producer prices led to only a slight increase in inflation in the EU. The inertia factor, i.e. the change in inflation in the previous periods, had the greatest impact on the inflation rate in the EU.

The next stage of the analysis was the measurement of the impact of the analyzed factors on the inflation rate in the EU in the period 2002–2022. This measurement was made using the so-called impulse response functions, i.e. the function of the reaction of the inflation rate to an impulse in the form of a unit change in import prices of intermediate goods, production prices of intermediate goods; import prices of capital goods; production prices of capital goods; import prices of consumer goods and producer prices of consumer goods in the EU.

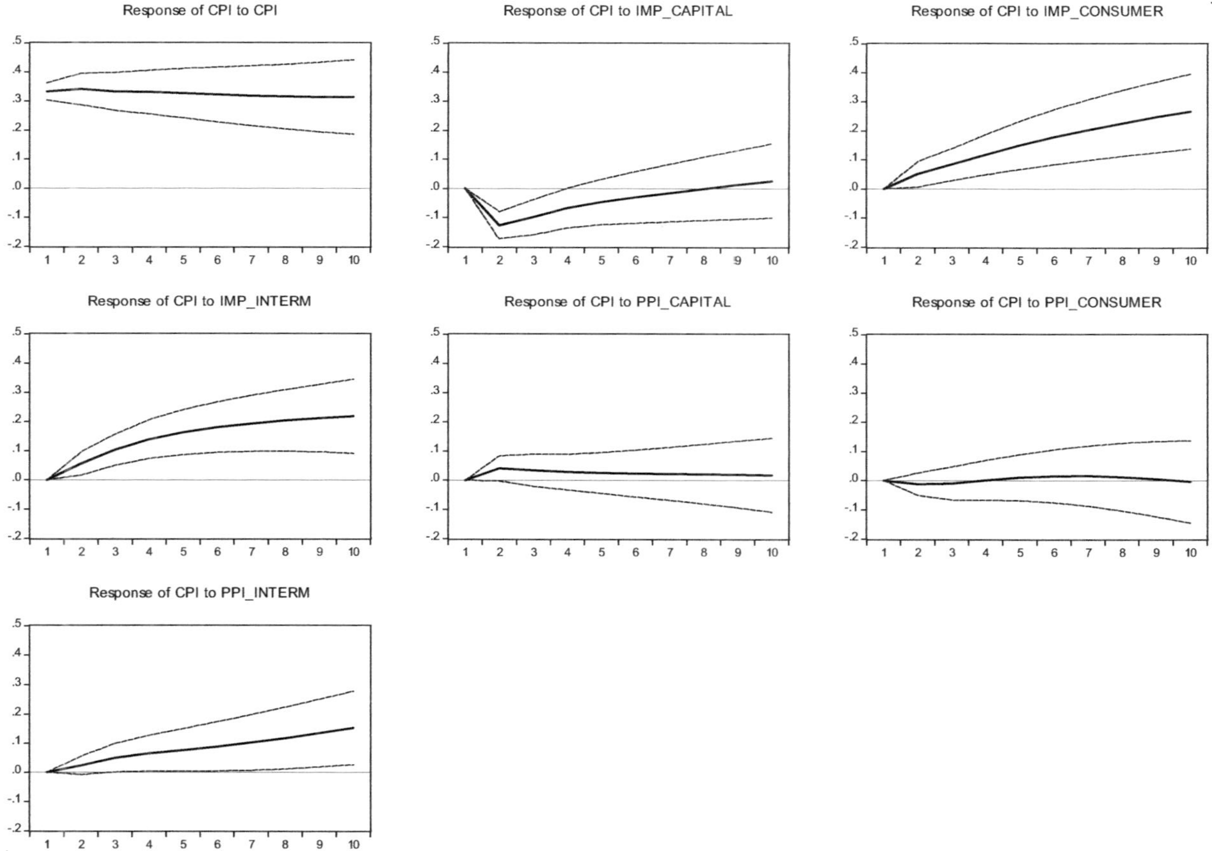

Figure 4. The impulse response function of the EU inflation index to an impulse caused by a single, unit change in import and production prices of intermediate, capital and consumer goods.

Source: Own study.

From the figures above, it was noted that the price shock of imported capital goods led to an immediate decline in the EU consumer price index in the two months following the price shock, followed by a stabilization in consumer prices after five months. On the other hand, a shock increase in the prices of imported consumer as well as intermediate goods in the EU led to an immediate increase in the consumer price index within ten months of the price shock, and then to its stabilization after this period.

The impact of a unit change in the consumer price index on further changes in this index in the EU was different. In this case, a shock increase in the consumer price index by one unit led to an immediate increase in inflation during the first month, and then to inflation stabilization after the fifth month from the moment of the shock.

The last stage of the analysis was the decomposition of the variance of the residual component of the consumer price index in the EU in the period 2002–2022, in order to estimate the impact of changes in the analyzed factors on the inflation volatility in the EU.

Table 3. Decomposition of the variance of the residual component of the inflation rate in the EU in the period 2002–2022

;Period	CPI	IMP_ CAPITAL	IMP_ CONSUMER	IMP_ INTERM	PPI_ CAPITAL	PPI_ CONSUMER	PPI_ INTERM
1	100.0	0.0	0.0	0.0	0.0	0.0	0.0
2	90.4	6.3	1.0	1.2	0.6	0.0	0.2
3	85.9	6.4	2.4	3.5	0.7	0.0	0.7
4	82.0	5.4	4.2	6.1	0.6	0.0	1.3
5	78.0	4.5	6.4	8.4	0.6	0.0	1.8
6	74.0	3.7	8.7	10.4	0.5	0.0	2.3
7	70.2	3.0	11.0	12.0	0.5	0.0	2.9
8	66.7	2.5	13.2	13.3	0.4	0.0	3.5
9	63.4	2.2	15.2	14.3	0.4	0.0	4.2
10	60.2	1.9	17.2	15.1	0.3	0.0	4.9
11	57.3	1.7	19.0	15.6	0.3	0.0	5.7
12	54.6	1.6	20.7	15.9	0.3	0.1	6.6

Source: Own study.

Based on the data in the Table 3 above, it can be seen that changes in the prices of imported capital goods explained about 1,6 % of the volatility of consumer prices in the EU one year after the shock. Moreover, changes in import prices of consumer goods explained almost 21 % of the volatility of consumer prices one year after the price shock. On the other hand changes in the prices of imported intermediate goods explained near 16 % of the volatility of consumer prices in the EU twelve months after price shock. For comparison, by far the largest contribution to explaining the volatility of consumer prices in the EU in the period 2002–2022 was made by the inertial factor, i.e. lagged changes in consumer prices. Thus, we were dealing with the phenomenon of inflation persistence in the EU. This phenomenon makes it significantly more difficult for the central banks to reduce inflation after a period of its increase, and adjustments take longer and are more costly for the economy in terms of output and employment volatility (NBP, 2009). Next, the speed and cumulative impact of import prices on changes in inflation in the EU were assessed. The results are shown in the Table 4 below.

Table 4. The speed and magnitude of the pass-through of import and producer prices to inflation

Change in:	**Speed (How much of the total pass-through is completed in %)**						**Magnitude (Accumulated pass-through in % point)**					
	Q1	**Q2**	**Q3**	**Q4**	**Q5**	**Q6**	**Q1**	**Q2**	**Q3**	**Q4**	**Q5**	**Q6**
IMP_CAPITAL	0	11	47	70	88	100	0.00	0.02	0.08	0.12	0.15	0.17
IMP_CONSUMER	11	39	60	79	93	100	0,05	0,17	0,34	0,40	0,40	0,43
IMP_INTERM	55	80	95	100	97	80	0,22	0,32	0,38	0,40	0,39	0,32
PPI_CAPITAL	42	85	100	85	0	0	0,03	0,06	0,07	0,06	0,00	0,00
PPI_CONSUMER	52	87	100	100	87	61	0,12	0,20	0,23	0,23	0,20	0,14
PPI_INTERM	43	65	78	89	98	100	0,20	0,30	0,36	0,41	0,45	0,46

Source: Own study.

On the basis on the data presented in table above, 10% increase in price of imported consumer goods causes a 4.3 percentage point rise in inflation at the end of the sixth quarter, and 10% increase in price of imported intermediate goods causes a 4.0 percentage point rise in inflation at the end of the fourth quarter. By contrast, a 10% change in the price of imported capital goods results in an increase in inflation of less than 1.7 percentage point after six quarters. When it comes to the speed of pass-through, it can be noticed that 100% of the pass-through of import prices to inflation is completed between fourth and sixth quarter after price change. Accordingly, it can be confirmed that there is a remarkable short-run pass-through from import prices to inflation in the EU.

4. Conclusions

The issue of the impact of import prices on inflation has not yet been the subject of a broad discussion among economic theoreticians and economic politicians. Economists were much more interested in the transmission of exchange rate changes to import, production and consumer prices. Despite the relatively small interest of researchers in the issue of transferring changes in import prices to inflation, this issue is particularly important from the point of view of a central bank conducting a monetary policy focused in particular on maintaining a stable price level in a given country. Import prices have a direct impact on inflation through the import of consumption and investment goods into the country and indirectly as a result of imports of intermediate goods which are inputs in the production process of enterprises.

The results of the conducted research revealed that the most important factors determining the dynamics of inflation in the EU in the period 2002–2022 were import prices of consumer goods and import prices of intermediate goods. Moreover, it should be noted that there was a negative impact of one-month lag prices of imported capital goods on inflation and a positive impact of import prices of consumer and intermediate goods on inflation. It should be also noted here that the pass-through of prices of imported consumer goods to inflation was higher than the share of imported consumer goods in total EU imports. This situation could be a consequence of the impact of changes in the prices of imported consumer goods on the prices of domestically produced consumer goods, directly competing with imports.

In general, taking into account the pass-through of changes in import prices of intermediate, capital and consumer goods to inflation, it can be seen that the general increase in the prices of imported goods led to an increase in inflation in the EU. This situation was a consequence of the largest share of intermediate goods in the total imports of the EU.

Moreover, the results of the conducted analysis also indicated that changes in consumer prices in the EU were explained to the greatest extent by changes in the prices of imported consumer goods, and least by changes in the prices of imported capital goods. However, apart from the prices of imported goods, the greatest contribution to explaining the volatility of consumer prices was made by the inertial factor (lagged consumer prices), which proved the existence of the phenomenon of inflation persistence in the EU.

Bibliography

Arsova, A. (2021). Exchange Rate Pass-Through to Import Prices in Europe: A Panel Cointegration Approach. *Empirical Economics,* No 61.

Borio, C., & Filardo, A. (2007). *Globalization and Inflation: New Cross-Country Evidence on the Global Determinants of Domestic Inflation.* Bank for International Settlements Working Papers, No 227.

Çağlar, Y. (2009). *Import Price Pass-Through into Inflation Indicators in Turkey* (Master's Thesis). Department of Economics, Middle East Technical University, Ankara.

Feyzioglu, T., & Willard, L. (2006). *Does Inflation in China Affect the United States and Japan.* IMF Working Paper, No 06/36.

IMF. (2006). *World Economic Outlook.* International Monetary Fund, April.

Kamin, S., Marazzi, M., & Schindler, J. (2004). Is China Exporting Deflation? *Board of Governors of the Federal Reserve System International Finance Discussion Papers,* No 791.

Korhonen, M. (2007). *Exchange Rate Pass-Through into Prices: Dependence on Inflation Regime.* University of Turku, Department of Economics, EEA-ESEM Congress.

McCarthy, J. (1999). *Pass-Through of Exchange Rates and Import Prices to Domestic Inflation in Some Industrialized Economies.* Bank for International Settlements Working Papers, No. 79.

Mortaza, M. G., & Rahman, H. (2008). *Transmission of International Commodity Prices to Domestic Prices in Bangladesh.* Policy Analysis Unit Working Paper Series, No 0807.

NBP (2009). Monetary Policy Guidelines for 2010. Warsaw.

Öğünç, F. Özmen, M. U., & Sarikaya, C. (2018). Inflation Dynamics in Turkey from a Bayesian Perspective. *Central Bank of the Republic of Turkey Working Paper,* No. 18/10

Syed, A. R., & Sahminan, S. (2020). Commodity Price and Inflation Dynamics: Evidence From BRIICS. *Bulletin of Monetary Economics and Banking, 23*(4).

Taylor, J. B. (2000). Low Inflation, Pass-Through, and the Pricing Power of Firms. *European Economic Review,* Vol. 44 issue 7.

Turkcan, K. (2005). Exchange Rate Pass Through Elasticities in Final and Intermediate Goods: The Case of Turkey. *Yonetim ve Ekonomi,* Vol.12, No.1.

Piotr Misztal and Vasili Kulakov

Investment Attractiveness of the Country and Methods of Measuring It on the Example of Belarus and Poland[1]

1. Introduction

As previously stated, the concept of a country's investment attractiveness is inextricably tied to the concept of its international competitiveness. Specifically, the country's high international competitiveness is a necessary but not sufficient requirement for the country to be an appealing destination for foreign direct investment by commercial entities. As a result, it is critical to examine an economy's investment attractiveness in the context of its competitiveness with other economies throughout the world.

Foreign direct investment (FDI) is defined as an investment made by a foreign institution or entity in a company registered in the country. According to the United Nations Conference on Trade and Development (UNCTAD), FDI can provide numerous other benefits to the host country, such as the entry of technology or the transfer of skills. The entrance of FDI in this manner has a favorable impact on the economy's competitiveness, enhancing the possibility of job growth. The findings of theoretical and empirical studies conducted by Behrman (1972), Findlay (1978), Blomström and Kokko (2003), Alfaro et al. (2004), Blomkvist (2009), and Sabir et al. (2019) support these benefits.

One of the variables influencing the country's economic growth is the policy of recruiting foreign capital. A country can provide a variety of incentives to encourage capital inflows in the form of FDI. Location considerations (access to the sales market), demographic factors (access to an educated workforce), and economic factors (dynamic economic growth) are examples of these. Furthermore, financial variables such as tax costs and institutional factors such as the quality of institutions in the host country are aspects that foreign investors consider when making investment decisions. The tax burden has a direct impact on the return on investment capital movements and has an indirect impact on company competitiveness (Bellak et. al. 2009). demonstrate that a high corporate

1 Project financed by the National Center for Research and Development "Solidarity with scientists" (SzN/2/129/MDCDPECBPB/2022).

income tax rate reduces the profitability of FDI investments. Economically underdeveloped countries are viewed as appealing destinations for FDI inflows due to their comparative advantage of low labor costs, favorable pro-investment policies implemented by their governments, rich mineral resources, and an abundance of raw commodities. However, due to limited financial resources and substantial pressure on budget deficits, it is apparent that these countries' governments adopt high tax rates to ensure enough budget revenues.

Poor institutional quality is today a global concern, affecting many aspects of the economy not only in individual countries but also across the developing world as a whole. Poor quality institutions are the root source of corruption. Corruption, in theory, is a "hand in hand" since it increases the risk of transaction costs and impedes the flow of FDI. Corruption, on the other hand, may act as a "helping hand" by helping to "oil" the flywheel in countries where institutions remain cumbersome and ineffective. As a result, corporations earn more by paying a little fee to obtain critical data and profits (Heckelman & Powell, 2010).

Tax rivalry between governments to attract FDI has become a worldwide challenge in the modern economy. Capital owners commonly compare tax costs in countries with comparable market size and geography. While international tax competition is increasing, these states' tax rates are seen as unavoidable. Nonetheless, there is no strong evidence that this tax drop will help impoverished countries recruit FDI. Reduced tax revenues will result in decreased infrastructure investment, which will result in a reduction in the provision of public goods and services as well as distortions in the distribution of public money. As a result, it is unclear whether these countries remain appealing to international investors.

Furthermore, low institutional quality might be one of the most significant barriers to economic growth and development. According to the World Bank and Transparency International, corruption has become more complex and prevalent in some rising countries. Many international empirical studies indicate that corruption and low institutional quality slow economic development by limiting private investment and diminishing the effectiveness of government investment (Gupta et al., 2002; Knack & Keefer, 1995; Mauro, 1995; Tanzi & Davoodie, 2001). However, Ehrlich and Lui (1999) argue that the repercussions of corruption are broad and have a significant economic impact. Corruption stifles economic growth in several African and South American countries. Corruption, on the other hand, does not appear to be limiting growth in many countries with significant regional disparities, including China and India. Foreign direct investment (FDI) has grown significantly in recent years, as has its share of overall capital flows in emerging markets, as has its contribution to economic growth.

2. Literature Review

The level of taxation in the host country is one of the elements influencing the entry of foreign direct investment into a country. While the influence of taxes on FDI inflows varies greatly depending on the type of tax, empirical evidence suggests that nations with high tax rates are less appealing to FDI inflows than those with low tax rates. Hartman (1984) was the first to demonstrate that certain forms of FDI inflows are less tax sensitive than others. This means that FDI investors in specific areas are immune from taxation in the host country.

Using a meta-analysis technique, De Mooij and Ederveen (2003) discovered a charge versatility for FDI of −3.3, which means that a 1 % decrease in the charge rate of the have nation will increase the influx of FDI to that nation by 3.3 %. Meanwhile, Bellak et al. (2009) conducted a comparison analysis, and the results of their investigation revealed that this flexibility is less than −1.45.

In addition, Stöwhase (2005) investigated the sensitivity of FDI to interest rates. He observed that the variety of FDI streams has a large impact on this affectability. As a result, this study shows that there is an underestimating or overestimation of FDI charge versatilities as compared to the average detailed in previous studies. The theory also posits that problems with information access, estimation, and estimating methodologies may have led to incorrect conclusions in previous studies. Furthermore, a regulatory number governing the influx of outside coordinate speculation to the country was envisaged. The World Bank defines debasement as the abuse of open control for individual pick up. Debasement is widely acknowledged to have a detrimental impact on FDI flows in many circumstances. Regardless, there is no clear link between debasement and FDI flows.

Wheeler and Mods (1992) investigated the impact of debasement on FDI in countries with poor regulatory quality. This is exemplified by sluggish authoritative techniques, excessive bureaucracy, and the necessity for the legal framework to be plain. According to the study, the effect of debasement on FDI is not statistically significant. In other words, debasement does not stifle FDI flows because of poor education in developing countries. In any event, Wei (2000) pointed out that the Wheeler and Mods (1992) consider has certain limitations and contributes to bias in the research outcomes. Wei (2000) claims that Wheeler and Mods (1992) included one debasement variable among 12 other factors used in the demonstration experiment. As a result, the assessment of the impact of debasement on FDI is ambiguous in this scenario. Wei (2000) did information mining from 45 countries in this method. The Tobit technique was used to show estimation. According to the findings of the investigation, debasement has a negative impact on FDI flows. Abed and Davoodi (2002) examined the impact of debasement levels on FDI per capita flows in transition economies using cross-sectional and board data. It appears that economies with lower levels of debasement attract more FDI investment.

In any case, when a control variable for organizational change was included within the appear, the degradation variable had to be immaterial, so this thought almost sheds light on the basic conclusion that organizational change is more important than reducing the level of degradation to draw in FDI streams to specific countries. Habib and Zurawicki (2002) examined the impact of debasement on reciprocal FDI flows in 7 subsidized countries and 89 countries tolerating coordinate speculation. In this scenario, the hypothesis was tested that if the level of corruption in the receiving country is higher than in the native country, the influx of FDI will be lower. As a result, the experimental design uses the difference in debasement levels between providing and receiving countries as an illustrative variable. It has been argued that FDI influx keeps a strategic distance from debasement because it is regarded as dishonest. Furthermore, Voyer and Beamish (2004) used a single source country (Japan) and 59 developing countries as target countries for these investments. The researchers discovered evidence that the influx of FDI from Japan had a negative link with debasement within the host country. Looking into remote coordinate speculation in Africa, Asiedu (2002) identified the most important factors influencing FDI inflows to Africa. It appears that both debasement and political insecurity have a negative impact on FDI inflows.

Mathur and Singh (2013) emphasized that international investors are more concerned with economic freedom than political freedom when deciding on capital flows. The paper investigates the factors that influence FDI inflows to 29 emerging markets. According to empirical findings, corruption has a substantial impact on the choice of destination for investors. FDI flows to developing countries, in particular, are extremely intertwined. The high level of corruption has a detrimental influence on foreign direct investment inflows into certain countries.

According to some studies, corruption has no negative influence on foreign direct investment. The premise is that corruption can help in some cases if other components of governance are missing or economic measures are deemed to be unsuccessful (Leff, 1964). In certain circumstances, corruption is advantageous since it allows investors to avoid impediments and take advantage of host-country benefits. Between 1995 and 1999, investigated the relationship between corruption and FDI inflows in 73 developed and developing countries, and their empirical findings show that corruption can promote FDI inflows by allowing entrepreneurs to avoid burdensome regulations and administrative procedures. They contended that corruption can increase efficiency by allowing businesses to remedy or eliminate government errors. Lui (1985) developed a queuing model to demonstrate how corruption might assist firms in avoiding the repercussions of inefficient rules, and the results demonstrated that bribes to officials can give an incentive to speed up the administrative process. Bayley (1966) claimed that corruption may overcome bureaucracy by enhancing institutional quality, and it can assist enterprises in avoiding public policy impediments that impede their operations, so assisting them in finding good and acceptable solutions.

Macroeconomic variables can also play a role in determining the amount of foreign direct investment that enters a country. Behrman (1972) produced one of the first comprehensive studies on the effects of these determinants on FDI inflows. According to a study of 72 U.S. enterprises with substantial foreign operations, FDI promoted growth not only in terms of money but also in terms of management and technical skills. Findlay (1978) established using the dynamic model that technological diffusion enhances the rate of technical improvement in a somewhat "less developed" location, enhancing the attractiveness of FDI. These previous findings imply that fast-growing countries attract more FDI. However, the relationship between FDI inflows and economic growth may be complex and varied between industrialized and developing countries.

According to Nunnenkamp (2002) and Blonigen (2005), FDI inflows are influenced by two major groupings of determinants. Market (traditional considerations) and efficiency are examples. Economic growth rate, population, tax load, and other market characteristics are examples. The impact of efficiency on FDI inflows, in turn, comprises the amount and dynamics of a country's cost of doing business, which includes tax charges, salaries, non-wage labor costs, and so on. The scholarship on the determinants of FDI inflows is currently focused on analyzing the shift in emphasis between the two groups of factors outlined above. Mottaleb and Kalirajan (2010) and Kumari and Sharma (2018) examined the impact of host nation market size on FDI inflows in recent publications. These studies give information on the macroeconomic factors influencing FDI inflows in both developed and developing nations, however the results are inconclusive.

The level of human capital development and costs are major predictors of FDI inflows to the country, according to research on the impact of efficiency on FDI flows. According to Noorbakhsh et al. (2001) and Braconier et al. (2005), lowering labor costs has a favorable impact on FDI inflows to a country, and human capital is one of the elements that trigger FDI inflows.

4. Measuring the Investment Attractiveness of Belarus and Poland

The so-called Pyramid of the country's investment attractiveness was developed to simplify the analysis of elements impacting the country's investment attractiveness. Here, the determining factors are divided into two basic groups. It is about political factors (*Policy Input*) and essential conditions of attractiveness (*Essential Conditions*). The first group includes the policy pursued in the area of broadly understood business, physical infrastructure and scientific knowledge infrastructure. On the other hand, the second group includes the economic situation, efficiency of production factors, price and cost developments, and labor force resources.

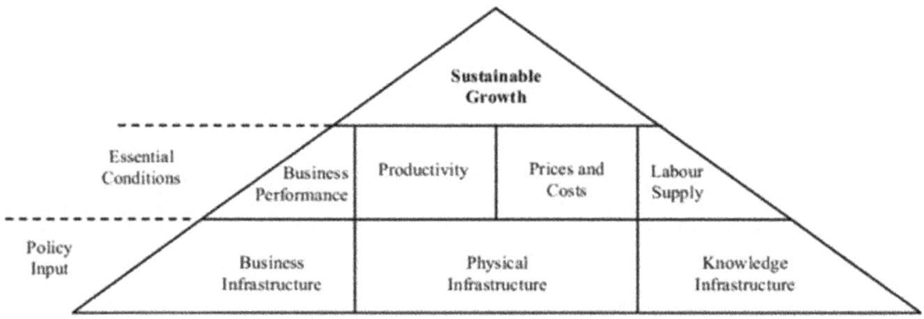

Figure 1. Pyramid of the country's investment attractiveness.
Source: Annual Competitiveness Report (2009).

The analysis of the basic macroeconomic indicators of the studied countries shows that in the case of Belarus there is an upward trend in GDP in absolute terms (in USD) and in relative terms (per capita). Only in 2015, negative economic growth was recorded due to the recession in Russia, the main trading partner of Belarus. Belarus' foreign trade balance was unstable in the period 2005–2021. While Belarus recorded a positive current account balance in 2005 and 2021, the current account was negative in 2010 and 2015, amounting to over -14 % of GDP in 2010. These changes were accompanied by a sharp depreciation of the Belarusian ruble against the U.S. dollar, which in 2021 will be almost 85 % of its 2005 value. The balance of capital turnover in the form of foreign direct investment was positive throughout the period under review, with the inflow of foreign direct investment into Belarus being at least a multiple of the outflow of foreign direct investment from this country.

Table 1. Macroeconomic situation in Belarus in 2005–2021

Indicators	**2005**	**2010**	**2015**	**2021**
GDP in million USD	31232	57232	56455	66970
GDP per capita in USD	3144	5881	5820	6992
Real GDP growth in %	9.44	7.75	−3.83	2.30
Current account balance to GDP in %	1.47	−14.47	−3.24	2.75
exchange rate (USD)	0.215	0.298	1.593	2,539
FDI inflow in USD million	306.60	1393.40	1667.90	1232.94
FDI outflow in USD million	2.50	50.60	122.20	−84.92

Source: UNCTAD (2023).

In turn, examining the main macroeconomic indicators in Poland in the period 2005–2021, it should be stated that there was a clear upward trend in terms of GDP in absolute and relative terms. Moreover, the dynamics of real GDP exceeded 3.5 % throughout the period under review, approaching almost 5 % in 2021. The current account balance in the entire analyzed period was characterized by a negative value, with a clear tendency to improve this balance. The Polish currency was stable against the US dollar. In 2021, a decrease in the value of the zloty against the dollar was recorded by almost 16 %. The balance of foreign direct investment flow was positive throughout the analyzed period, with the inflow of FDI to Poland several times higher than the outflow of FDI from this country.

Table 2. Macroeconomic situation in Poland in 2005–2021

Indicators	2005	2010	2015	2021
GDP in million USD	306146	479834	477812	668183
GDP per capita in USD	7936	12432	12394	17443
Real GDP growth in %	3.51	3.74	4.24	4.75
Current account balance to GDP in %	−2.89	−5.56	−0.91	−0.58
exchange rate (USD)	3.235	3.015	3,770	3.862
FDI inflow in USD million	8203.22	12796.27	15270.83	24815.95
FDI outflow in USD million	1346.74	6147.18	4995.54	5178.27

Source: UNCTAD (2023).

Foreign trade can also be a factor affecting a country's investment attractiveness. The method for measuring investment attractiveness in this case is to determine the country's comparative advantage in foreign trade. Revealed Comparative Advantage (RCA) is based on Ricardo's trade theory, which assumes that trade flows between countries are determined by their relative productivity differences. While such productivity differences are difficult to observe, the RCA metric can be easily calculated using trade data to "uncover" such differences. While this indicator can be used to assess a country's export competitiveness in general, it is important to note that internal policies that affect competitiveness, such as tariffs, non-tariff measures, subsidies, and so on, are not included in the RCA statistic.

A country A is said to have a manifest comparative advantage in a specific product i if its product exports to total exports of all goods (products) surpasses the global average.

$$RCA_{Ai} = \frac{\frac{X_{Ai}}{\sum_{j \in P} X_{Aj}}}{\frac{X_{wi}}{\sum_{j \in P} X_{wj}}} \geq 1$$

where: _

- P is the set of all products (z $i \in P$),
- X_{Ai} is the export of product *and country A*,
- X_{wi} is the world export of the product *i*,
- $\Sigma\, j \in PX_{Aj}$ is the total exports of country *A* (all products $_{j \text{ in } P}$), and
- $\Sigma\, j_{\in}\, PX_{wj}$ is the total world exports (of all products *j* in *P*).

If a country has a demonstrable comparative advantage for a certain product (RCA > 1), it is assumed that it is a competitive producer and exporter of that commodity in comparison to a country that produces and exports that commodity at or below the global average. A country with a comparative advantage in a product is thought to have a good export performance in that product. The bigger a country's RCA for product i, the greater its product i export power. The numbers below are intended to provide a thorough picture of each of the countries studied's demonstrated comparative advantage in the manufacture and export of a wide range of items in a particular year. The products shown are commodity groups at the three-digit level of the SIT C categorization. According to the SITC classification, the various sectors of the economy are depicted in distinct colors and with different titles. Figures for all product groups show the amount of advantage and comparative advantage of exported products.

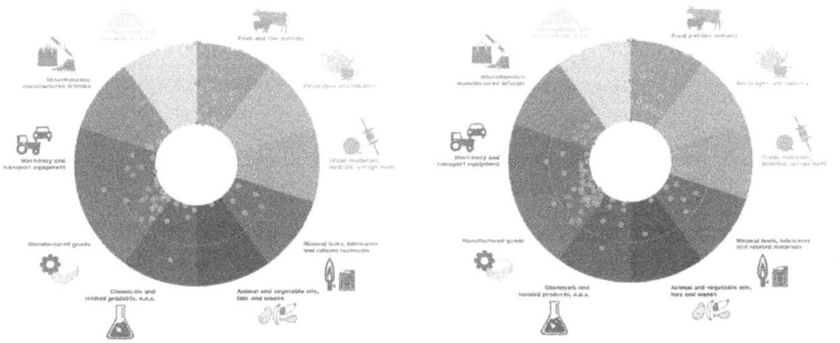

Figure 2. RCA of Belarus in 2010 and 2021.
Source: UNCTAD (2023).

According to the data presented in the Figure 2 above, it can be seen that Belarus has the largest revealed relative advantage in the export of products included in the commodity groups food and live animals, inedible raw materials except fuels and chemicals. This situation did not change significantly throughout the period considered.

In turn, in the case of Poland, the highest relative advantage was found in the export of products classified into such commodity groups as mineral fuels, lubricants and related products, food and live animals, as well as beverages and tobacco. Also in this case, there were no significant changes in relative advantage over the entire period under review. In addition, it is worth noting that in the case of Polish exports, there were definitely more goods in the case of which there was a revealed relative advantage compared to Belarusian exports.

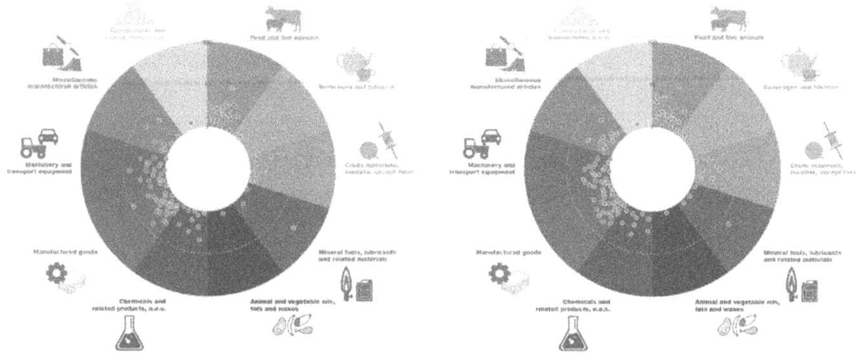

Figure 3. RCA of Poland in 2010 and 2021.
Source: UNCTAD (2023).

The Productivity Index created by the United Nations Conference on Trade and Development (UNCTAD) (PCI) is another indicator used to analyze a country's investment attractiveness. PCI is a dynamic and practical technique that assists developing countries in understanding and improving their productive potential. It is based on an examination of the productive capacities required for equitable and sustainable growth and development. The United Nations Conference on Trade and Development defines productive capacity as "productive resources, entrepreneurial capacities, and productive linkages that together determine a country's ability to produce goods and services and enable it to grow and develop." This encompasses both financial and physical capital, with the latter consisting of machinery and equipment (often at the enterprise/farm level) as well as infrastructure. Firms' entrepreneurial competencies include their skills, expertise, and information. Entrepreneurship, entrepreneurial abilities, and technological skills are among them. They encompass the necessary abilities for investing, producing, and making relationships at the enterprise/farm level. Productive linkages are the exchange of commodities and services, knowledge, technology, and information, as well as productive resources (including human resources) between production units (firms/operations). They include exchanges between different sizes of production units (microenterprises, small and medium-sized firms, and large enterprises) and ownership structures (domestic/foreign, public/private) functioning in various sectors. The overall index computes values ranging from 0 to 100 to assess the condition of productive capacity in economies around the world. PCI gives results at the country level, which aids in understanding the roots of economic systemic flaws and identifying economic growth drivers, such as progress toward national and global development goals. The overall indicator PCI is further subdivided into the following eight categories for statistical and measuring purposes: ICT, structural change, natural capital, human capital, energy, transport, private sector, and institutions.

Capital comprises the population's educational, skill, and health status, as well as the overall integration of research and development into the fabric of society as measured by the number of researchers and research spending. The gender component is mirrored in the fertility rate, which decreases the value of human capital as it rises.Natural capital assesses the availability of mining and agricultural resources, including rents received from natural resource extraction less the cost of extraction. Natural capital declines as material intensity rises, capturing commodity reliance.

The category of energy examines the availability, durability, and efficiency of energy sources. As a result, it covers the GDP generated by each unit of oil, as well as energy consumption and access, distribution losses, and renewable energy components and sources, to underline the necessity of effective energy systems. Transportation assesses a system's ability to transport people or things from one location to another. It refers to the combined capacity of the road, rail, and air networks. The accessibility and integration of communication networks within a population are assessed using information and communication technologies. Users of landlines and cell phones, Internet access, and server security are among them. Institutions involve assessing political stability and performance based on the effectiveness of regulation, the success of the battle against crime, corruption, and terrorism, and the protection of freedom of expression and association.

The private sector decides cross-border trade facilitation, which includes the time and monetary expenses of exports and imports, as well as business support in the form of domestic finance, the speed with which contracts are enforced, and the time it takes to start a business. The movement of labor and other productive resources from low-productivity industries to high-productivity industries is referred to as structural transformation. The sophistication and diversity of exports, the intensity of fixed assets, and the weight of industry and services in total GDP now reflect this trend. Structural changes can also occur inside a specific sector if the sector's binding restrictions are identified and appropriately addressed.

Table 3. Productive capacity index in Belarus in 2005–2018

Category	2005	2010	2015	2018
Productive capacity index	28.5	31.4	33.5	34.4
Human capital	51.6	51.6	51.6	51.7
Natural capital	49.0	48.7	48.2	48.1
Energy	30.5	31.1	31.6	31.8
Transport	15.3	15.5	15.6	15.7
Information and communication technologies	8.1	14.3	19.6	22.0
Institutions	32.3	33.6	40.1	41.7
Private sector	73.6	78.6	78.2	77.7
Structural changes	19.4	20.5	21.2	22.1

Source: UNCTAD (2023).

The index can assist identify areas where countries are leading or underperforming, as well as where policies are working and where changes are needed. It proposes a strategy for future policies and interventions in eight areas: human capital, natural capital, information and communication technologies, structural transformation, transportation, institutions, and the private sector. Throughout the reporting year, the capacity index in Belarus increased. The private sector, human capital, natural capital, and institutions have the highest values in the production capacity index in Belarus. It should also be highlighted that the highest increase in the PCI index occurred in the sphere of information and communication technologies, with an almost threefold increase from 2005 to 2018.

Table 4. Productive Capacity İndex in Poland in 2005–2018

Category	2005	2010	2015	2018
Productive capacity index	35.4	37.6	38.9	39.6
Human capital	56.1	57.6	60.6	61.1
Natural capital	52.7	51.4	51.1	50.8
Energy	31.1	31.8	32.0	32.2
Transport	18.1	18.3	18.3	18.4
Information and communication technologies	10.4	14.3	17.0	20.3
Institutions	67.7	73.2	74.6	72.3
Private sector	78.2	80.1	81.2	81.3
Structural changes	27.0	27.8	28.1	27.9

Source: UNCTAD (2023).

Also in Poland, the index of productive capacity was characterized by an upward trend throughout the analyzed period, and it was significantly higher in Poland than in Belarus. The highest values of the PCI index were found in the private sector, institutions, human capital and natural capital, with the largest (almost two-fold) increase in the productive capacity index in the case of information and communication technologies. Thus, the situation in this case was similar in Belarus and Poland.

The performance of the PCI is closely related to economic growth. As a result, a higher PCI value is frequently connected with a greater GDP per capita. The highly positive correlation coefficient between PCI and GDP per capita demonstrates the close relationship that might exist between support for productive capacity and overall GDP, boosting GDP per capita growth. The ability of the economy to generate goods and services is largely determined by production capacity.

Another way to measure the investment attractiveness of a country is also attractiveness indicators and rankings of investment attractiveness of countries, which are compiled by renowned research institutes based on them. Country rankings of investment attractiveness are collections of information on various aspects of the socioeconomic situation of the countries studied, which are then aggregated into overall indices using various subjective methods. Based on these indices, corresponding rankings are finally compiled, which are called rankings of investment attractiveness of countries.

One of the rankings of investment attractiveness of economies is the Global Attractiveness Index (GAI) developed by The European House. Ambrosetti is an Italian designer. It compares 148 economies from around the world, accounting for 95 % of the global population and 99 % of global GDP, using four macro areas of attractiveness (openness, innovation, endowment, and productivity) and four additional indices (dynamism, sustainability, growth expectations, and conflict vulnerability). The GAI measures a country's attractiveness primarily through quantitative indicators that map various aspects of a country's attractiveness, dynamism, and sustainable development, and analyzes attractiveness from two perspectives:

- internal – the ability to retain resources already owned;
- external – the ability to attract new resources from outside.

Table 5. Global attractiveness ındexes of Belarus and Poland in 2021–2022

	Place in GAI (2022)	Points in GAI (2022)	Place in GAI (2021)	Points in GAI (2021)	Dynamics	Sustainable development	Growth expectations	Exposure to conflict
Belarus	68	27.5	66	29.1				
Poland	33	49.5	32	50.7				
Legend								
Horizontal:	High			Medium		Small		Critical

Source: The European House – Ambrosetti (2023).

Of the 148 countries, only 7 have high attractiveness (4.7 % of countries), 9 have medium attractiveness (6.1 % of countries), 47 have low attractiveness (31.8 % of countries), and the remaining 85 have marginal (critical) attractiveness (57.4 % of countries) . Thus, Belarus ranks among the economies with the lowest investment attractiveness with simultaneous prospects for strong economic growth, in conditions of high exposure to armed conflict between Russia and Ukraine. On the other hand, Poland is among the economies of medium-low attractiveness, with prospects for further, dynamic economic growth.

5. Conclusion

The obtained test results show the main determinants of countries' investment attractiveness. They also underline a clear upward trend in the investment attractiveness of Belarus and Poland, which means that the economies of these countries may become particularly interesting for potential investors in the near future. However, it should be remembered that investment decisions are made not only on the basis of assessing a country's investment attractiveness, but also, and perhaps most importantly, on the basis of the risk associated with the investments made. In the current situation, the armed conflict in Ukraine, caused by Russia and supported to some extent by the Belarusian authorities, leads to the imposition of economic and political sanctions against Russia and Belarus. These sanctions have resulted, among other things, in industrialized countries significantly limiting their investment activities in Belarus.

However, after the end of the armed conflict and the stabilization of the political situation in Belarus, foreign investors will certainly return to Belarus. The results of the conducted research show that the mere analysis of the country's macroeconomic indicators is not sufficient to properly assess the investment attractiveness of the country. Therefore, in practice, domestic and foreign investors use many additional tools to properly assess the attractiveness of the country. These tools include the revealed relative advantage of the country (RCA), the index of the country's productive capacity (PCI) or the global country attractiveness index (GAI). It should be understood that all tools for assessing the investment attractiveness of countries in the form of various indicators, indexes, and rankings have their advantages and disadvantages.

Nevertheless, they can be an important decision-making aid for potential investors. the investment attractiveness of a country is therefore a useful tool for investors, both domestic and foreign. They can also be used by representatives of national authorities to encourage foreign companies to invest in a particular country, in particular sectors or areas of the economy, and in the longer term they can serve the development of the economy as a whole.

References

Abed, G. and Davoodi H. (2000). Corruption, Structural Reforms and Economic Performance in the Transition Economies, *IMF Working Paper* No. 132.

Alfaro, L., Chanda, A., Kalemli-Ozcan, S., & Sayek S. (2004) . FDI and Economic Growth the Role of Local Financial Markets. *Journal of International Economics*, *64*(1), 89–112.

Annual Competitiveness Report. (2009). National Competitiveness Council.

Asiedu, E. (2002). On the Determinants of Foreign Direct Investment to Developing Countries. *Is Africa Different?. "World Development"*, *30*(1), 107–119.

Bayley, D. H. (1966). The Effects of Corruption in a Developing Nation. *The Western Political Quarterly*, *19*, 719–732.

Behrman, J. R. (1972). Sectoral Investment Determination in a Developing Economy. *The American Economic Review*, *62*(5). 825–84 5.

Bellak, C., Leibrecht, M., & Damijan, J. P. (2009). Infrastructure Endowment and Corporate Income Taxes as Determinants of Foreign Direct Investment in Central- and Eastern European Countries. *The World Economy*, *32*(2), 267–290.

Blomkvist, K. (2009). Reverse Technology Diffusion . On the Diffusion of Technological Capabilities from Advanced Foreign Subsidiaries to Headquarters of the MNC. In *Proceedings of EIBA Conference.* Reshaping the Boundaries of the Firm in an Era of Global Interdependence, 13–15 December, Valencia.

Blomstrom, M., & Kokko, A. (2003). Human Capital and Inward FDI. *CEPR Discussion Paper* R 376 .

Blonigen, B. A. (2005). *A Review of the Empirical Literature on FDI Determinants*. NBER Working Paper Series, 11.

Braconier, H., Norback, P. J., & Urban, D. (2005). Reconciling the Evidence on the Knowledge-Capital Model. *Review of International Economics, 13*, 770–786.

De Mooij, R. A., & Ederveen, S. (2003). Taxation and Foreign Direct Investment a Synthesis of Empirical Research. *International Tax and Public Finance, 10*, 673–693.

Ehrlich, I., & Lui, F. (1999). Bureaucratic Corruption and Endogenous Economic Growth. *ournal of Political Economy, 107*, 54–76.

Findlay, R. (1978). Relative Backwardness Direct Foreign Investment and the Transfer of Technology a Simple Dynamic Model. *Quarterly Journal of Economics, 92*, 1–16.

Gupta, S., Davoodi, H., & Alonso Terme, R. (2002). Does Corruption Affect Income Inequality and Poverty? *Econ Governance, 3*(1), 23–45.

Habib, M., & Zurawicki, L. (2002). Corruption and Foreign Direct Investment. *Journal of International Business Studies, 33*(2), 291–307.

Hartman, D. G. (1984). Tax Policy and Foreign Direct Investment. *Journal of Public Economics, 26*, 107–121.

Heckelman, J. C., & Powell, B. (2010). Corruption and the Institutional Environment for Growth. *Comparative Economic Studies, 52*(3), 351–378.

Knack, S., & Keefer, P. (1995). Institutions and Economic Performance Cross-Country Tests Using Alternative Institutional Measures. *Econ Politics, 7*(3), 207–227.

Kumari, R., & Sharma, A. K. (2017). Determinants of Foreign Direct Investment in Developing Countries and Panel Data Study. *International Journal of Emerging Markets, 12*(4), 658–682.

Leff, N. H. (1964). Economic Development through Bureaucratic Corruption. *American Behavioral Scientist*, 8, 8–14.

Lui, F. (1985). An Equilibrium Queuing Model of Bribery. *Journal of Political Economy, 93* , 760–781.

Mathur, A., & Singh, K. (2013). Foreign Direct Investment Corruption and Democracy. *Applied Economics, 45*(8), 991–1002.

Mauro, P. (1995). Corruption and Growth. *The Quarterly Journal of Economics, 110*(3), 681–712 .

Mottalab, K. A., & Kalirajan, K. (2010). *Determinants of Foreign Direct Investment in Developing Countries . A Comparative Analysis*. ASARC Working Paper 13.

Noorbakhsh, F., Paloni, A., & Youssef, A. (2001). Human Capital and FDI Inflows to Developing Countries. *New Empirical Evidence of World Development, 29*(9), 1593–1610.

Nunnenkamp, P. (2002). *Determinants of FDI in Developing Countries . Has Globalization Changed the Rules of the Game?* Kiel Working Paper, 1122.

Sabir, S., Rafique, A., & Abbas, K. (2019). Institutions and FDI Evidence From Developed and Developing Countries. *Financial Innovation, 5*(1), 126–138.

Stöwhase, S. (2005). Asymmetric Capital Tax Competition with Profit Shifting. *Journal of Economics Springer, 85*(2), 175–196.

Tanzi, V., & Davoodi, H. (2001). *Corruption Growth and Public Finances.* IMF Working Paper 182.

The European House - Ambrosett and. (2023). *Global Attractiveness Index.*

United Nations Conference on Trade and Development. (2023). Switzerland.

Voyer, P. A., & Beamish, P. W. (2004). The Effect of Corruption on Japanese Foreign Direct Investment. *Journal of Business Ethics, 50*(3), 211–224.

Wei, S.J. (2000). How Taxing is Corruption on International Investors?, *Review of Economics and Statistics*, 82 (1), 452-486.

Wheeler, D., & Mods, A. (1992). International Investment Location Decisions The Case of US Firms. *Journal of International Economics, 33*, 57–76.

Ersi-Iliana Savvopoulou*

Higher-Order Beliefs and Self-Fulfilling Sovereign Debt Crises: A Review

1. Introduction

As in the famous Keynes' (1936) newspaper beauty contest, "higher-order" beliefs refer to the process via which each investor tries to "guess what other investors try to guess about what other investors try to guess"... (and so on, to the n-th order) "about what other investors guess" about something (usually fundamentals or returns). It is a device that describes the updating of beliefs under rational expectations based on the reception of some signal or approximate information (Rangvid et al., 2009,2013). When financial markets are fragmented and heterogeneous signals are possible, the average belief for pricing may differ from each individual investor's belief. Heterogeneity of information implies that the law of iterated expectations does not hold for the determination of average expectations (Rangvid et al., 2009).

Higher order beliefs[1] models have been applied as an additional explanation to self-fulfilling crises described via the multiple equilibria apparatus, as extended to include the mutually reinforcing actions of market participants and the effect of small differences in the information across such agents (Morris & Shin, 1998a). These two features are shown to remove the "indeterminacy of beliefs". As such, contingent on the type of crisis and payoffs assumed in each case, they give rise to policy recommendations in preventing a self-fulfilling crisis.[2]

---

* **Disclaimer:** *The views and positions of the author do not necessarily reflect the views and positions of the Greek Ministry of Finance"*

1 The higher-order beliefs framework was built based on the game-theoretical concept of 'higher-order uncertainty' and the works of Aumann (1976), Rubinstein (1989), Carlsson and Van Damme (1993), Morris et al. (1995). Kajii and Morris (1997) provide a relevant survey. More recently, the market pricing impact of higher-order expectations has been examined by Allen et al. (2003), Bacchetta and van Wincoop (2006), Nimark (2008), Rangvid et al. (2009).

2 For example, the Morris and Shin (1998b) currency crisis model proposes increased 'transparency' in financial markets, highlights the importance of public announcements as remedies to uncertainty in privately held beliefs by market participants, while also showing that capital controls impose transaction costs which limit capital flight and, thus, create some friction to the self-fulfilling onset of a crisis.

Higher order beliefs have been used to explain bank runs, risky corporate debt and the onset of currency crises, yet no study has focused on government debt, except Hattori (2004). As with sunspots (Cass & Shell, 1983; Shell, 2007), higher-order beliefs may provide some insight in answer to the central question about whether equilibria on sovereign debt pricing in crisis arise due to fundamentals or whether expectations and additional external influencing factors may affect the eruption of a government debt crisis. Unlike sunspot-driven outcomes, which bear no correlation to fundamentals, higher order beliefs would point to an answer that lies somewhere in-between the two extreme viewpoints.

2. Self-Fulfilling Debt Crises

Self-fulfilling crises are distinguished from fundamentals-based crises, as in the latter, it is a deterioration in fundamentals and a "sequence of bad productivity shocks" which usually render the debt unsustainable (Chamon, 2004). In contrast, the self-fulfilling literature emphasizes the role of expectations and beliefs propagation in financial markets. In this strand of literature, sovereign default arises due to a coordination failure among current investors or between current and future investors in government bonds, for which they expect a risk premium to be compensated for the coordination risk they face. Intertemporal coordination affects investor beliefs as follows: current investors expect future investors not to buy the country's debt; the expectation of a future rollover crisis induces current investors not to lend to the country; hence, the initial expectations become self-fulfilling (Chamon, 2004).[3]

Self-fulfilling expectations were first introduced by Calvo (1988), who proved the non-uniqueness of equilibria for two-period domestic debt under a lack of fiscal policy commitment. The occurrence of a confidence crisis automatically induces a regime switch. In contrast, in a model with exchange-rate dynamics, Giavazzi and Pagano (1989) add imperfect public information about the government's preferences in a model where a crisis increases the probability of a regime shift (as opposed to Calvo's certain regime shift). In this confidence crisis model, "sunspot-type beliefs" induce a speculative attack. Factors that are associated with the probability of crisis include the level of debt outstanding, short average maturities and a concentration of maturities around certain dates. Similarly, Alesina et al. (1989) were the first to propose a "coordination failure

3 A relevant, simple model of sovereign debt crises is provided in Romer (2012, pp. 632–639).

among investors at different dates" (Chamon, 2004). Their model follows a tripartite classification of outcomes based on the deadweight cost of taxation, where two equilibria are possible: a default occurs in the first period, or debt is rolled over and repaid in the second period. Cole and Kehoe (1996, 2000) propose an infinite horizon model in which a "crisis zone" is defined beyond some threshold of debt, and in which the default outcome arises when the incidence of some random shock (sunspot) is sufficient to induce a rollover crisis.

International investors are assumed to coordinate on this sunspot variable, demanding a risk premium for the probability of default and associated loss in their investment (Chamon, 2004). Maturity structure and the level of private capital stock are critical in addition to the level of debt outstanding. Detragiache (1996) extends the link of such expectations-based models to the real economy by proposing a model with endogenous output. As such, two channels may give rise to the multiplicity of outcomes and result in crisis: the effect of beliefs on debt-servicing costs and financial market disruption. Pessimistic investor expectations about future outcomes increase the risk premium required by bondholders, thereby increasing the debt-servicing burden on the government, precipitating a liquidity crisis via "surprise inflation"; alternatively, pessimistic investor beliefs may reduce the proceeds from a government bond sale, inducing the government to cut investment, which in turn, reduces output and imposes a strain on debt dynamics without having directly increased the cost of debt-servicing (Detragiache, 1996). Coordination failures in the presence of multiple small market players reinforce the liquidity crisis in this rational expectations framework (Detragiache, 1996). Chamon (2007) portrays sovereign default as a coordination failure between market participants and explicitly suggests a role for "higher order beliefs" (namely, beliefs of each market participant regarding the beliefs of other market players to the nth order) as in Morris and Shin (1998a).

Chamon (2004) offers a concise review of the self-fulfilling debt crises literature, alongside solutions, such as contingent bids as a remedy for intertemporal investor coordination or state-contingent debt securities and maturity extensions to remedy the time inconsistency of fiscal policy. Alternative sources of multiplicity in debt equilibria include "rollover multiplicity" (Cole & Kehoe, 2000); or "Laffer-Curve Multiplicity" (Lorenzoni & Werning, 2013, 2019) whereby there are multiple equilibria for the maximum sustainable debt level. Aguiar and Amador (2013) provide an overview of more recent relevant models and policy solutions. More recently, Auclert and Rognlie (2016), prove the *uniqueness of equilibrium* under an Eaton-Gersovitz (1981)-type model for sovereign debt, and attribute the sources of multiplicity of outcomes in sovereign debt models to modelling assumptions: timing and commitment assumptions, the introduction of long-term debt, the assumption of low international interest rates.

The role of expectations is central in currency crisis models, such as the Jeanne and Masson (2000) "escape clause" or "second generation" approach to currency crises, which follows in the light of Obstfeld (1994) and Jeanne (1997). Jeanne and Masson (2000) are associated with the broad class of "second generation currency crisis models", in which both economic fundamentals and market expectations drive exchange rate dynamics, unlike the first-generation rationale (e.g. Krugman, 1979) that crises are the outcome of deteriorated fundamentals only. Strategic complementarities in the behavior of financial markets are shown to lead to multiple equilibria and provide the link to the class of models used in this paper.

Within the broad class of second-generation currency crisis models, substantial controversy has arisen with respect to the number of possible equilibria (unique vs. multiple) and the time at which market expectations affect the policymaker's decision-making (Jeanne & Masson, 2000). In his seminal paper, Krugman challenged the multiplicity of equilibria by showing that when expectations (of devaluation) are formed during a crisis, the outcome is unique. In response, Kehoe (1996) and Obstfeld (1996b) defended the multiplicity of equilibria when devaluation decisions are taken prior to the crisis. The Jeanne and Masson (2000) hybrid reduced-form model offers a solution to the apparent puzzle via a "hybrid" reduced-form model of the above, in which both current and previous-period expectations affect outcomes (Jeanne & Masson, 2000). They suggest that although multiple equilibria are not the case with stochastic economic fundamentals or when fundamentals follow a deterministic trend as in Krugman (1996), an "arbitrarily large number of equilibria" is still possible due to the indeterminacy of financial market expectations (Jeanne & Masson, 2000).

3. Self-Fulfilling Crises and Informational Asymmetries

While acknowledging the results of the above seminal papers, this review focuses on a more niche literature that has elaborated on the role of informational asymmetries with respect to perceived fundamentals in the ignition of financial crises. Noting certain unexplained shifts of investor sentiment in financial markets, or the difficulty in fundamentals-based predictions of the timing of certain crises, this research focuses on speculative beliefs of multiple investors (as opposed to a single representative investor) in anticipation of a crisis. These models show how belief propagation under imprecise information, whether private or public, results in a coordination problem, which ultimately gives rise to a unique crisis or panic outcome. "Information structure" and "market characteristics" drive the multiplicity or uniqueness of outcomes (Hellwig et al., 2006). Investors update their beliefs about whether or not to invest in government bonds based on their expectations about other investors' actions and about their expectations of the state of fundamentals. Morris and Shin (1998a) pioneered this strand of research in macroeconomics for the modelling of self-fulfilling events, based on the game-theoretic results of Carlsson and Van Damme (1993). Morris and Shin (1998a) argue that the multiplicity of macroeconomic equilibria arises due to the simplifying assumption of common knowledge. In reality, common knowledge, as defined in Aumann (1976), never holds.[4] Failure of common knowledge occurs when agents "merely know each other's posteriors" (Aumann, 1976). Differences in posteriors may arise due to differences in subjective probabilities, even when these cannot be directly traced back to differences in information. Kahneman and Tversky (1974) use systematic biases or heuristics to explain the above. Morris and Shin (1998a) challenge that multiple equilibria models of self-fulfilling crises fail to provide an account for the shift in beliefs that sends the economy from one equilibrium to another.

In their first static model of self-fulfilling events, applied to currency crises, Morris and Shin (1998a) show how the breakdown of some imperfection in the information signals received by financial markets may send the economy to the single crisis outcome. In their model, fundamentals follow the multiple equilibria framework of tripartite classification, and emphasis is placed on the intermediate "ripe for attack" region, where the interplay of speculative beliefs and fundamentals leads to the devaluation outcome.

Higher-order beliefs are introduced precisely to explain the process of expectation formation in financial markets once the economy is in some intermediate zone of fundamentals, called the "ripe for attack region," in which a crisis is precipitated. This framework is used to explain how among the multiple equilibria suggested by models such as in Jeanne & Masson (2000), when in the "ripe for attack" region and when uncertainty implies unclear market signals, speculators' actions will lead to the unique self-fulfilling outcome of a debt crisis (as empirically proxied by an increase in the probability of sovereign default).

---

4 "If two people have the same priors, and their posteriors for a given event A are common knowledge, then these posteriors must be equal…. In brief, people with the same set of priors *cannot agree to disagree*….When we say that an event is "common knowledge," we mean more than just that 1 knows it, 1 knows that 2 knows that 1 knows it, 2 knows that 1 knows it, and so on." (Aumann, 1976).

Subsequently, Heinemann (2000) challenged the characterization of the equilibrium solution for the limiting case, where informational signal uncertainty approaches zero, and presented a "Revised Theorem" for the relevant subsection, such that the switching thresholds are not independent of the critical mass of speculative attacks, even when uncertainty is close to zero. Morris and Shin (1998b)[5] build a more elaborate dynamic continuous-time framework as a theory for the onset of a currency attack, in an attempt to resolve the "indeterminacy in the theory" of the shifts across equilibria. In their model, the actions of multiple diverse economic agents are mutually reinforcing and agents are well-informed about the state of fundamentals, albeit with small informational disparities. Uncertainty about fundamentals leads to some degree of "indeterminacy in beliefs," which in turn removes the indeterminacy about the crisis outcome. This framework enables some correlation of the crisis outcome with deteriorated fundamentals, yet also shows how the probability of such an outcome increases more than proportionately to the deteriorated fundamentals.

Morris and Shin (2000) extend the discussion on the "indeterminacy in beliefs" to macroeconomic outcomes, noting that indeterminate beliefs leave a role for "sunspots." However, over and above sunspot-induced crises, shifts in beliefs preserve the correlation of outcomes with fundamentals.[6] In a bank-run model, they show how private and public signals received by depositors interact with the state of fundamentals, resulting in a bank run. Rey (2000), unconvinced by the uniqueness of equilibrium, counterargues that the number of equilibria in this setup depends on both relative precision and absolute precision of private and public information signals, which in reality, is impossible to gauge. Atkeson (2000) also disputes the basis of the Morris and Shin (2000) argument by asserting that asset prices in a dynamic market economy serve to coordinate the beliefs across heterogeneous agents. According to the Atkeson (2000) critique, market prices serve as public signals which dynamically incorporate all publicly

---

5 Morris and Shin (1998b) introduced such higher-order beliefs to re-examine multiple equilibria models. They note that agents' beliefs are indeterminate due to two simplifying modelling assumptions in related literature: 1. Fundamentals are common knowledge; and 2. Agents are certain about others' behavior in equilibrium (Morris & Shin, 1998b). In turn, these give rise to perfect coordination of actions and beliefs. Morris and Shin (1998b) note that "even a small amount of idiosyncratic uncertainty" may give rise to a "unique set of self-fulfilling beliefs."

6 In essence, higher order beliefs may substitute for the effect of sunspots in such models; however, the application of higher order beliefs differs from sunspots in that the former preserve a relationship with fundamentals, whereas the latter are assumed to be payoff-irrelevant random shocks.

available information. Essentially, this critique reformulates the Efficient Market Hypothesis, which the Morris and Shin (2000) setup implicitly challenges, albeit under a rational expectations crisis equilibrium setup.

Using financial market asset pricing by risk averse, short-lived traders, Allen et al. (2003) show how even in a rational expectations model, market prices deviate from those prescribed by the martingale measure of asset pricing; the law of iterated expectations for average beliefs fails under asymmetric information. This failure of public signals in the presence of uncertainty suggests there is scope for a role for noisy private signals, which undergird the higher-order-beliefs crisis-outcome. The authors comment that the weight placed by market participants on the private signal is non-monotonic, as the shorter the timespan or time-to-maturity of a bond, the greater the weight on private signals. This occurs due to a lower number of "layers of average expectations," such that the agent's average forecast increasingly resembles his own forecast of fundamentals in lieu of the iterated average expectations (Allen et al., 2003).

Naturally, the breakdown of the law of iterated expectations and the role of private beliefs about fundamentals and about the beliefs of others becomes even more pronounced with myopic traders. Tirole (1982) and De Long et al. (1990), among many, have related the myopic traders' forecasting of the beliefs of rational traders to the breakdown of backward induction and the formation of financial market bubbles. As such, the higher order beliefs argument in this line of research is bound to be robust and reinforced under a behavioral finance approach to government debt crises. However, as cautioned by Allen et al. (2003), irrationality is not a necessary condition for the higher order beliefs framework to be valid.

Like Morris and Shin (1998a), Hattori (2004) provides an application of the "higher order beliefs" concept to sovereign debt crises. Hattori (2004) adopts a market-based perspective and in its distinction between a case of common knowledge and a case of uncertainty for financial markets. Nevertheless, the application, methodology and insights are entirely different from Morris and Shin (1998a). For example, Hattori (2004) considers two types of investors in government bonds ("specialist" and "final investor"). In contrast, Morris and Shin (1998a) are not concerned with the actual auction dynamics between the government and primary dealers. Secondly, by applying Morris and Shin (2002b), the relative precision of distinct signals of fundamentals is considered in Hattori (2004), from which Morris and Shin (1998a) abstract. Thirdly, Hattori (2004) parametrizes a loss function for the government, such that tax considerations enter the game, on which the seminal Morris and Shin (1998a) paper is agnostic due to the emphasis placed on market sentiment, given some set of fiscal fundamentals. More importantly, a global game setup is developed in Hattori (2004) and a distinction between short-term and long-term debt is the underlying focus, with the ensuing policy implication that an extension of maturities is required to flatten average repayment schedules, and, thus, reduce rollover risk. Lastly, unlike the proposed application in Morris and Shin (1998a), Hattori (2004) includes cross-default among categories of sovereign debt and comments on the possibility of debt monetization.

More recently, currency crisis models in this literature have pondered over the role of interest rates. By focusing on the information content of interest rates during currency crises, Tarashev (2003) further elaborates on the process of information aggregation via market prices, using an endogenous "learning" relationship between private and public information ("endogenous public signal"). Tarashev's (2003) model enriches the analysis on the relative precision of private and public signals. Failure in common knowledge among market participants is generated via informational heterogeneity, as agents avail themselves of slightly perturbed non-identical information sets. The market provides a medium via which agents communicate their beliefs to the market and learn of others' beliefs.

Following the literature on global games and information aggregation (Angeletos et al., 2006; Angeletos & Werning, 2006, *inter alia*), Hellwig et al. (2006) refute the premise of the Morris & Shin (1998a, 2000) apparatus, by elaborating on the Atkeson (2000) critique on the informational role of markets, as applied to the informational role of interest rates. Hellwig et al. (2006) show that the number of equilibria in currency crises depends on market characteristics and not on the information structure. The Morris and Shin (1998a, 2000) uniqueness arises as a special case of strong market-clearing due to a perfectly elastic bond supply at a fixed and, thus, uninformative interest rate, in which case private information signals drive the uniqueness of the outcome (Hellwig et al., 2006). Interest rates affect traders' contingent bids via two channels: first, they influence traders' expectations about the probability of devaluation; second, they affect traders' payoffs from domestic bonds (Hellwig et al., 2006). By endogenizing the interest rate, they refute the claim by Morris and Shin (1998a) that multiplicity or uniqueness arises due to the coordination problem, and instead show that it is the result of multiple market-clearing interest rates.

4. Forthcoming Research

While the above explanations and models of sovereign debt self-fulfilling crises offer some contribution to the literature, an element that is certainly lacking relates to a description of a chaotic world. What does chaos theory have to teach economists about market beliefs, expectations, and sunspots to explain sovereign debt crises? What are the implications for market efficiency? Could chaos resurrect the traditional prescriptions of finance when in crisis, or would a fractal interpretation of financial markets make more sense to provide an explanation for self-fulfilling debt crises? The latter perplexing questions could shed new light on an old debate, which in the current "polycrisis" landscape could prove more relevant than ever.

References

Aguiar, M., & Amador, M. (2013). Sovereign Debt: A Review. *National Bureau of Economic Research*. NBER Working Papers 19388, National Bureau of Economic Research, Inc.

Alesina, A., Pratti, A., & Tabellini, G. (1989). *Public Confidence and Debt Management: A Model and a Case Study of Italy*. National Bureau of Economic Research, NBER Working Papers. 3135, Inc.

Allen, F., Morris, S., & Shin, H. S. (2003). Beauty Contests, Bubbles and Iterated Expectations in Asset Markets. Cowles Foundation Discussion Papers 1406, *Cowles Foundation for Research in Economics, Yale University.*

Angeletos, G. M., Hellwig, C., & Pavan, A. (2006). Signalling in a Global Game: Coordination and Policy Traps. *Journal of Political Economy*, *114*(3), 452–84.

Angeletos, G. M., & Werning, I. (2006). Crises and Prices: Information Aggregation, Multiplicity and Volatility. *American Economic Review*, *96*(5), 1720–36.

Atkeson, A. (2000). [Rethinking Multiple Equilibria in Macroeconomic Modelling]: Comment. *NBER Macroeconomics Annual*, *15*(2000), 162–171.

Auclert, A., & Rognlie, M. (2016). Unique Equilibrium in the Eaton-Gersovitz Model of Sovereign Debt. *Journal of Monetary Economics*, *84*, Dec 2016, 134–146.

Aumann, R. (1976). Agreeing to Disagree.*The Annals of Statistics*, 4(6), 1276–1239.

Bacchetta, P., & Van Wincoop, E. (2006). Can Information Heterogeneity Explain the Exchange Rate Determination Puzzle? *American Economic Review*, *96*(3), June, 552–576.

Calvo, G. (1988). Servicing the Public Debt: The Role of Expectations. *American Economic Review, American Economic Association*, *78*(4), 647–661.

Carlsson, H., & E. Damme. (1993). Global Games and Equilibrium Selection. *Econometrica, 61*(5), September, 989–1018.

Cass, D., & Shell, K. (1983). Do Sunspots Matter? *Journal of Political Economy*.

Chamon, M. (2004). *Can Debt Crises Be Self-Fulfilling? International Monetary Fund*. IMF Working Paper No. 04/99.

Chamon, M. (2007). Can Debt Crises Be Self-Fulfilling? *Journal of Development Economics, 82*(1), 234–244.

Cole, H., & Kehoe, T. K. (1996). Self-Fulfilling Debt Crises. *Federal Reserve Bank of Minneapolis*. Research Department Staff Report No. 211.

Cole, H., & Kehoe, T. (1998). A Self-Fulfilling Model of Mexico's 1994–1995 Debt Crisis. *Journal of International Economics, 41*(3–4), 309–330.

Cole, H., & Kehoe, T. (1998). Self-Fulfilling Debt Crises. *Federal Reserve Bank of Minneapolis*, Research Department, Staff Report 211.

Cole, H., & Kehoe, T. (2000). Self-Fulfilling Debt Crises. *The Review of Economic Studies, 67*(1), 91–116.

De Long, J. B., Shleifer, A., Summers, L., & Waldmann, R. (1990). Noise Trader Risk in Financial Markets. *Journal of Political Economy, 98*(4), 703–38.

Detragiache, E. (1996). *Rational Liquidity Crises in the Sovereign Debt Market: In Search of a Theory*. International Monetary Fund. IMF Working Paper, April 1996.

Eaton, J., & Gersovitz, M. (1981). Debt with Potential Repudiation: Theoretical and Empirical Analysis. *The Review of Economic Studies,* 48(2), April, 289–309. Oxford University Press.

Giavazzi, F., & Pagano, M. (1989). *Confidence Crises and Public Debt Management. National Bureau of Economic Research*. NBER Working Paper No. 2926, April 1989.

Hattori, M. (2004). *A Theory of Sovereign Debt Roll-Over Crisis*. Discussion Paper (488). Financial Markets Group, London School of Economics and Political Science, London, UK.

Heinemann, E. (2000). Unique Equilibrium in a Model of Self-Fulfilling Currency Attacks: Comment. *The American Economic Review, 90*(1), March, 316–318.

Hellwig, C., Mukherji, A., & Tsyvinski, A. (2006). Self-Fulfilling Currency Crises: The Role of Interest Rates. *The American Economic Review, 96*, 5, December, 1769–1878.

Jeanne, O. (1997). Are Currency Crises Self-filfilling? A Test. *Journal of International Economics, 43*(1997), 263–286.

Jeanne, O., & Masson, P. (2000). Currency Crises, Sunspots and Markov-Switching Regimes. *Journal of International Economics, 50*(2), 327–350.

Kahneman, D., & Tversky, A. (1974). Judgement under Uncertainty: Heuristics and Biases. *Science*, New Series, *185*(4157), September 27, 1124–1131.

Kajii, A., & Morris, S. (1997). The Robustness of Equilibria to Incomplete Information, *Econometrica*, 65, 1283(1309).

Kehoe, T. (1996). Comment on Krugman, Are Currency Crises Self-Fulfilling? *NBER Macroeconomics Annual*, MIT Press, Cambridge, MA.

Keynes, J. M. (1936). *The General Theory of Employment, Interest and Money*. London: Macmillan.

Krugman, Paul. (1979). A Model of Balance-of-Payments Crises. *Journal of Money, Credit, and Banking* 11, 311–325.

Krugman, Paul. (1996). Are Currency Crises Self-fulfilling? *NBER Macroeconomics Annual*, 11, 345-378, The University of Chicago Press.

Lorenzoni, G., & Werning. I. (2013). *Slow-Moving Debt Crises*. NBER Working Paper No. 19228. National Bureau of Economic Research.

Lorenzoni, G., & Werning, I. (2019). Slow Moving Debt Crises. *American Economic Review, 109*(9), September, 3229–63.

Morris, S., Rob, F., & Shin, H. S. (1995). p-Dominance and Belief Potential. *Econometrica, 63* (1), January, 145–157.

Morris, S., & Shin, H. S. (1998a). Unique Equilibrium in a Model of Self-Fulfilling Currency Attacks. *The American Economic Review*, *88*(3), June, 587–597.

Morris, S., & Shin, H. S. (1998b). A Theory of the Onset of Currency Attacks. *Oxford Review of Economic Policy*, *15*(3).

Morris, S., & Shin, H. S. (2000). *Rethinking Multiple Equilibria in Macroeconomic Modelling*. No 1260, Cowles Foundation Discussion Papers from Cowles Foundation for Research in Economics, Yale University.

Morris, S., & Shin, H. S. (2002b). Global Games: Theory and Applications. *Advances in Economics and Econometrics, the English World Congress*. Cambridge University Press.

Nimark, K. (2008). Dynamic Pricing and Imperfect Common Knowledge, *Journal of Monetary Economics*, Elsevier, *55*(2), March, 365–382.

Obstfeld, M. (1994). Models of Currency Crises, NBER Working Paper No. 4640. *Cahiers Economiques et Monetaires, Bank of France*, *43*, 189–213.

Obstfeld, M. (1996). Models of Currency Crises with Self-Fulfilling Features, *European Economic Review, vol. 40 (3-5), 1037-1047.*

Rangvid, J., Schmeling, M., & Schrimpf, A. (2009). *Higher-Order Beliefs Among Professional Stock Market Forecasters: Some First Empirical Tests*. Working Paper, Department of Finance, Copenhagen Business School.

Rangvid, J., Schmeling, M., & Schrimpf, A. (2013). What Do Professional Forecasters' Stock Market Expectations Tell Us about Herding, Information Expectation and Beauty Contests? *Journal of Empirical Finance*, *20*(1), 109–129.

Rey, H. (2000). Comments on "Rethinking Multiple Equilibria in Macroeconomic Modelling" by Morris and Shin, *NBER Macro Annuals, 2000.*

Romer, D. (2012). *Advanced Macroeconomics*, Fourth Edition, McGraw Hill.

Rubinstein, A. (1989). The Electronic Mail Game: Strategic Behavior Under 'Almost Common Knowledge…'. *American Economic Review*, *79*(3), June, 385–91.

Savvopoulou, E. (2021). *Quantitative Models of Sovereign Risk and State-Contingent Debt*. (Doctoral Thesis). National and Kapodistrian University of Athens, Greece.

Shell, K. (2007). Sunspot Equilibrium. *The New Palgrave: A Dictionary of Economics*.

Tarashev, N. (2003). *Currency Crises and the Informational Role of Interest Rates*. Bank for International Settlements, BIS Working Papers No 135, Monetary and Economic Department, September 2003.

Tirole, J. (1982). On the Possibility of Speculation under Rational Expectations. *Econometrica*, 50(5), September, 1163–1181.

Săseanu Andreea Simona, Ghiță Simona Ioana and
Gogonea Rodica-Manuela

E-Commerce and Its Determinants – Behavior Patterns of European Countries in COVID-19 Times

1. Introduction

The last pandemic has changed many aspects of our lives, some of the activities we used to do by travelling to different locations (work, shopping, theaters or cinemas, leisure) are now moving to the online environment (Lestari, 2019, Pastiu et al. 2020). Online shopping exploded in the year of the pandemic. It has changed not only the behavior of consumers, but also their profile, which has an effect on e-commerce and economy overall (Abu-Shamaa & Abu-Shanab, 2015; OECD, 2020a).

The ease, with which online channels can be used for e-commerce, is even greater as consumers have stronger, above-average digital knowledge and skills, accompanied by higher degree of trust in such e-commerce technologies. Panda and Swar (2013) identified among the determinants of consumer behavior using digital environment to purchase necessary products and services: anxiety, ease of use, utility and price, and others found that a combination of education and income can influence the intention of buying, using modern technologies, while gender, occupation or activity sector are less important in shaping behavior (Malik & Guptha, 2013; Zaharia, 2020; Zaharia & Bălăcescu, 2020).

Other authors (Anvari & Norouzi, 2016; Zatonatska, et al., 2018) analyzed the impact of e-commerce activity and Research & Development sector on economic development using panel data. Their results show positive and significant impact of the first two variables on GDP per capita, with higher e-commerce effect than R&D. Empirical research of He and Wang (He & Wang, 2019; Valarezo et al. 2018) led to conclusion that GDP has significant effect on the activity of "cross-border e-commerce trade".

The aim of this study is to highlight and analyze two significant aspects of e-commerce activity under the influence of the current pandemic crisis. The first aspect refers to the main factors that had an impact on individuals' participation in purchasing goods and services through Internet, but also to the magnitude and direction of this influence. The second aspect aims at identifying behavioral patterns of European countries from e-commerce perspective, under the impact of its influencing factors, in COVID-19 context.

The pandemic restrictions have led both companies and individual shoppers to turn to online, which has created a real opportunity for developing e-commerce. The present research – through the selected variables from a wide range of potential economic and social factors of e-commerce activity – takes into account both the similarities and differences of countries, contributing to the development of behavioral patterns that have been very little addressed so far in the literature. The innovative nature of the research consists both in the variables selected for the analysis and in the original way of combining them, in order to identify complex factors significantly influencing the phenomenon of internet purchases by individuals (Welfare, digital skills and internet access; Employment and education; Importance of ICT sector in economy). From a methodological point of view, three main methods are applied in a logical chain, in order to form a clear and complete picture for individuals' shopping online activity, on the one hand, and for the behavior of European countries in this respect – on the other hand. The study starts with a presenting data set and the main methods used in their processing (Section 2). The actual processing and presentation of results (Section 3) has three stages: firstly, the initial set of potential factors influencing e-commerce activity is summarized in a small number of main, complex components (Section 3.1); next, the variation of individuals' participation in e-commerce activity is modeled under the action of complex components previously identified (Section 3.2). The next section (Section 4) includes discussions on the results and conclusions.

2. Data and Methodology

The coronavirus pandemic has exposed even more clearly than ever the rising role of digitalization in our lives. Digitization has made it possible to continue to carry out activities that otherwise could hardly have taken place due to the restrictions imposed by the pandemic. One of the sectors that has benefited most from the advantages of digitalisation has been the trade.That is why we believe it is necessary to analyze this phenomenon in more detail, to find out what could be the factors that favored its development in European countries during the pandemic, which are the factors whose influence explained to a greater extent the changes in the online shopping phenomenon and whether there are certain patterns of behavior of European countries from the perspective of this phenomenon. In this sense, our research has the following objectives:

1. To identify potential factors influencing e-commerce activity in the context of the coronavirus pandemic
2. To analyze and compare the impact of these factors on e-commerce activity.
3. To identify behavioral patterns in European countries based on the individuals' involvement in e-commerce activity and its influence factors, in the context of the current pandemic.

Thus, from a methodological point of view, the analysis is carried out in three main directions:

Principal Component Analysis.The initial set (established based on the results of specialized studies presented above, on the correlation of e-commerce activity with other macro or micro-economic variables) included 19 variables that characterize the level of development of a country, material and financial situation of the population, social exclusion, size and contribution of the IT sector to the economy, the level of digital skills of individuals, digital infrastructure, accessibility of modern technologies, the importance of research and development, the level of employment, the level of education, gender inequalities, severity of COVID-19 pandemic. The complete list of these variables can be found in Table 1.

Table 1. List of variables included in the study

Variable Name	Measurement Unit	Label
Real GDP per capita, Chain linked volumes (2010=100)	thousand EUR per capita	GDP_PER_CAP
Mean equivalized net income	Thousand EUR	MEAN_INCOME
Low-wage earners as a proportion of all employees (Size classes in number of employees: 10 employees or more)	%	LOW_WAGE
Employed persons with ICT education (% in total labor force with ICT education)	%	EMPL_ICT_ED
People at risk of poverty or social exclusion	%	POVERTY_RATE
Percentage of the ICT sector in GDP	%	ICT_CONTRIB
Percentage of the ICT personnel in total employment	%	ICT_ PERSONNEL
Households – level of internet access	% of households	INTERNET_ ACCESS
Individuals who have above basic overall digital skills	%	DIGITAL_SKILLS
Gross Expenditure on Research&Development	% of GDP	GERD
Employment rate – females (15–64 years)	%	EMPL_FEMALE
Employment rate – males (15–64 years)	%	EMPL_MALE
Gender pay gap in unadjusted form	%	GPG
Gender employment gap	%	GEG
Excess mortality	%	EXCESS_MORT
Internet purchases (mobile internet users – Last online purchase: in the 12 months)	% of individuals	MOBILE _INTERNET_ USERS
Participation rate in education and training (25 to 64 years)	%	TRAINING
Employment with Upper secondary and post-secondary non-tertiary education (levels 3 and 4) (20 to 64)	% of total population	EMPL_3_4_ ISCED
Employment with tertiary education (20–64)	% of total population	EMPL_5_8_ ISCED
Internet purchases (Last online purchase: in the 12 months)	% of individuals	INTERNET_ PURCHASES

Source: Authors' own selection

The data were taken from the EUROSTAT database (Eurostat database, 2021), covered 28 European countries and the last year available was considered (mainly 2020, to capture the pandemic evolutions).

Following the analysis of the correlation matrix between the variables, there were eliminated the ones with deterministic or very weak correlations. In order to select the optimal number of main components, several criteria were used – for more objectivity – such as: Kaiser's criterion (or greater-than-one-eigenvalue rule), Cattell's criterion (slope criterion – Scree Plot) and Benzecri criterion (covering percentage criterion). In order to optimize the solution, the rotation of the main components was performed through the VARIMAX method, which allows an easier interpretation of the identified factors. At the same time, the conditions to be fulfilled for a proper application of the method were verified: the character of continuous numerical variables, sampling adequacy (using the Kaiser-Meyer-Olkin (KMO) Measure of Sampling Adequacy), suitability for data reduction (using the Bartlett's test of sphericity); the non-existence of outliers (using exploratory descriptive analysis applied to the variables).

Multiple Regression and Correlation Analysis. In the present study, this method was applied to analyze the correlation between internet usage for online shopping and the complex factors previously identified by Principal Component Analysis, but also to measure and compare the impact of these factors on the variable summarizing the e-commerce activity of individuals. Therefore, the chosen endogenous variable was Internet purchases by individuals (% of individuals), and the exogenous variables were represented by the three main components previously created, the model having the following general form:

$$Y_i = \beta_0 + \sum_{j=1}^{k} \beta_j \cdot Comp_j^i + \varepsilon_i \qquad (1)$$

where:

i stands for the country, N = 28 (the sample size);

Y_i represents the value of the explained, response variable for country i;

$Comp_j^i$ represents the value of the explanatory variable (the Principal Component) j for country i;

$\beta_0, \beta_1, \ldots, \beta_k$, are the regression model parameters (β_0 is the intercept parameter, while $\beta_1 - \beta_k$ are the slope parameters);

k is the number of explanatory variables included in the model;

ε_i represents the value of the residual variable for country i.

All variables are numerically continuous, measured on a ratio scale. In order to verify the quality of the model and to make sure that it is the "best fit" model that interconnects the four variables, the following hypotheses were verified: the existence of outlier values, residuals' normality, residuals' independence, residuals' homoscedasticity, collinearity of the explanatory variables, the validity of the regression model, the statistical significance of the model parameters. Using the correlation matrix and the standardized regression coefficients, the impact of each complex factor on the use of the Internet for online shopping activities was compared, in order to establish the sensitivity of the latter to the variation of the studied factors. The results can be useful for decision-makers to determine which levers can be pushed to stimulate and streamline e-commerce activity, what economic and social policy measures can be taken in the context of a possible extension of the pandemic period beyond estimates.

Taking into account the results of the specialized studies regarding the elements that can sensitize to a higher degree the individuals' behavior in making purchases of goods and services through the digital environment, the following working hypotheses were formulated:

H1: The size of the online shopping phenomenon is positively and significantly influenced by income level, digital skills and infrastructure.
H2: Employment and education level have a direct and significant impact on the online shopping phenomenon.
H3: The use of the Internet for online shopping is directly and significantly correlated with the importance of the ICT sector in the economy.

3. Results

Internet users who bought or ordered goods or services for private use (as a percentage of individuals who used the internet) experienced in 2020 a large variation in territorial profile. Thus, developed countries in northern or central Europe such as the Netherlands, Denmark, Germany, Sweden or Ireland lead the ranking in terms of this criterion, with percentages of over 80 % of total Internet users in the last 12 months. The last ranked countries are less developed countries, such as Romania or Bulgaria (with less than 50 %), preceded by countries in southern Europe (Cyprus, Italy, Portugal and Greece), with shares between 52–59 %. The top 5 countries exceeded in 2020 the European average level, with values between 10–25 %, while the last ranked countries are below the European average by about 40 % (Figure 1).

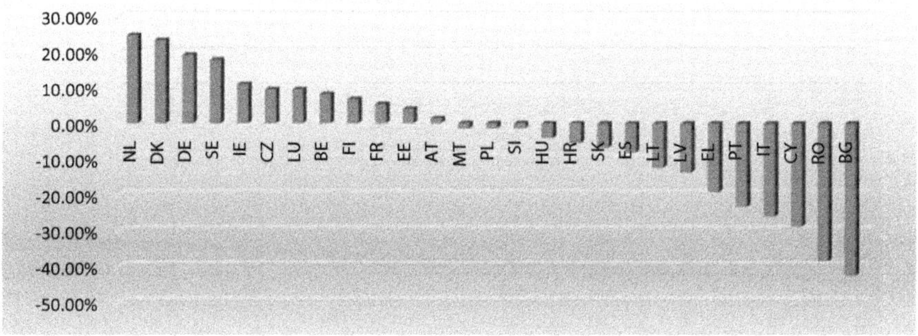

Figure 1. Internet users who bought or ordered goods or services for private use – 2020 (%, EU_level=100 %).

Source: Authors' results, based on data provided by Eurostat [43].

There is a more pronounced increase in the share of individuals who used internet in Europe, in order to buy goods and services for private use, in the pandemic year 2020 compared to the previous year (2019), especially for those aged 25–54 and 55–74. Among young people, growth was lower in 2020 than in 2019. In 2020, across the EU, most internet users who shopped online were young (25–34 years old), highly educated, working as employees or self-employed. The 1 % gender gap from this point of view is insignificant (73 % – men, 72 % – women), basically almost three quarters of the male or female internet users bought/ordered goods or services via internet. The preferences of those who acquired products online were directed towards clothes, shoes and accessories (63 %), furniture, home accessories or gardening products (29 %) and deliveries from restaurants, fast-food chains, catering services (28 %) (Figure 2).

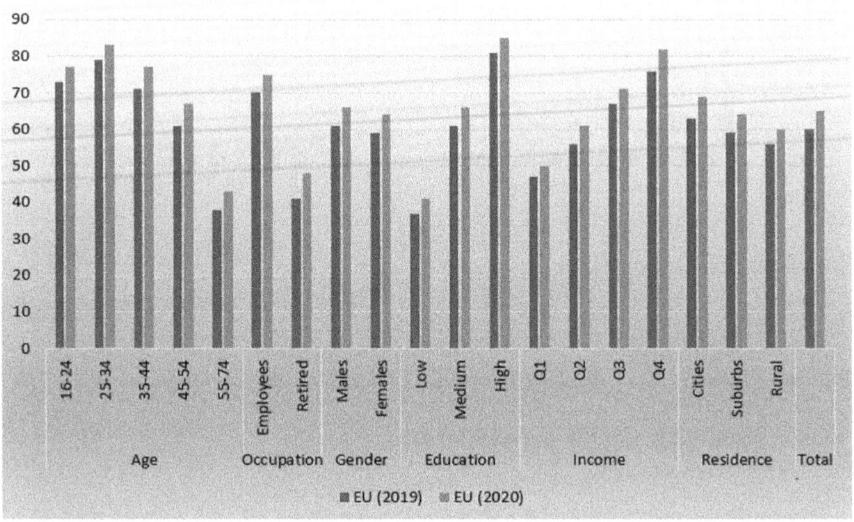

Figure 2. Internet purchases (% of individuals), EU level, 2019 and 2020.

Source: Authors' results, based on data provided by Eurostat [43].

35 % of the online shoppers have ordered products 3–5 times in the last 3 months 44 % of them spent between 100 and 500 EUR on online shopping (Eurostat, 2021).

3.1. Identifying the Main Influencing Factors of E-Commerce Activity

The Main Component Analysis aims to refine and synthesize the picture of these variables (potentially determining the behavior of individuals to shop online) in a small number of main components, which should, however, retain an important part of the information brought by the initial data. For this, we first analyzed the correlation matrix between all these variables, eliminating the ones between which there are deterministic or very weak correlations, statistically non-significant. Following this step, the initial set of variables was reduced to 13 variables in the economic and social area of European countries.

Table 2. KMO and Bartlett's test

Kaiser-Meyer-Olkin Measure of Sampling Adequacy.		**.661**
Bartlett's Test of Sphericity	Approx. Chi-Square	339.577
	df	78
	Sig.	.000

Source: authors' results, based on data provided by Eurostat [43]

All variables included in the analysis are continuous numerical, measured on a ratio scale. The adequacy of the data for the application of the Principal Component Analysis Method was first tested using the Kaiser-Meyer-Olkin (KMO) Measure of Sampling Adequacy and the Bartlett's Test of Sphericity. Since the KMO indicator has exceeded the limit value 0.6 (KMO = 0.661), and the minimum level of significance Sig. < 0.05, we conclude that the data sample is suitable for the application of this method (Table 2).

Table 3. Total variance explained

Com.	**Initial Eigenvalues**			**Extraction Sums of Squared Loadings**			**Rotation Sums of Squared Loadings**		
	T.	**% of Var.**	**Cum.%**	**T.**	**% of Var.**	**Cum.%**	**T.**	**% of Var.**	**Cum.%**
1	6.73	51.745	51.745	6.73	51.745	51.745	5.18	39.810	39.810
2	2.33	17.945	69.690	2.33	17.945	69.690	3.50	26.922	66.731
3	1.58	12.174	81.864	1.58	12.174	81.864	1.97	15.133	81.864
4	.556	4.279	86.143						
5	.466	3.587	89.730						
6	.384	2.956	92.685						
7	.309	2.375	95.060						
8	.237	1.822	96.883						
9	.156	1.204	98.086						
10	.118	.909	98.995						
11	.072	.553	99.549						
12	.041	.314	99.862						
13	.018	.138	100.000						

Extraction Method: Principal Component Analysis.
Note: Comp. = Component; T = Total; Var. = Variance; Cum. = Cumulative.
Source: authors' results, based on data provided by Eurostat [43].

In addition, the shares of the variation of each variable that will be explained by the main components are significant, ranging between 72.7 % and 91.2 %.

In order to maximize the variance shared among items, the Varimax rotation method was applied (Allen, 2017).

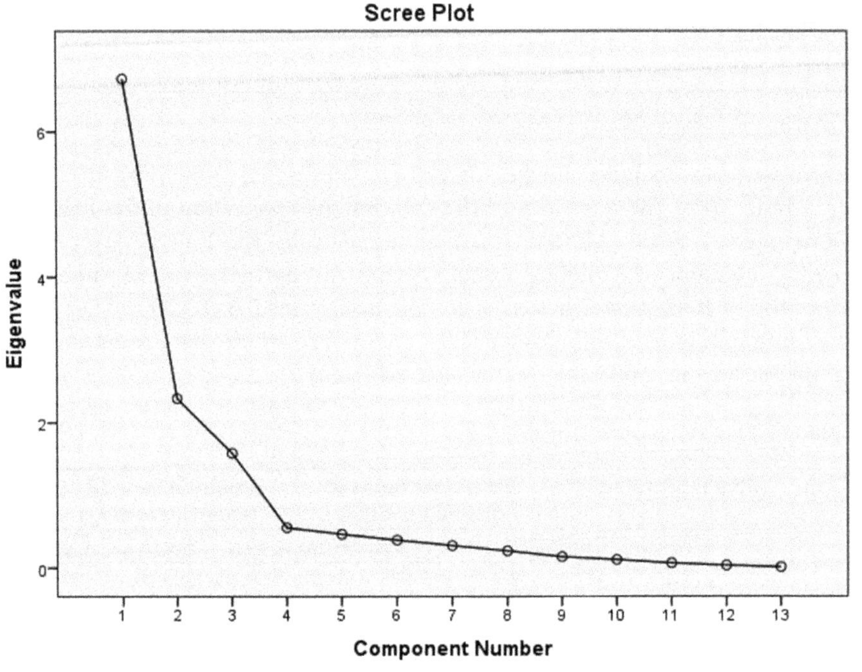

Figure 3. Scree plot.

Analyzing the factor loadings and the Eigenvalues, a three main component solution was identified, whose Eigenvalues are higher than 1 and which keep 81.86 % of the variability in the initial dataset (Table 3, and Figure 3).

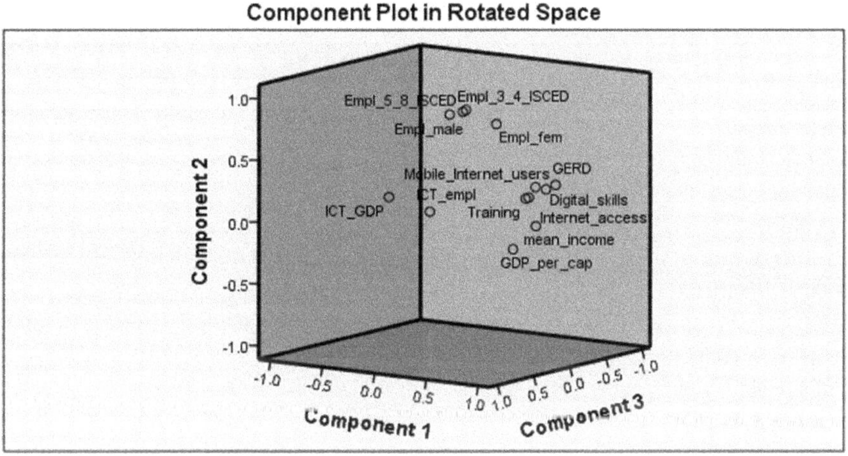

Figure 4. Component in rotated space.

Rotated Component Matrix reveals the structure of the three principal components (Figure 4, and Table 4).

The conclusion is that the initial set of variables was restricted to 3 complex components (Table 5). The first component (Component_1) combines factors related to the individuals' well-being, their digital skills and internet access, including mobile phones. The second component (Component_2) related to the labor market reflects the employment and education level of employees. The importance and contribution of the ICT sector in the economy – as added value and number of employees – are combined into the third component (Component_3).

Table 4. Rotated component matrix[a]

	Component		
	1	**2**	**3**
Mean_income	.912		
Digital_skills	.873	.301	
GDP_per_cap	.819		.372
Training	.813		
Internet_access	.807		
Mobile_Internet_users	.799	.319	
GERD	.730	.275	-.344
Empl_3_4_ISCED		.908	
Empl_male		.886	
Empl_5_8_ISCED		.845	
Empl_fem	.456	.804	
ICT_GDP		.281	.891
ICT_empl	.359		.863

Extraction Method: Principal Component Analysis.
Rotation Method: Varimax with Kaiser Normalization.
a. Rotation converged in 5 iterations.
Source: authors' results, based on data provided by Eurostat (Eurostat, 2021)

All the variables included in the principal components are strongly and directly correlated to them (correlation coefficient between 0.73 and 0.912).

Table 5. The structure of the main components

Component	Name of the main component	Variables included in the main component
Component_1	Welfare, digital skills and internet access	Mean income Individuals who have above basic overall digital skills Households' level of internet access GDP per capita Participation rate in education and training Mobile internet users Gross Expenditure on Research&Development
Component_2	Employment and education	Male/Female employment rate Employment with Upper secondary and post-secondary non-tertiary education Employment with tertiary education
Component_3	Importance of ICT sector in economy	Percentage of the ICT sector in GDP Percentage of the ICT personnel in total employment

Source: authors' results, based on data provided by Eurostat (Eurostat, 2021).

Next, the study aims to examine whether these three complex variables can have a significant influence on the degree of Internet use for online shopping.

3.2. Analysis of the Impact of Key Determinants of E-Commerce Activity

In order to explain the individuals' behavior regarding online shopping based on the complex factors previously identified, the multiple linear regression method was applied. The dependent variable is given by the share of individuals who have made online purchases (Internet purchases by individuals), while the independent variables are represented by the three main components: Welfare, digital skills and internet access (REGR_COMP_1), Employment and education (REGR_COMP_2) and Importance of ICT sector in economy (REGR_COMP_3).

The results of applying the multiple linear regression model are presented in Table 6 and Eq. (2).

Table 6. The results of the multiple linear regression model

Variable	Est. coeff.	Std. error	Std. Coeff.	t – sts	Sig.	Collinearity Statistics	
						Tolerance	VIF
C	64.071	1.109		57.75	.0000		
REGR_COMP_1	12.602	1.203	.796	10.48	.0000	.854	1.170
REGR_COMP_2	4.788	1.124	.303	4.26	.0002	.978	1.022
REGR_COMP_3	2.388	1.018	.180	2.35	.0275	.839	1.192
R^2		.882	*Prob(F-statistic)*				0
Adjusted R^2		.867	*Dependent variable mean*				64.536
Standard error of the Estimate		5.776	*Standard error for dependent variable*				2.990
Sum of squares residuals		800.8	*Akaike criterion*				103.633
F Statistics		59.53	*Durbin-Watson statistic*				2.299

Nota: Est. coeff. = Estimated coefficients (unstandardized); Std. error = Standard error; Std. coeff. = Standardized coefficients; t-sts = t-statistics;
Source: authors' results, based on data provided by Eurostat (Eurostat, 2021).

The model equation is the following:

$$y_i = 64.074 + 12.602REGR\_COMP\_1 + 4.788REGR\_COMP\_2 + 2.388REGR\_COMP\_3 + \varepsilon_i \quad (2)$$

where: $i = \overline{1,28}$

The evaluation of the quality of the regression model was done by testing the following hypotheses: the linear functional form hypothesis; the normal distribution of the residuals; the residuals homoscedasticity; the residuals non-autocorrelation; the hypothesis of no correlation between the explanatory variables and the error term; the hypothesis of non-existence of multicollinearity between the exogeneous variables.

Model Summary

Target	Internet_purchases
Automatic Data Preparation	On
Model Selection Method	Best Subsets
Information Criterion	103.633

The information criterion is used to compare to models. Models with smaller information criterion values fit better.

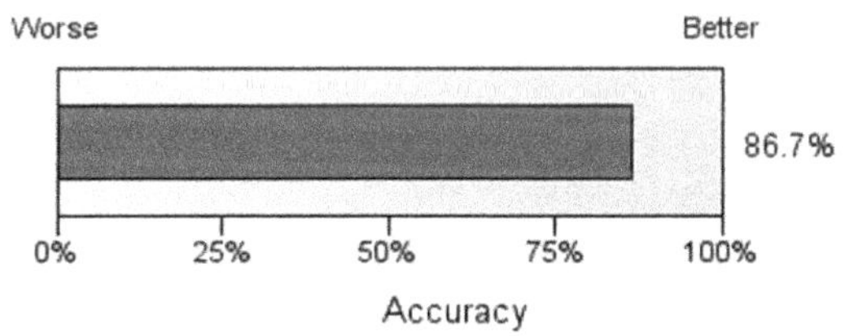

Figure 5. Model summary.

Source: Elaborated by the authors.

The efficiency of all models with subset predictor of the initial set was also compared.

Model Building Summary

Target: Internet_purchases

		Model							
		1	2	3	4	5	6	7	8
Information Criterion		103.633	106.678	116.664	119.576	149.007	149.187	154.932	155.774
Effect	REGR_COMP_1_transformed	✓	✓	✓	✓				
	REGR_COMP_2_transformed	✓	✓			✓		✓	
	REGR_COMP_3_transformed	✓		✓		✓	✓		

The model building method is Best Subsets using the Information Criterion.
A checkmark means the effect is in the model.

Figure 6. Model building summary.

Source: Elaborated by the authors.

The model with all the three main components as predictors proved to be the best, (Figures 5, 6, 7, 8).

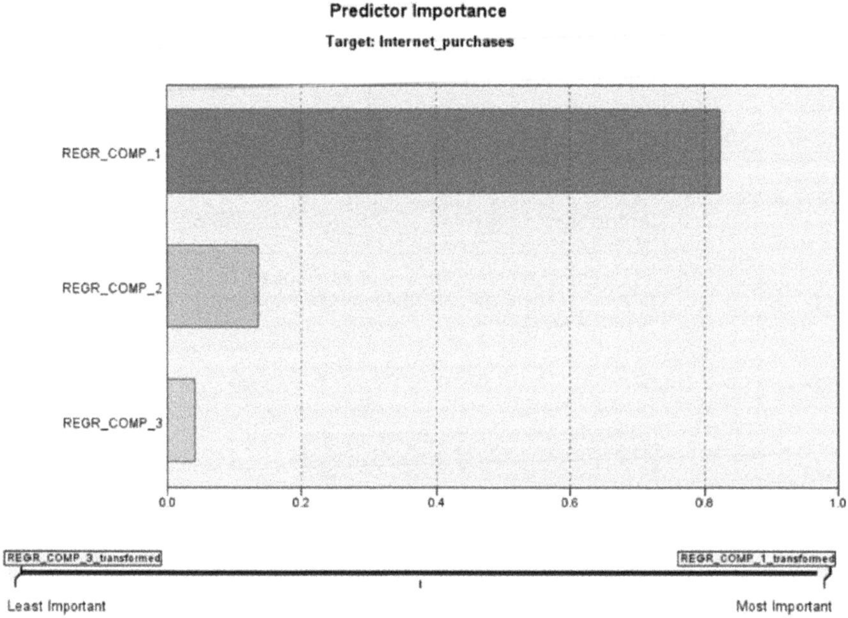

Figure 7. Predictor importance.
Source: Elaborated by the authors.

Akaike criterion less than 103.63 (Table 6, Figure 5, 6, 7, 8) confirms the validity of the model with the three components.

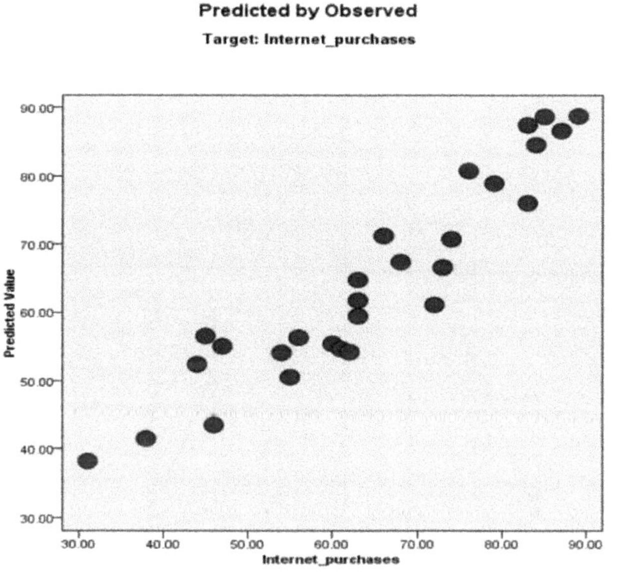

Figure 8. Model prediction quality.
Source: Elaborated by the authors.

The Durbin-Watson statistic used in testing the non-autocorrelation hypothesis (2.23) leads to the acceptance of the null hypothesis and therefore to the validation of this assumption.

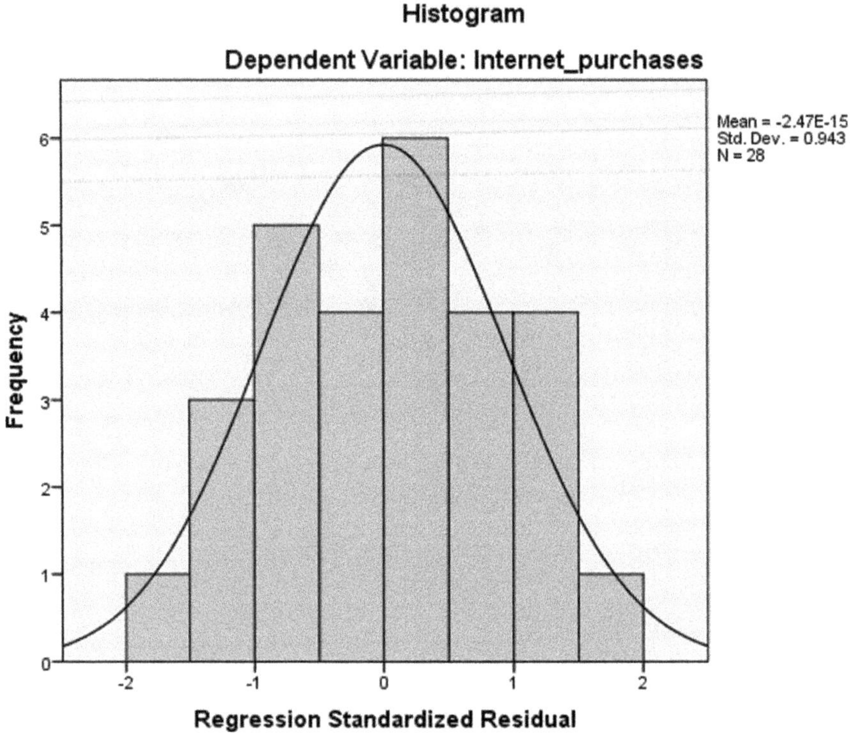

Figure 9. Histogram of standardized residuals.

Source: Elaborated by the authors.

Histogram and Normal P-P Plot of the Standardized Residuals indicates that the errors generated by the regression model are normally distributed (Figures 9 and 10).

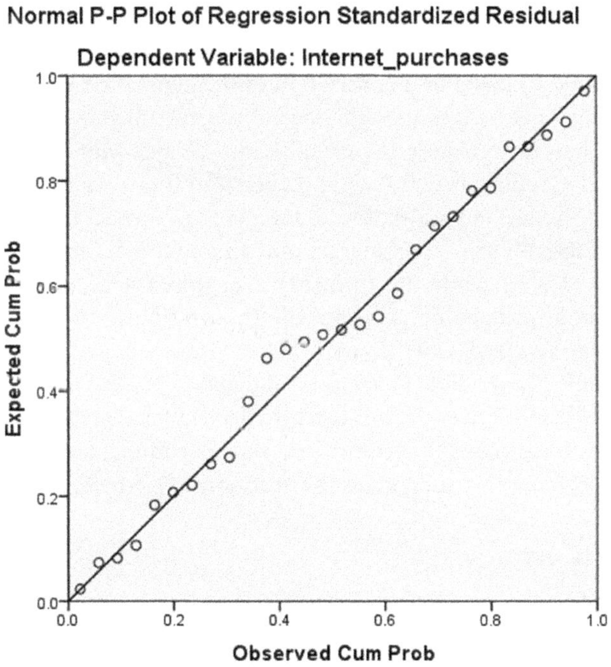

Figure 10. Normal P-P plot of standardized residuals.
Source: Elaborated by the authors.

Testing the validity of the regression model using the Analysis of Variance (ANOVA) method and Fisher's test led to the rejection of the null hypothesis and to the conclusion that the regression model is statistically significant, having a high explanatory power on the variability of the dependent variable. Thus, the model explains 86.7 % of the variation of the Internet use for making online purchases of products and services (F Statistics = 59.53, Significance level very close to 0 – lower than 0.05) (Table 6). Applying Student's test to verify the statistical significance of the model parameters confirmed their validity, for significance levels below the 0.05 threshold (Sig.1 = 0.000, Sig.2 = 0.000, Sig.3 = 0.0002, Sig.4 = 0.0275) (Table 6). According to the same table, all three main components that also fulfill the role of regressors have a direct influence on the variation of online purchases (all three slope estimators of the regression model are positive).

Comparing the absolute values of the standardized regression coefficients of the model, we can make general assessments regarding the importance of the three complex factors on the variation of the dependent variable. Thus, the component that synthesizes the influence of income, digital skills and internet accessibility has the greatest importance on the behavior of digital buyers (Standardized Coefficient = 0.796) and therefore the working hypothesis H1 is validated. The second most important place is owned by the population employment rate on the labor market and the education level (Standardized Coefficient = 0.303), while the third place in importance on the use of the Internet for online shopping is owned by the contribution of the IT sector in economy (Standardized Coefficient = 0.18). Therefore we can sustain that working hypotheses H2 and H3 are also validated.

Good knowledge of these factors can help decision makers to develop policies and strategies to encourage e-commerce and m-commerce activities, for the benefit of both society members and the economy as a whole.

4. Conclusions

At European level, e-commerce is considered to be one of the most important channels that can be optimized, offering unique features that help individuals to promote and sell their products online, but also to buy them, especially in the context of the COVID-19 pandemic. Thus, understanding individual behavior in order to use e-commerce can be seen as a powerful tool to help managers develop a superior strategy to compete and formulate specific policies in the future. In this context, behavioral patterns of European countries from the perspective of e-commerce have been established, given that the manifestation of the COVID-19 pandemic is a favorable framework, thus becoming an interesting topic to examine.

The analysis of the individuals' behavior in Internet shopping was based on a set of 19 variables which, subsequently – following the application of the Principal Component Analysis Method – was reduced to three complex components: Welfare, digital skills and internet access, Employment and education and Importance of ICT sector in economy.

Next, the highlighting of their behavior according to these complex factors was done by applying the multiple linear regression model. The determined model has the advantage of making it possible to explain the behavior of individuals to purchase products and services online based on a component of financial well-being, digital skills and Internet access, on the component of employment and education, as well as the contribution of the IT sector to the economy.

Regarding the effect induced by the first component on the Internet use for shopping, indeed, we can expect that with the increase of income, with the improvement of the digital skills of the population and the access of households to the Internet, the share of individuals shopping online will also increase. Macro and microeconomic well-being creates the financial resources individuals need to engage in such activities

Regarding the correlation of component 2 with the e-commerce activity described through the dependent variable, we can sustain that the higher the employment rate of the population on the labor market and the education level of employees, we can expect a higher participation of the population to the online shopping process. The impact of component 3 on e-commerce activity is explained by the fact that the successful use of the online environment for the purchase of goods and services by the population also depends directly on the importance of the IT sector in the economy, on its contribution to obtaining gross value added and on the share of labor employed in this sector in the total employed population.

By the magnitude of the effect that these three complex components have on the internet shopping process, it turned out that the first component has the strongest effect on the variation of the endogenous variable, followed by the second and third components. This order is natural, as the first two components refer to personal characteristics of individuals or their households, which have a direct influence on the behavior of Internet shopping, while the third component has a macroeconomic dimension, the IT sector being considered as a whole and having a smaller influence on this behavior. People are more inclined – especially under pandemic conditions – to buy more and more frequently using modern communication technology (computers, mobile phones, etc.) if they have the necessary income, if they have adequate digital competences of using these devices and if they also have a high quality access to the internet. Of course, these conditions are related to the status on the labor market (employed / unemployed) and the level of education. At the same time, it is important for a country to have a well-developed ICT sector, which ensures a high-level, reliable infrastructure and well-trained specialists, as a precondition for ensuring a significant increase in e-commerce activity (AL-Hawari, et al., 2021; Bălăcescu,2021; Ilkin 2003; Kumar et al., 2014; OECD, 2020b).

Pointing out the main characteristics of behavioral patterns in European countries, their strengths and weaknesses may be the basis for the future development of a set of specific measures to boost and streamline e-commerce, thus encouraging the involvement of as many people as possible in purchasing products and services through various digital channels.

References

Abu-Shamaa, R., & Abu-Shanab, E.(2015). Factors Influencing the Intention to Buy from Online Stores: An Empirical Study in Jordan – *IEEE 8th GCC*, Muscat, Oman, 1–4 February. https://ieeexplore.ieee.org/abstract/document/7060022

AL-Hawari, A. R. R. S., Balasa, A. P., & Slimi, Z. (2021). COVID-19 Impact on Online Purchasing Behaviour in Oman and the Future of Online Groceries. *European Journal of Business and Management Research*, *6*(4), 74–83. ISSN: 2507-1076, http://dx.doi.org/10.24018/ejbmr.2021.6.4.923, https://www.ejbmr.org/index.php/ejbmr/article/view/923.

Allen, M. (2017), The SAGE Encyclopedia of Communication Research Methods, https://methods.sagepub.com/reference/the-sage-encyclopedia-of-communication-research-methods; https://doi.org/10.4135/9781483381411

Anvari, R. D., & Norouzi, D. (2016). The Impact of E-Commerce and R&D on Economic Development in Some Selected Countries. *Procedia-Social and Behavioral Sciences*, *229*, 354–362. https://doi.org/10.1016/j.sbspro.2016.07.146, https://www.sciencedirect.com/science/article/pii/S1877042816310813

Bălăcescu, A. (2021). Visibility and Communication of Small NGOs in the Context of Digital Transformation. *Journal of Research and Innovation for Sustainable Society (JRISS)*, *3*(2), 201–208. ISSN: 2668-0416. https://jriss.4ader.ro/pdf/2021-02/22_Ec.pdf, https://doi.org/10.33727/JRISS.2021.2.22:201-208.

Eurostat. (2021). *E-Commerce Statistics for Individuals, Statistics Explained*. Available online: https://ec.europa.eu/eurostat/statistics-explained/index.php?title=E-commerce_statistics_for_individuals

Eurostat database. (2021). Available online: https://ec.europa.eu/eurostat/data/database

He, Y., & Wang, J. (2019). – A Panel Analysis on the Cross Border E-commerce Trade: Evidence from ASEAN Countries. *Journal of Asian Finance, Economics and Business*, *6*(2), 95–104. https://doi.org/10.13106/jafeb.2019.vol6.no2.95. https://www.koreascience.or.kr/article/JAKO201915658234895.page

Ilkin, M.(2003). Impact of E-Commerce and Use of Information and Communications Technology on Promotion and Development of Intra-OIC Trade. *Journal of Economic Cooperation*, *24*(4), 81–128.

Kumar, V., Arif, T., & Malik, M. B. (2014). Role of ICT in Driving E-Commerce Business in Developing Countries. *Conference: National Conference on Recent Innovations and Advancements in Information Technology-RIAIT*, November, ISBN: 978-93-5212-284-4.

Lestari, D.(2019). Measuring E-Commerce Adoption Behaviour Among Gen-Z in Jakarta, Indonesia. *Economic Analysis and Policy*, *64*, 103–115, https://doi.org/10.1016/j.eap.2019.08.004.

Malik, G.; Guptha, A.(2013). An Empirical Study on Behavioral Intent of Consumers in Online Shopping. Business Perspectives and Research, July-December, p. 13-28, https://doi.org/10.1177/2278533720130102

OECD. (2020a). E-Commerce in the Time of COVID-19 in *Tackling CORONAVIRUS (CODIV-19): Contributing to a Global Effort*, October 2020. Available online: https://www.oecd.org/coronavirus/policy-responses/e-commerce-in-the-time-of-covid-19-3a2b78e8/

OECD. (2020b). *Digital Economy Outlook*. Available online: https://www.oecd.org/digital/oecd-digital-economy-outlook-2020-bb167041-en.htm

Panda, R., & Swar, B. N. (2013).Online Shopping: An Exploratory Study to Identify the Determinants of Shopper Buying Behaviour. *IJBIT*, *7*(1), 52–59.

Pastiu, C. A., Oncioiu, I., Gardan, D. A., Maican, S. S., Gardan, I. P., & Muntean, A. C. (2020). The Perspective of E-Business Sustainability and Website Accessibility of Online Stores. *Sustainability, 12*(22), 9780. https://doi.org/10.3390/su12229780, https://www.mdpi.com/2071-1050/12/22/9780/htm.

Valarezo, Á., Pérez-Amaral, T., Garín-Muñoz, T., García, I. H., & López, R.(2018). Drivers and Barriers to Cross-Border E-Commerce: Evidence from Spanish Individual Behavior. *Telecommunications Policy*, *42*(6), 464–473

Zaharia, M.(2020). An Image of the Loss of Pre-University School Enrollment during the Education Levels. *Journal of Research and Innovation for Sustainable Society (JRISS)*, *2*(1), 51–60, ISSN: 2668-0416. Thoth Publishing House, https://doi.org/10.33727/JRISS.2020.1.8., http://jriss.4ader.ro/pdf/2020-01/08_Zaharia.pdf.

Zaharia, M., & Bălăcescu, A. (2020). Evolutions and Structural Changes in Secondary Vocational Education in Romania during the Last Three Decades. *Journal of Research and Innovation for Sustainable Society (JRISS)*, *2*(2), 65–78. http://jriss.4ader.ro/pdf/2020-02/09_article_ec.pdf.

Zatonatska, T., Rozhko, O., & Tkachenko, N. (2018). Modern Trends of Impact on Economic Development of Countries: E-Commerce and R&D. *Marketing and Management of Innovations*, *4*, 129–135. http://doi.org/10.21272/mmi.2018.4-12

Alexandru Trifu

One More Problem to Solve for Entrepreneurs and CEOs: The Generational Peculiarities of their Employees

1. Approach to the Complexity of the Problem

We make the introduction by starting from the trends that are manifested currently on the labor market and that impact *the person/HR position* within any company/organization.

Each generation has its own unique set of peculiar traits, characteristics and values that they bring to the workplace. This is important to recognize because these differences impact how people communicate and how they want to be managed.

There are five generations in the existence and operation of today's workforce (www.knowledgecity.com/blog/ 2022):

Generation Z: born between 1996 and 2012*;

Millennials: Born between 1981 and 1996/1997;
Generation X: born between 1965 and 1980;
Baby Boomers: born between 1946 and 1964; In Romania, as an exception for example, the "Baby Boomers" do not coincide with the generation born after the World War II, but they are the oversized generation after 1967.
Silent Generation: born between 1925 and 1945.

- This is the right range for Gen Z (see also Dimock, 2019).

In order to highlight the features of these generations, a psychological profile thereof is needed. We will use the psychological profile that the psychologist Daniel David, Rector of the Babeş-Bolyai University in Cluj-Napoca, Romania, drew up for this country, but this is certainly valid at a general level as well (Răducanu, 2023).

Professor David claims that the "Baby Boomers", the "Millennials", the "Gen Z" and the "Alpha" are the generations that have made the switch and transition from key questions such as "What can I offer?" to "What can I get from here?". Daniel David claims that, psychologically speaking, today's generations are no longer so afraid of unpredictability, but rather, (we might add) they know how to look for opportunities in the uncertainties and risks to which they are exposed.

Thus, the "Baby Boomers" followed a work ethic and they were very responsible for their actions, often at their own request.

The "generation X" was considered to be more autonomous, perhaps more rebellious and which emphasized the getting of results.

The "Millennials" are those who have experienced various activities, processes, and we believe that they should be rewarded for the mere fact that they worked, even if they did not reach the set goals. They have very high expectations, and the recent events, the pandemic and the war in Ukraine have kind of shattered their expectations. They are those who have penetrated the political and leadership structures and who, together with Gen Z, will try to change the paradigm.

Gen Z has a higher dose of pragmatism and its members want innovation and new approaches in the economy and society (as it is almost always the case with younger generations in their early stages). They would be followers of the "no bosses" activity, or without such an obvious concentration of power. This is the reason why a working atmosphere without pressure and fear and without bossing or bullying, is what Gen Z wants.

We will focus on the Millennials and the Gen Z, that is, the two generations that currently dominate the current labor market.

Thus, we also consider the following assessments to be eloquent: the Millennials are eager for rapid career advancement; they want a clear career path and enough opportunities for internal promotion (Wong et al., 2017). They have a greater inclination towards leadership and they believe that the social environment is important in the workplace, as they prioritize the work-life balance; through work they want profit and they are open to professional advancement. They define themselves as reliable workers, they admit they like competition and they believe there must be competition among employees in the labor market. The balance between the professional life and the personal life is somewhat more pronounced among Millennials, while the members of the Gen Z are looking for other opportunities to work after 5 p.m, so to speak.

By comparison to the previous Generation Y (Millennials), whose multitasking ability is recognized, Generation Z has an even greater ability to multitask while it is even more productive. This ability is related to their greater access to information and social networks from an early age, with Generation Z having a higher capacity to process a large amount of information.

The key aspect in this analysis is that a company/organization/entity that works with five generations together, must understand very well the generational differences that set them apart. Workers of variousgenerations bring different expectations and life experiences to the workplace. This can be especially difficult for managers trying to lead teams made up of workers of various generations. It is not just about getting the most out of your employees but it is about making sure everyone has a satisfying workplace experience.

After the general presentation of the current situation of *the labor market* and the importance of studying the characteristics of each generation that acts in business and society, we focus on the more in-depth analysis of the Generation Z, Gen Z in short, i.e. the generation born between 1996 and 2012 (this is its largest definition), a generation that is experiencing the full process of high school and university education.

Gen Z was born in the era of the digitization, so 45 % of them already had a smartphone or other smart devices at the ages 10–12. An interesting thing and worthy of consideration by the management of companies/organizations is the sensitivity of these young people who want to be told stories through storytelling. Hence the fact that they are more attracted to influencers, Youtubers, Instagram and Tik Tok stories. Also, they break with the tradition so far and they are self-confident, having the idea that they can achieve what they set out to do even through more work as their credo.

The World Economic Forum's 2023 Future of Jobs report estimates that approximately a quarter of the jobs will undergo radical transformations in the next 5 years or even sooner (https://www.weforum.org/agenda/2023/04/future-jobs-2023-fastest-growing-decline/).

The digitization, the ecological transition and the disruption of the global supply chains will also make 2 % of these jobs disappear.

In the conditions of this divergent labor market, faced with multiple challenges, the issues related to the quality of work and its results return to the foreground. The transformations that can occur are related to the people's willingness to change employers. About 1/3 of those interviewed in this regard stated that they do not think they would work for the same employer in two years' time, and 50 % of employees actively explore the activity of other companies (Zahidi, 2023).

So, all the more, rational, balanced measures are required, so that employees can be best rewarded according to their performance, knowledge, skills that ensure the progress of firms/companies and also for the appropriate satisfaction of those who contribute to a common effort.

2. Methodology

In this paper, we first conducted a review of the existing literature and practice on the HR field and the interpersonal relationships in the workplace, while planning to conduct a qualitative analysis of the people working in the field about their actual experiences. Thanks to the analysis of the specialized literature and the accumulated experiences, including our own experience working with students, we provide a picture of what is happening in the labor market and the causes of the labor force movements over time.

Also, there is the impact of new methods and activities in the workplace and a few best practices for the HR professionals and managers helping them effectively prevent any negative incidents to take place in their departments and organizations.

We used *the synthesis* to extract the current trends and characteristics of the labor market of Gen Z that we are most interested in, which is key for the operation of entities, their development and also the development of national economies. Last, but not least, finding the most appropriate ways to reach a *modus in rebus*, the optimality both for entrepreneurs/CEOs and for workers.

3. Deepening the Analysis

We will deal with the post-pandemic labor market strongly impacted by the phenomenon of "The Great Resignation" and which involved a very large number of employees from the USA and also from other countries in Europe and the world. Most of them were "captured" by other entities, or they no longer found the salary they received stimulating; in some cases even the career prospects were no longer those from the time they got employed alongside the fatigue, the stress and even the weak involvement of the general management of the companies. Let's also talk about *the quiet quitting*, but especially about *the career cushioning*. This is not a new phenomenon, so it is not a new concept, but after these important movements on the labor market, employees have to protect their jobs, or to preserve the upward path of their careers (Juncu, 2022).

The idea is actually the provision of each employee in finding in due time the possibilities to continue the activity, something like theme used in the specialized works- *you come first your job comes second*, continue the current job, but think about the next steps.

After such opinions and experiences, following discussions with students who have children within Gen Z, or from the statements of people we work with, we have selected the following characteristics/information for the Gen Z people, even before they actually enter the labor market.

As they acquired more knowledge, especially through real-time information, as they were born in the years when new technologies developed and they grew up playing with them instead of playing with the classic toys, they will try to act without calculating the risks arising from their actions, but they will simply take risks, in an atmosphere they want (and which often does not overlap with what entrepreneurs and CEOs want).

One the one hand, the most effective leaders and managers understand that different generations bring unique strengths to the workplace. Therefore, it is important that line managers and supervisors adapt their management styles and learn how to motivate each generation. The first thing *the Millennials* look for in a job is how well they'll get along with a manager. If they don't like their boss, they are less likely to stay in their current position. This can lead to high job rotation rates for companies that have not learned to effectively manage various generations.

On the other hand, *Gen Z* believes in organizational culture values and happiness and less in the pecuniary side of life. About the career and the possibilities to progress and accumulate skills, knowledge, they are welcome. According to surveys conducted and published (Chirciu, 2022; Deloitte, 2022), the cost of living is the main problem, both for Millennials and for Gen Z. The unemployment is at a low rate of 20 % for both generations; Gen Z is interested in taking an additional job to the first, or a part-time job for about 43 %, and the Millennials for about 33 %.

If we focus on Gen Z alone, over 60 % of it want to live by their values and be happy; approx. 50 % of those surveyed stated that they leave the workplace without regrets, if they cannot grow professionally, or if the environment is "harmful"; around 50 % of them are currently using IC technology and they are looking in online and offline groups for job offers.

They resemble the peoples of Northern Europe, i.e. those who are always in the top list of happiness worldwide (Kalkunte, 2020):

(a). The GDP/capita;
(b). The life expectancy;
(c). The unemployment rate;
(d). The population density/square km;
(e). The share of the population in cities;
(f). The atmospheric pollution, in micrograms/mc.

So it can be seen which quantitative and qualitative indicators are the basis for the preparation of this ranking.

Qualitatively speaking, how is Gen Z shaping the workplace and also shaping itself?

These young people, representatives of Gen Z, believe that the trust in a company/organization rests on a triangular basis (Banov, 2022):

(a). The first and most important aspect is *its purpose*. The economic purpose – The profit, the quality of service to consumers and the employee satisfaction – are the defining elements of purpose;
(b). The sincerity and honesty in achieving the flourishing of the business in question;
(c). *The transparency* of activities and decisions.

Thus, once the internal climate is optimal, the activity takes place in good conditions and it will be successful as the customers and incomes increase and, as a result, the wages of those who work in these conditions, regardless of the generation to which they belong increase as well.

The attraction of the the members of Generation Z who do not mainly pursue monetary gains, but finding motivations and adapting to the goals of the a particular company (just like the Millennials), leads through training and the use of knowledge and skills, to the career development and improvement of the individual and collective performance.

That is, this Gen Z starts from the employment in the desired firms/ companies after having graduated their studies to the demonstration of what they can achieve and fit into the respective economic-social gear. Then there are the responsibilities and the space or context in which to evolve as they wish and in which they feel good and in which to demonstrate, perhaps, that the world belongs to them .

As a partial conclusion, companies that own recognized brands and significant market share are reluctant to hire the Gen Z members. Why? Precisely because they are the ones who want to introduce innovations, who respond to challenges and then:

(a). Either ideas that provide nuances and fine touches to the brand are accepted, so as not to reduce its prestige and therefore its economic strength;
(b). Or, another company can be opened within a holding company, if need be and then a free field for ideas and efforts for a strong brand is provided;
(c). Whether, if the forecasts and analyzes are correct and they take into account possible disruptive factors, even the well-known and already strong brands may undergo changes, here and there and, after a possible or certain decline, be reborn under a new form.

The problem cannot be considered to be analyzable if we do not show what the generational weight on the current labor market is, not only in the European Union, but also in the states that contribute the most to the world economic development.

For instance in the US, the Millennials still have the highest share in the labor market, around 30 %, and through the migrant inputs occurred in recent years (Fry, 2018), as they are strongly competed by young people, i.e. the Gen Z members, which brings not only the age-specific momentum, but also a new approach to the staffing are, able to unite in a single (mainstream) effort the beneficial features of these two generations.

These two generations are also the most important on the labor market in the European Union. And, in order to support entrepreneurs, CEOs, HR managers to reduce the pressure generated by this problem that we have tried to highlight, here are some similarities and differences between the two basic generations. We bring this issue to the fore to see how these generations can work and make efforts together (EURES, March 2023):

Similarities

(a). They rely on technology → both generations are used to learning and using modern technologies and devices for a large scale digitization;
(b). The emphasis is placed on supporting the CSR, the great common good and they want to work for companies which share their values;
(c). The recognition of their workplace achievements as quickly as possible. More specifically, studies show that lower earnings through a performance-based scheme can be motivating for employees;
(d). The consistent and open communication is the desire of both generations, but also the achievement of effective feedback to help correct possible mistakes and the ease in taking the following steps. Here, some remarks are required that slightly differentiate the Millennials from Gen Z members. The latter prefer the direct and clear feedback, while the Millennials are more sensitive to criticism and, therefore, they would prefer a feedback accompanied by encouragement and a positive attitude.

Differences

(a). The work-life – personal life balance, with a career development in mind. Gen Z is more applied to career achievements, however also considering financial issues/advantages;
(b). The adaptability to the job versus the job stability, which for Millennials translates into a change as often as needed (we are in "The Great Resignation" paradigm), while the Gen Z members want stability where they feel comfortable and they can contribute to the smooth operation of the entity;

(c). The physical, direct communication versus the virtual/online communication. Even if the Millennials want face-to-face communication, they also use platforms like Facebook and the Gen Z members who can't live without digitization uses platforms like TikTok and YouTube, in the sense of shortening communication as much as possible (saving time).

Certainly, the task of recruiting and placing employees in the proper places falls on the HR department, but because the workforce is the determining factor in a business, the CEO and even the owner decide on this topic. So, they need to know briefly the traits of the generations working in the company, for their harmonization (patience and wisdom shared by the older employees with the young dynamic employees, knowledge in digitalization and enthusiasm towards everything new) and ensuring an effective communication between the leadership/management of the company and its employees.

In general, if leaders want to create high-performing, inclusive and multigenerational firms, they must let go of the prejudices that linger in business and society about older generational workers and they must admit that (www.weforum.org/agenda/2023/):

1. The talent speaks for itself, regardless of age;
2. To attract younger talent does not mean discarding skilled, high-performing, older employees;
3. The age various helps provide the diverse perspectives, knowledge, skills and social connections that help firms to gain a competitive advantage and meet today's complex challenges.

4. Conclusions

Since our analysis focused mainly on the Gen Z members, let us reinforce the idea that the members of this generation which are the employees to be. By the way they think and act especially through modern devices and the avoidance of socialization, can be a new facet of business activities and also challenges for entity leaders, as we have seen.

The defining element, the synthesis of the present analysis, is that it is necessary to harmonize the characteristics of employees, who are part of several generations, so that:

(a). On the one hand, we need to create a more relaxed, collaborative and supportive working atmosphere. Companies need strategies, and specific tactics, for attracting Gen Z members as their employees, as well as their integration, development and inclusion in the core projects and actions;

(b). On the other hand, the entire energetic, motivational and even emotional flow should be channeled to achieve the goals of the activity of the respective entity: obtaining profit and continuing to perform in the specific market, as well as the satisfaction, even the happiness of those who work there.

(c). But, above all, we believe that capturing the specific traits and abilities of each employee are decisive in using them where the most suitable place requires them (not necessarily taking into account the general traits of the respective generations).

And in the everyday practice we have also noticed the paradox whereby certain young people with special abilities and knowledge, considered perhaps to be little who stood out noticed since the graduation year of high school, do not manage to become accepted by the faculties they would like to attend, maybe because of stricter regulations of the subject to be prepared or because of their disregard related to the stipulated requirements. They are more sensitive people and they wish the stages to be followed were as they wanted them to be, without a higher degree of coercion and thus they do not fit into a certain higher education profile.

But, the employment in a firm/company based on their profile can be achieved, with the result that, along the way, that particular young person will succeed in finalizing their vocational or professional training.

The generational diversity creates more understanding and more perspectives and managers/leaders must ensure that the departments as well as the employees are well managed, capable, motivated and that they combine all the strengths of the representatives of the existing generations in the company.

References

Banov, Nevena. (2022). *How Gen Z Is Shaping the Future of Business*. Retrieved May 4th, 2023 from www.moonshotpirates.com

Chirciu, Simona. (2022). *What Gen Z Wants from the Labor Market: Values and Happiness First, Not Money and Career (orig. in Rom)*. Mediafax, Retrieved April 28th, 2023 from www.mediafax.ro/social

Dimock, Michael. (2019). *Defining Generations: Where Millennials End and Generations Z Begins*. Pew Research Center. Retrieved April 20th, 2023 from www.pewresearch.org/short-reads/2019

Fry, Richard. (2018). *Millennials are the Largest Generation in the U.S. Labor Force*, Retrieved April 29th, 2023 from www.pewresearch.org/short-reads/2018

Juncu, Raluca. (2022). *After "The Great Resignation" and "Quiet Quitting", a New Trend Appears Amongst Employees (orig. in Rom)*. Retrieved April 27th, 2023 from www.wall-street.ro/articol/Careers/

Kalkunte, Vee. (2020). *What Makes Countries Happy? Predicting Country-Level World Happiness Report Results*. Retrieved May 2nd, 2023 from www.medium.com/@valkunte/

Răducanu, Mara. (2023). *From "Baby Boomers" to "Gen Z" (orig. in Rom)*. Retrieved May 6th, 2023 from www.gandul.ro/actualitate/

Wong, IK., A., et al. (2017) *How to Attract and Retain Generation Y Employees? An Exploration of Career Choice and the Meaning of Work*. Tourism Management Perspectives. Retrieved May 5th, 2023 from www.researchgate.net/publication/

Zahidi, Saadia. (May 2023). Future of Jobs Report 2023. *World Economic Forum*. Retrieved May 10th, 2023 from www3.weforum.org/docs.

*** EURES. (March, 2023). https://eures.ec.europa.eu/millennials-and-gen-z-workplace-similarities-and-differences-2023-03-02_en

***. (February, 2023). *Why Older Talent Should Be a Consideration for Today's Inclusive Leader*. World Economic Forum. Retrieved May 6th, 2023 from www.weforum.org/agenda/2023/

*** Deloitte. (2022). *Striving for Balance, Advocating for Change*

*** KnowledgeCity. (2022). *Generational Differences in the Workplace: A 2022 Guide*. Retrieved April 19th, 2023 from www.knowledgecity.com/blog/

Zhou S., Chimucheka T., Ayandibu A., and Masuku M

Economic Policy Responses to the COVID-19 Pandemic: A Review of Literature[1]

1. Introduction

Economic policy responses to the COVID-19 pandemic were wide and varied as countries fought to ameliorate the impact of the pandemic on their economies and societies. Whilst no country foresaw the socio-economic devastation that was going to be caused by the pandemic, particularly the recession it induced, policy makers in most countries swiftly responded to the pandemic. The differences in the scope of the responses requires attention and the available literature shows unequal capacity to respond to the pandemic between developing and advanced economies (Cantillon et al., 2021; World Bank, 2021; Mohajan, 2020). World Bank (2021) shows that expenditure of advanced economies rose to slightly above 9 % of Gross Domestic Product (GDP) compared to only 1.8 % in developing economies. Many authors have undertaken to highlight responses that were used by different countries to fight the recession triggered by lockdowns related to the pandemic (Azad et al., 2021; Béland et al., 2021; Cantillon et al., 2021; Craven et al., 2020). Whilst the South African government, including the central bank took steps to lessen the impact of the pandemic (De Villiers et al., 2020), the spirit of this Chapter is to provide a comparison of the policy stance taken by different countries to South African policy responses.

In the South African case, the government anticipated economic consequences of the pandemic as early as March 2020 when the pandemic was initially declared (Shipalana, 2021; World Health Organization, 2020). Specifically, the South African government formulated a tri-phased economic response strategy over a two-year period. The first phase was promulgated at the beginning of the lockdown in March 2020. The policies used during this time included tax cuts, provision of a special social grant of R350, release of disaster relief funds for business support, UIF applications for workers who lost their jobs and several funding opportunities for small businesses. During the second phase, which was a follow up to the measures announced in March, the government availed the R500 billion financial stimulus for both managing the health crisis and

1 Funding Statement: This work is based on the research supported by the National Institute for the Humanities and Social Sciences (NIHSS).

the economic consequences of COVID-19 pandemic. The financing was to be done by redirecting government expenditure, providing banks with guarantees and external borrowing from multilateral financial institutions. The last phase of the intervention is found in several speeches given by the President, Cyril Ramaphosa and other cabinet Ministers. Unlike both phase 1 and phase 2, the 3rd phase focused on economic recovery as opposed to relief interventions.

The South African responses were in line with developments in major economies (Junior et al., 2021). In the United States of America (US), the federal reserve bank (Fed) and the government-initiated policy responses to the pandemic. Interest rate cuts, which left the US interest rate at zero and unlimited bond purchases were used by the Fed, whilst bank loan guarantees, tax cuts and other subsidies were also allocated for consumers and small businesses (Bernoth et al., 2020; Zhang et al., 2020). In Lacalle (2021) the authors argue that COVID-19 carried both a supply and demand shock, hence t needs a response that addresses both demand and supply deficiencies. Unlike Danielli et al. (2021) who lists the different kinds of policy interventions for different countries, we focus on synthesizing literature available on Government interventions during the pandemic. This Chapter seeks to achieve the following objectives:

- To review literature on economic responses to the COVID-19 pandemic.
- To compare responses from advanced economies with the South African case.
- To evaluate the adequacy of South African policy responses to the COVID-19 pandemic.

2. Theoretical Perspective

The theory underlying government intervention into market economies can be traced back to Keynes (1936)'s General Theory of Employment, Interest and Money. Intervention by government is premised on failure of the market to allocate resources efficiently and equitably (Barro, 1979). Le Grand (1991) argues that in a pure market economy, the economy frequently fails to deal with socio-economic challenges without the intervention of the government. Whilst economic inefficiencies in the market can be addressed through regulation, a slump in general economic activity requires a government to inject funds to stimulate demand and avoid further economic deterioration. The tools of the government in the Keynesian theory include both fiscal and monetary instruments (Barro, 1979). With this in hindsight, governments around the world responded to the Coronavirus pandemic as a threat both to humanity and the global economy. Similar to other governments, the South African government used both fiscal and monetary policy in fighting against the pandemic (Bernoth et al., 2020; Jinjarak et al., 2020).

According to Romer and Romer (2021) governments have two basic/conventional instruments of fiscal policy at their disposal, cutting of taxes and increasing government spending. However, during the pandemic, governments have employed a vast number of other non-conventional fiscal measures, including tax deferrals, social contributions holidays, special social grants and credit guarantees. In both Anderson et al. (2020) and Romer and Romer (2021) the majority of developed countries have used a higher proportion of non-conventional fiscal policy interventions compared to their use of tax cuts and direct government expenditure. Chen et al. (2021) uses a three-dimensional analysis and show that comparatively, countries have used fiscal policy at different scales depending on the envisaged target population and the instruments at their disposal. Their first dimension relates to the size of the fiscal response/stimulus, which in the South African context was initially estimated at R500 billion. The second dimension relates to the targets of the intervention, which could be consumers or specific economic sectors. Lastly, the third dimension are the tools of fiscal policy employed by a specific government, which include both conventional and non-conventional tools.

In addition to the Keynesian view, the pandemic has demonstrated the need for supply-side policies to support production and labor. However, this requires an understanding of the two-dimensional shock exerted by the pandemic (Lacalle, 2021; Baqaee & Farhi, 2020). Firstly, the pandemic has reduced household income, propagating a demand shock of the Keynesian version. Responses through stimulating aggregate demand could be useful in boosting economic activity against such a shock. Secondly, the pandemic has exerted a supply-side shock on the economy, which is identifiable in disruption of global value chains. In some instances, firms have exited the market, resulting in loss of output and at the same time increasing unemployment and decreasing household income. Thus, other contributors have argued that the COVID-19 supply shock resulted in further Keynesian demand shocks (Guerrieri et al., 2020). In response to the supply-side shock, various government subsidies have been widely used, consisting of direct production subsidies, tax reliefs and payroll subsidies.

3. Economic Policy Responses to the COVID-19 Pandemic – Stylized Facts in Advanced Economies

The typical economic interventions used by governments during the pandemic were both fiscal and monetary in nature. Fiscal measures included both direct and indirect interventions targeted at cushioning business and households, and stimulus packages meant to stimulate economic activity. On the other hand, conventional and unconventional monetary policy measures were used. However, as argued by Levin and Sinha (2020) monetary policy is limited when it comes to dealing with depressions and recessions. Thus, fiscal and quasi-fiscal interventions became the major forms of intervention. This section analyses the approaches to intervention adopted by advanced economies.

3.1. Monetary Interventions

Unlike emerging markets and developing economies, a characteristic of advanced economies is lower interest rates, which limits the use of conventional monetary policy (Lepetit & Fuentes-Albero, 2020). In extreme cases such as Japan, the interest rate has been below the zero lower bound for a protracted period of time. However, monetary policy remains one of the major tools for policy interventions that is used by the governments in these regions. This is due to the fact that responses to monetary interventions have been observed to be quicker than economic responses to fiscal interventions. In general, monetary policy has become an immediate policy option for responding to business cycles and short-term economic slumps. Fiscal policy on the other hand is particularly useful but suffers from time lags (Krysovatyi et al., 2019; De Cesare & Sportelli, 2012).

Bernoth et al. (2020) discusses the interventions by the FED and ECB (European Central Bank) during the first waves of the pandemic. They identify interest rate cuts and bond purchase programmes as main tools used. In the United States of America and China, the initial response to the pandemic was to cut interest rates. The FED reduced the interest rate by 50 basis points on the 3rd of March 2020. In addition, on the 16th of March 2020 the bank also cut the rate with 100 basis points. No further cuts were feasible. Lowering the interest rate reduces the interest payable on credit, encourages borrowers to take up new credit and should be able to reduce the burden on creditors. Furthermore, low interest rates encourage investment as firms find it cheaper to borrow for expansion or growth of their businesses. In turn this is expected to stimulate economic activity as both investment and consumption increases. In Japan and the EURO, the rates were already below zero and rate cuts were not a feasible option.

In addition to cutting interest rates, central banks engaged in direct credit support to firms. Credit guarantees were extended through the banking sector to provide firms with more access to credit. Niedźwiedzińska (2021) highlights the use of credit support mechanisms in 11 advanced economies including the US, Japan and the Euro area. These mechanisms were meant to provide support to the banking system to continue issuing credit. However, in contrast to the 2009 Global financial crisis, there has been an increase in the use of credit support mechanisms during the pandemic.

3.1.1. Non-Conventional Monetary Policy

Unconventional monetary policy describes monetary interventions other than the normal interest rate cuts and are varied in nature. Due to lower interest rates in advanced economies, central banks face limited options in using monetary policy tools. For instance, the US dropped its interest rate to zero on the 15th of March 2020 and could not further implement any rate cut. To ensure flexibility in policy options, central banks adopted lesser conventional interventions. In the US, Japan and the Euro Quantitative Easing was adopted from the beginning of the pandemic (Bernoth et al., 2020). This (QE) involved systematic purchase of government bonds. However, the distinctive feature of QE during the pandemic was the large scale at which the purchases were being done (Pinshi, 2020; Zaremba et al., 2021). In Canada for instance, Azad et al. (2021) highlights several programmes aimed at purchasing government bonds, commercial paper, short-term government provincial bills and corporate bonds.

3.1.2. Liquidity Support

The US FED announced alterations to banks' liquidity coverage ratio and encouraged banks to use their capital and liquidity buffers to support credit extension to distressed firms and households during the pandemic. In the case of the US, banks have enough reserves of high-quality liquid assets, which could be used for this purpose. In the EURO area, the ECB also temporarily lowered the LCR to below 100 %, allowing banks to lend more. Liquidity buffers were also used to support the economy. Both the bank of Japan and the ECB initiated support for the money market to increase liquidity in the money market through purchase of money market instruments. Other major economies including China and the Republic of Korea also put into place measures to support liquidity targeted at specific industries and financial markets.

3.2. Fiscal Interventions

World Bank (2021) noted that there were about 4000 policy actions taken by different countries in trying to mitigate the pandemic. They measure the fiscal intervention using common criteria such as reversibility, targetability and cost recovery. Advanced economies were found to have used approximately 9 % of their GDP on average in responding to the pandemic compared to 3.4 % and 1.8 % for emerging markets and developing economies, respectively. Governments have used interventions ranging from tax cuts, tax holidays, tax deferrals, social welfare support for households, business subsidies and direct injection of funds into businesses. Furthermore, most governments provided loan guarantees to businesses through the banking sector. In the UK, France and Japan tax deferrals were a common policy, whilst tax cuts were only implemented in a few countries.

In the literature, we find 4 strands of works on fiscal policy relating to the COVID-19 pandemic: firstly, there are studies that proffer possible policy direction, papers that outline the interventions made, studies that evaluate the potency of used policy (Gourinchas et al., 2021), and lastly those who investigate the interaction between fiscal and monetary policy during the pandemic.

The first strand of literature consists of propositional studies meant to give policy direction at the onset of the COVID-19 focused on determining the correct policy responses by governments (Dzigbede & Pathak, 2020; Zeidy, 2021). The second strand of literature includes many studies that have documented the interventions taken by different governments (Brodeur et al., 2021; World Bank, 2021; Tahajuddin & Sulaiman, 2021). World Bank (2021) categorises the interventions into three forms, interventions to fight the COVID-19 pandemic, interventions to protect households and interventions to stimulate economic activity through providing grants to business. The fiscal interventions were both direct and indirect, with direct interventions encompassing direct grants paid to specific industries, businesses, households or individuals. Indirect interventions were in the form of tax deferrals, tax cuts and different types of subsidies (Brodeur et al., 2021; Gourinchas et al., 2021; World Bank, 2021).

Other studies focused on evaluating the effectiveness of fiscal policy interventions used to ameliorate the COVID-19 pandemic (Gourinchas et al., 2021; Tahajuddin & Sulaiman, 2021; Faria-e-Castro, 2021; Chudik et al., 2021). Chudik et al. (2021) analyse the effectiveness of global discretionary fiscal policy measures and finds that these actions were successful in stabilising the global economy and financial markets. Lacalle (2021) and Azad et al. (2021) supports this finding but notes also that the policy stabilisation actions may only stabilise the economy in the short-term, but the pandemic could still have detrimental long-term effects. Castro uses a non-linear DSGE model to assess the effectiveness of different policy actions in the US. The study found that unemployment benefits were the most effective way to stabilise the economy. The fourth strand of literature has focused on assessing the balance between monetary and fiscal policy, and their use during the pandemic (Tahajuddin & Sulaiman, 2021; Azad et al., 2021; Bartocci et al., 2020; Riza & Wiriyanata, 2021). The limit of the zero lower bound is noted in most studies as reducing the effectiveness of monetary policy and favouring fiscal policy (Bartocci et al., 2020; Lacalle, 2021).

4. Responses from South Africa and Other Developing Economies

In principle, responses from South Africa and other developing economies were similar to those of advanced economies. In particular, the South African reserve bank (SARB) announced a raft of policy responses at the beginning of the pandemic (Khambule, 2021; Shipalana, 2021). These were complimented by an announcement of a fiscal stimulus package, initially amounting to R500 billion. The interventions were targeted at addressing the three components of policy objectives, firstly to provide resources to deal with the health-related costs arising from the spread of the virus. The second objective was to shield consumers, whilst the last of the three broad objectives was to provide an economic stimulus to sustain and boost economic activity. The major difference in monetary policy stance came on the backdrop of high interest rates in emerging markets and developing economies. South Africa, together with other developing economies had more flexibility in using conventional monetary policy tools. Thus, the SARB embarked on a series of interest rate cuts, totalling 275 basis points within 1.5 years. Similar to advanced economies, the bank offered liquidity support in the interbank market and also through purchases of bonds. Forward guidance also emerged as an important component of the monetary policy implementation.

The use of fiscal policy was also largely similar to the policies previously discussed for advanced economies. Transfer payments in the form of grants were paid to household (new COVID-19 income grant (Social Relief of Distress) and increases in existing income grants), unemployment insurance, subsidies for SMMEs, tax deferrals, credit guarantees, further grant support to municipalities and allocations for infrastructure development (Burger & Calitz, 2021; Chitiga-Mabugu et al., 2022; Shipalana, 2021). However, a major argument that has arisen on the policy front is that the policies used, whilst relevant and potent, were at a lower scale compared to advanced economies (Estmann et al., 2021; Makgetla, 2021). For instance, the COVID-19 grant in South Africa was only R350 per month, whereas unemployment grants for Canadian workers out of employment was C$300 (about R3510) per week. The initial stimulus package of Australia was 15,75 % of GDP, which included 1 % of GDP as health response. This is high compared to 5,46 % average for developing economies (Carpentier et al., 2021).

Furthermore, Burger and Calitz (2021) analyse the impact of increasing government expenditure on economic growth in the context of the COVID-19 pandemic shock. They show that increasing government expenditure without curbing government debt would not result in the desired outcome and therefore suggest a debt ceiling. This point resonates with argument that emerging market economies already had a constraining fiscal space before the pandemic (Alberola et al., 2021; Burger & Calitz, 2021). South Africa in particular entered the pandemic with a high debt to GDP ratio, sluggish economic growth and high unemployment. Further comparison in terms of specific interventions is documented by the World Bank (2020), who identify differed taxes, cash transfers and credit guarantee as major interventions used by Sub-Saharan countries in addition to health expenditures.

5. Conclusion

This Chapter presents the main literature on policy responses to the COVID-19pandemic economic shocks. We review literature covering advanced economies and compare this with works covering emerging markets and developing economies. Specifically, our approach makes comparison of the policy strategies used in advanced economies to those used in the South African context. We find differences in use of conventional and non-conventional monetary policy instruments in responding to the pandemic between developing and advanced economies. In developing economies, monetary responses were conventional, with additional aspects such as liquidity support and credit guarantees. On the other hand, monetary policy in advanced economies was restricted by the zero lower bound as interest rates are lower. Thus, advanced economies depended on large scale quantitative easing and credit guarantees.

There were no stark differences in the nature of fiscal interventions between advanced and developing economies. Fiscal policy interventions were primarily aimed at addressing the health crisis, protecting households and workers, and protecting business. The emphasis on the later was however on small businesses and specific sectors that suffered greater consequences from the lockdown measures. Such sectors include airlines and the hospitality industry. The major difference in fiscal measures was in the size or scale of the interventions. Advanced economies used approximately eight times as much resources compared to developing economies. For South Africa, the lower spending was largely due to a stagnant economy and a constrained fiscal space due to high debt to GDP ratio even prior to the pandemic.

The work covered in this Chapter demonstrate the need to reign force economic growth in developing economies, stabilise debt and improve budget positions. There is scant empirical literature in the African context, which provides an opportunity for further inquiry into the policy dynamics of the COVID-19 era.

References

Alberola, E., Arslan, Y., Cheng, G., & Moessner, R. 2021. Fiscal Response to the COVID-19 Crisis in Advanced and Emerging Market Economies. *Pacific Economic Review, 26*, 459–468.

Anderson, J., Bergamini, E., Brekelmans, S., Cameron, A., Darvas, Z., Jímenez, M.D. and Midões, C. (2020). The fiscal response to the economic fallout from the coronavirus. *Bruegel datasets*.

Azad, N. F., Serletis, A., & Xu, L. (2021). COVID-19 and Monetary–Fiscal Policy Interactions in Canada. *The Quarterly Review of Economics and Finance, 81*, 376–384.

Baqaee, D., Farhi, E. (2020). Supply and demand in disaggregated Keynesian economies with an application to the covid-19 crisis. NBER Working Paper 27152, National Bureau of Economic Research, Cambridge, MA.

Barro, R.J. (1979). Second thoughts on Keynesian economics. *The American Economic Review*, *69*(2), pp.54-59.

Bartocci, A., Notarpietro, A. and Pisani, M. (2022), June. COVID-19 shock and fiscal-monetary policy mix in a monetary union. In *Economic Challenges for Europe After the Pandemic: Proceedings of the XXXII Villa Mondragone International Economic Seminar, Rome, Italy, 2021* (pp. 233-266). Cham: Springer International Publishing.

Béland, D., Dinan, S., Rocco, P., & Waddan, A. (2021). Social Policy Responses to COVID-19 in Canada and the United States: Explaining Policy Variations Between Two Liberal Welfare State Regimes. *Social Policy & Administration, 55*, 280–294.

Bernoth, K., Dany-Knedlik, G., & Gibert, A. (2020). ECB and Fed Monetary Policy Measures against the Economic Effects of the Coronavirus Pandemic Have Little Effect. *Deutsches Institut für Wirtschaftsforschung (DIW), Berlin.* DIW Focus No. 3.

Burger, P., & Calitz, E. (2021). Covid-19, Economic Growth and South African Fiscal Policy. *South African Journal of Economics, 89*, 3–24.

Brodeur, A., Gray, D., Islam, A. and Bhuiyan, S. (2021). A literature review of the economics of COVID-19. *Journal of economic surveys*, *35*(4), pp.1007-1044.

Cantillon, B., Seeleib-Kaiser, M., & Van Der Veen, R. (2021). The COVID-19 Crisis and Policy Responses by Continental European Welfare States. *Social Policy & Administration, 55*, 326–338.

Carpentier, C., D'alelio, D., Zuccolo, B., Combe, O., & Landveld, R. (2021). Unprecedented COVID-19 Stimulus Packages Are Not Being Leveraged to Accelerate SDG Investment. New York: UNCTAD.

Chen, C., Shi, Y., Zhang, P. and Ding, C. (2021). A cross-country comparison of fiscal policy responses to the COVID-19 global pandemic. *Journal of Comparative Policy Analysis: Research and Practice*, *23*(2), pp.262-273.

Chitiga-Mabugu, M., Henseler, M., Mabugu, R., & Maisonnave, H. (2022). The Impact of the COVID-19 Enforced Lockdown and Fiscal Package on the South African Economy and Environment: A Preliminary Analysis. *Environment and Development Economics*, *27*(3), 209–222.

Chudik, A., Mohaddes, K. and Raissi, M. (2021). Covid-19 fiscal support and its effectiveness. *Economics Letters*, *205*, p.109939.

Craven, M., Liu, L., Mysore, M., & Wilson, M. (2020). COVID-19: Implications for Business. *McKinsey & Company*, 1–8.

Danielli, S., Patria, R., Donnelly, P., Ashrafian, H. and Darzi, A. (2021). Economic interventions to ameliorate the impact of COVID-19 on the economy and health: an international comparison. Journal of Public Health, 43(1), pp.42-46.

De Villiers, C., Cerbone, D., & Van Zijl, W. (2020). The South African Government's Response to COVID-19. *Journal of Public Budgeting, Accounting & Financial Management*, *32*(5), 797–811.

Dzigbede, K.D. and Pathak, R. (2020). COVID-19 economic shocks and fiscal policy options for Ghana. *Journal of Public Budgeting, Accounting & Financial Management*, *32*(5), pp.903-917.

Estmann, C., Hansen, H., & Rand, J. (2021). *Fiscal Policy Responses to COVID-19in Danida Priority Countries in Sub-Saharan Africa.* Development Economics Research Group Working Paper Series, 09-2021.

Faria-e-Castro, M. (2021). Fiscal policy during a pandemic. *Journal of Economic Dynamics and Control*, *125*, p.104088.

Gourinchas, P.O., Kalemli-Özcan, Ş., Penciakova, V. and Sander, N. (2021). *Fiscal Policy in the Age of COVID: Does it 'Get in all of the Cracks?'* (No. w29293). National Bureau of Economic Research.

Guerrieri, V., Lorenzoni, G., Straub, L. and Werning, I. (2022). Macroeconomic implications of COVID-19: Can negative supply shocks cause demand shortages?. *American Economic Review*, *112*(5), pp.1437-1474.

Jinjarak, Y., Ahmed, R., Nair-Desai, S., Xin, W. and Aizenman, J. (2021). Pandemic shocks and fiscal-monetary policies in the Eurozone: COVID-19 dominance during January–June 2020. *Oxford Economic Papers*, *73*(4), pp.1557-1580.

Junior, C. J. C., Garcia-Cintado, A. C., & Junior, K. M. (2021). Macroeconomic Policies and the Pandemic-Driven Recession. *International Review of Economics & Finance, 72*, 438–465.

Keynes, J.M. (1937). The general theory of employment. *The quarterly journal of economics, 51*(2), pp.209-223.

Khambule, I. (2021). COVID-19 and the Counter-Cyclical Role of the State in South Africa. *Progress in Development Studies, 21*, 380–396.

Krysovatyi, A., Lutsyk, A. and Synyutka, N. (2019), June. Influence of Time Lags on the Efficiency of Fiscal Poolicy in Ukraine. In *2019 9th International Conference on Advanced Computer Information Technologies (ACIT)* (pp. 380-383).

Lacalle, D. (2021). Monetary and Fiscal Policies in the COVID-19 Crisis. Will They Work? *Journal of New Finance, 2*(1), 4.

Le Grand, J. (1991). The theory of government failure. *British journal of political science, 21*(4), pp.423-442.

Lepetit, A. and Fuentes-Albero, C. (2022). The limited power of monetary policy in a pandemic. *European Economic Review, 147*, p.104168.

Levin, A.T. and Sinha, A. (2020). *Limitations on the effectiveness of monetary policy forward guidance in the context of the COVID-19 pandemic* (No. w27748). National Bureau of Economic Research.

Makgetla, S. (2021). *The COVID-19 Pandemic and the Economy in Southern Africa*. WIDER Working Paper.

Mohajan, H. K. (2020). Covid-19–The Most Fatal Pandemic Outbreak: An Analysis of Economic Consequences. *Annals of Spiru Haret University. Economic Series, 20*(2), 127–145.

Niedźwiedzińska, J. (2021). Initial monetary policy response to the COVID-19 pandemic in inflation targeting economies. *Gospodarka Narodowa. The Polish Journal of Economics, 308*(4), pp.125-165.

Pinshi, C.P. (2020). Monetary policy, uncertainty and COVID-19. *Journal of Applied Economic Sciences (JAES), 15*(69), pp.579-593.

Riza, F. and Wiriyanata, W. (2021). Analysis of the viability of fiscal and monetary policies on the recovery of household Consumption expenditures because of the Covid-19 pandemic. *Jambura Equilibrium Journal, 3*(1).

Romer, C.D. (2021). The fiscal policy response to the pandemic. *Brookings Papers on Economic Activity*, pp.89-110.

Shipalana, P. (2021). Macroeconomic Policy Development: Lessons Learnt from South Africa during COVID-19.

Tahajuddin, S. and Sulaiman, N.N. (2021). Malaysian government choice of fiscal and monetary policies during covid-19 pandemic: Preliminary insight.

International Journal of Advances in Engineering and Management, 3(1), pp.248-253.

World Bank. (2020). *The COVID-19 Pandemic: Shocks to Education and Policy Responses*. World Bank.

World Bank. (2021). A Review of Fiscal Policy Responses to COVID-19. *MTI Insight*. World Bank, Washington, DC. License: Creative Commons Attribution CC BY 3.0 IGO. https://doi.org/10.1596/35904

World Health Organization. (2020). *Coronavirus Disease (COVID-19): Situation Report*, 182.

Zaremba, A., Aharon, D. Y., Demir, E., Kizys, R., & Zawadka, D. (2021). COVID-19, Government Policy Responses, and Stock Market Liquidity around the World: A Note. *Research in International Business and Finance, 56*, 101359.

Zhang, D., Hu, M., & Ji, Q. (2020). Financial Markets under the Global Pandemic of COVID-19. *Finance Research Letters, 36*, 101528.

Andrew Enaifoghe

Exploring the Impact of Entrepreneurship and Small and Medium Enterprises in Advancing Local Economic Growth in South Africa

1. Introduction

The objective of this chapter examine the impact of entrepreneurship and small and medium enterprises in advancing local economic growth in South Africa. The impact of entrepreneurship on economic growth. The contribution of entrepreneurship to economic growth is significant. After all, entrepreneurs contribute to the economy by founding new enterprises, increasing their own wealth, opening new markets for their goods and services, and fostering innovation. This chapter provides a thorough explanation of the function that "entrepreneurship plays in the economic growth of a nation" (Enaifoghe & Vezi-Magigaba, 2023, p. 3). Scholars argued that "the economy is fueled by entrepreneurship, which also helps to create wealth and diversify the economy" (Enaifoghe & Vezi-Magigaba, 2023). The study summarizes the importance of entrepreneurship before delving into the nuances of its function in enhancing economic growth.

The following are reasons why entrepreneurship is significant in advancing local economic growth. It increases economic growth and jobs; "by introducing fresh concepts, goods, and services to the market, promotes innovation; creates goods or services that lessen people's reliance on antiquated technologies", and helps drive societal transformation (Enaifoghe & Vezi-Magigaba, 2022; Fatoki & Garwe, 2010). It fosters competition, which enhances company efficiency and decreases prices for consumers. Addresses social and economic challenges by developing solutions that fulfil the needs of people. Recognizing the role that "small and medium-sized firms play in their efforts to contribute to economic growth and offering potential solutions to those hurdles, the study also tries to locate and establish its purpose" (Enaifoghe, 2022).

2. Entrepreneurship's Contribution to Economic Development

Global policymakers, representatives of civil society, and academia continue to debate the importance of local economic development (LED) in local government (Enaifoghe, 2023). Given that essential services are supplied at the local level of government, this is particularly true (Ocloo et al., 2014). The debate over LED in local government is being triggered, among other things, by problems with financing, backlogs in infrastructure, and unemployment (Enaifoghe & Magigaba, 2022). Therefore, there is agreement among all these parties that LED may have an impact on socioeconomic development programs, particularly in poor nations like South Africa's rural regions (Mukwarami et al., 2020).

The local level of government in South African municipalities, among other issues, is found to be incapable of supplying the fundamental services and the required infrastructure (Enaifoghe, 2022; Durokifa et al., 2022). There is a growing understanding that a thriving small, medium, and micro-sized enterprises (SMMEs) sector is essential in tackling the socio-economic problems that plague most of the world's economies today, despite contradictions in the empirical data that is currently available. Most of these problems have to do with economic growth, wealth redistribution, poverty, and unemployment.

The majority of nations' development agendas would include SMME development as long as these problems persisted (Brierley, 2021). Ramadani et al. (2015) and Mahembe (2011) appear to agree that emphasizing SMME development is a viable strategy for achieving sustainable development. The aforementioned factors can affect the size of the SMME sector, depending on the nation and approach employed (Ramadani et al., 2015). For instance, SMMEs make up 60 % of all firms in countries like India, the Philippines, Malaysia, and Brazil but have significantly less impact there than in the USA, which has a sizable SMME sector that accounts for 90 % of all jobs there (Soni, 2005). Returning to South Africa, the literature contends that the agenda for SMMEs is being advanced due to the country's worsening socioeconomic issues (Mutyenyoka & Madzivhandila, 2014).

3. Entrepreneurship's Contribution to Economic Growth

The study presents some of the key lessons to learn about how entrepreneurship affects economic growth in the Table 1 below.

Table 1. Contribution of entrepreneurship to economic growth

Improves Quality of Life	*One of the most important roles that entrepreneurship plays in economic growth is its capacity to considerably increase the standard of living for individuals and communities by starting industries, making money, and creating new job possibilities.*
Financial Self-reliance	*Entrepreneurship can result in monetary autonomy for both a country and a person. It fosters independence and reduces the reliance of the country on imports of goods and services. Exporting the manufactured goods and services will encourage development, independence, money inflow, and financial stability.*
Advantages of New Companies and Businesses	*In order to start their firm, entrepreneurs research the needs of the market and develop alternatives using their products and services. By establishing new businesses and enterprises, entrepreneurs play a critical role in altering the economy and promoting a more lively and diverse business environment.*
Job Creation	*Entrepreneurship plays a crucial role in creating jobs. Managing the operations of new businesses and meeting customer expectations results in the creation of new employment opportunities.*
Promotes the Formation of Capital	*Capital creation is the process of accumulating assets, such as savings and investments, to finance new business endeavors and promote economic growth. Entrepreneurship can encourage capital formation by enticing investment.*
Development of Communities	*Capital creation is the process of accumulating assets, such as savings and investments, to finance new business endeavors and promote economic growth. Entrepreneurship can encourage capital formation by attracting investment.*
The end of poverty	*Entrepreneurship has the ability to help people escape poverty by generating jobs and stimulating the economy. Additionally, business ownership boosts the local economy and general living standards.*
Per capita income and the gross national product	*Growth in the economy and prosperity are significantly impacted by increases in the Gross National Product (GNP) and Per Capita Income (PCI) that can be linked to entrepreneurship. GNP measures a country's total economic output, while PCI examines its average per-capita income.*

Furthermore, the ability of entrepreneurship can offer large-scale employment opportunities and means of money generation, entrepreneurship can enhance people's quality of life by creating services and goods that are useful to them, safe to use, and inexpensive. Entrepreneurship also produces novel products and services that solve the problem of a lack of essentials. Business owners have entire control over their financial future in terms of financial independence. "Through their persistence and resourcefulness, they generate income and accumulate wealth, allowing them to achieve economic independence and financial stability" (Enaifoghe, 2023).

Entrepreneurship stimulates creativity and rivalry, which leads to new and improved goods and services that support economic expansion, which is a benefit for new enterprises and businesses. Entrepreneurship encourages innovation and competition, which encourages the employment of new employees across a range of industries, from manufacturing and construction to services and technology, in terms of job creation. According to Enaifoghe and Ramsuraj (2023), entrepreneurs can encourage the generation of investment, and the growth of a more diverse and

The creation of new businesses and the growth of existing ones can help create a dynamic economy that encourages capital formation and opens the door to a wide range of investment options. Entrepreneurship can help people escape poverty by generating jobs and stimulating the economy. Additionally, entrepreneurship boosts regional economies and general living standards. Entrepreneurship can accelerate community development. According to academics, entrepreneurship stimulates economic growth, expands access to products and services, and boosts standard of living overall (Brierley, 2021).

4. The Crucial Role of Small Enterprises in Job Creation

Small enterprises have a reputation for having the ability to produce wealth and job possibilities in developing regions on a global scale. Many African nations, including Togo, Uganda, Ghana, Cote d'Ivoire, Nigeria, Kenya, Malawi, and Burkina Faso, have acknowledged the significance of small enterprises (Brierley, 2021). SMEs in Africa generally are important for fostering economic growth, job creation, and poverty alleviation. According to Ogubazghi and Muturi , SMEs account for up to 90 % of all firms, more than 50 % of all jobs, and 33 % of the global GDP.

Additionally, according to Scheers (2011), SMEs account for over 90 % of African company operations and generate over 50 % of the continent's employment and Gross demestic product. Positive developments in the SMEs sector have been observed in North Africa, Mauritius, and Southern Africa. According to the European Commission (2005), SMEs are the driving force behind the development of the European economy since they are a significant contributor to the creation of new jobs, stimulate innovation and entrepreneurship in the member states of the European Union, and help to increase national competitiveness and employment levels.

5. SMMEs in South Africa in Job Creation

SMMEs in South Africa can considerably "address the issues of job creation, economic growth, and equity in the country". In March 1995, the government published the White Paper on National Strategy for the Development and Promotion of SMMEs in South Africa, which contained policies to foster an enabling environment to address the country's high unemployment rate. Additionally, Cass (2012, p. 5) asserts that;

> *Plan was developed to reduce unemployment and promote economic growth by assisting SMMEs to compete more successfully on the international market, the development of SMMEs becomes even more important for achieving social stability through creating jobs to solve South Africa's high unemployment rate.*

Krönke, Mattes, and Naidoo (2022) claim that SMMEs have been seen as a tool for fostering sustainable development and economic growth. According to Bruwer (2012, p. 2),

> *3,830,511 SMMEs were active and made a considerable contribution to the economy in 2012, this given that there are over 2.2 million SMMEs in South Africa (including both official and informal businesses), the SMME sector's contribution would be quite substantial if everything remained the same.*

On the other hand, it is challenging to determine the genuine contribution of SMMEs to the national economy in the context of South Africa due to uneven reporting and data. SMEs account for 91 % of South Africa's official enterprises, according to Abor and Quartey (2010), and they contribute up to 57 % of the GDP of the nation. According to Statistics South Africa (2015),

> *SMMEs can only contribute 40% of the GDP. The South African SMME industry has the potential to considerably contribute to job creation, poverty reduction, and socioeconomic upliftment despite its inconsistencies* (Tengeh, 2013).

One may argue that the poor performance of South Africa's SMMEs is not due to a lack of pro-SMME growth initiatives. Perhaps because, despite the numerous pro-SMMEs growth strategies that have been implemented over the past few years, the performance of the SMMEs sector remains lacklustre. The result shows that "SMME sector continues to perform poorly despite the multiple pro-SMME growth plans implemented by the South African government over the past few years" (Meyer, 2014; OECD, 2015; Mukwarami & Tengeh, 2017). Local economic development (LED) initiatives are one of the strategies used to encourage the growth and development of SMMEs (Nyawo & Mubangizi, 2015; Meyer, 2014).

The evidence at hand suggests that "roughly 40 % of new business ventures fail in their first year, 60 % fail in their second year, and 90 % fail in their first ten years of operation" (Tengeh & Mukwarami, 2017), despite the positive effects of the government's LED initiatives on the expansion of SMMEs (Mukwarami & Tengeh, 2017). Smaller businesses may fail because various stakeholders are unsure of how SMMEs may be used to successfully reduce poverty on purpose (Lekhanya, 2015).

6. South African Government Initiatives to Support the Growth of SMMEs

The government of South Africa has over the years responded to the advancement of local economic growth. The expansion of SMMEs has taken primacy since apartheid in South Africa was abolished. SMMEs, the country's economic growth engine, have the potential to eradicate poverty in rural areas by creating jobs, claim Chimucheka and Mandipaka (2015). Particularly, it is believed that SMMEs can have an impact on the economy that lessens poverty and generates employment at the local level (Small Enterprise Development Agency, 2016). One way to ensure that local communities benefit from the pro-SMME movement is to design and enforce appropriate LED policies.

One of the duties of the government is to boost economic growth, and some governments achieve this via supporting SMMEs. Through legislation, the government enacts laws and other regulations (Chimucheka & Mandipaka, 2015; Asoba & Tengeh, 2016). The government of South Africa enacts laws and policies to promote the growth of SMMEs. These legislation include the Local Government Transition Act of 1993, which was updated in 1999, the Broad-Based Black Economic Empowerment (BBE) Act 53 of 2003, and the National Small Business Act 102 of 1996. These laws have greatly aided in the expansion of the SMME sector, particularly the BBE Act of 2003, which was the first to provide historically underprivileged individuals with unrestricted opportunities to make significant contributions to the economy (Department of Trade and Industry, 2014).

The government has also tried to address the difficulties of the skills deficit among current and potential SMME operators through Sectorial Education and Training Authorities (SETAs), which manage the upskilling of the workforce (World Bank, 2007). Due to the localization of SMMEs, local governments' LED programs are essential to their growth (Chimucheka, 2015). Considering this, the Department of Cooperative Governance and Traditional Affairs (DCOGTA,

2015) hypothesizes that LED policies encourage people to recognize local economic potential. The government tries to close any capacity gaps that might appear in the environment of small businesses.

LED projects that target electrification, improved service delivery, transportation difficulties, and regulatory framework have been given priority to address socioeconomic challenges (OECD, 2015). Three government agencies have primarily focused on the SMME sector in the nation's fight against economic inequality. According to Tengeh (2013), Chimucheka and Mandipaka (2015), SMMEs provide employment possibilities and lessen the negative consequences of poverty on the economically disadvantaged. SMMEs are increasingly viewed as a key tool in the fight against poverty because of the pervasive socioeconomic gaps in South Africa's polarized communities (Mukwaramie et al., 2017).

The government offers a number of support programs in the form of funding for particular industries, R&D, and the development of young people's skills through special organizations (OECD, 2015). "The National Development Plan (NDP), one of the government's most recent programs, aims to eradicate poverty by 2030, the encouragement of SMME development inside the defined local economic zones is one of NDP's main goals". "The NDP aspires to boost yearly economic growth by 5 % by 2030, and SMMEs will play a significant role in assisting them in achieving this goal" S(OECD, 2015).

7. Breakdown of the Government's Initiatives Towards Economic Growth

In an effort to address the problems of socioeconomic injustice, the South African government has launched a number of economic development programs since 1994. One of these programs is the Reconstruction and Development Programme (RDP), which was established in 1994 and worked to improve the socioeconomic conditions of disadvantaged communities by ensuring that they had access to necessities like housing and water. With the same socioeconomic objectives as the RDP, the Growth, Employment and Redistribution (GEAR) program was established in 1996, but with a focus on boosting the economy, creating jobs, and redistributing wealth. The Accelerated and Shared Growth Initiative (AsgiSA) framework was introduced after 10 years to promote economic growth through the planned sharing of economic growth advantages.

The 2010 New Growth Plan aims to provide workable plans for revitalizing the economic development agenda. When the NDP was put into effect in 2012, one of its objectives was to eliminate socioeconomic disparities by encouraging company growth in specific areas. The NDP did, however, include provisions for the Industrial Policy Action Plan, the National Industrial Policy Framework

(NIPF), and other supplemental economic measures. The NIPF aimed to promote industrialization "by promoting diversification, developing labour-intensive industries, increasing production in the industries, and integrating historically disadvantaged South Africans into the mainstream economy through LED programs" (OECD, 2015; National Planning Commission, 2011).

8. Research Findings and Discussion

According to estimates made by the OECD (2015), SMEs create 75 % of all new gross jobs globally and employ an average of 65 % of the labor force. SMMEs are significant and contribute significantly to South Africa's economy;

> *"even though the nation's unemployment rate continues to be excessively high by international standards at 26% and above"*(Mukumba, 2014).
> *"In order for South Africa to advance economically and in terms of socioeconomic development, SMMEs will be crucial"* (OECD, 2015; Edwards and Rankin, 2015).

The Department of National Planning and Evaluation projects that SMEs would generate 90 % of new jobs through the NDP by 2030. However, the South Africa Institute of Chartered Accountants (SAICA, 2015) claims that until the Government policy is changed, such a lofty goal cannot be reached on the growth of SMMEs changes. A quick look at the situation as of the second quarter of 2015 reveals an increase in the number of people carrying out entrepreneurial activities. Although it is difficult to quantify their contribution, the associated growth in employment over this period could be attributable to persons working in the informal sector (Statistics South Africa, 2015).

In a different direction, the GDP contribution of SMMEs increased steadily over time (Figure 1). If everything else were equal, this might be interpreted as a sign of how well the pro-SMME policies are working. SMMEs encounter several difficulties, and as a result of their influence on the economy, these problems have become more prominent over time. Despite this, SMMEs face numerous obstacles to the success of SMEs to thrive, never mind development. In this regard, SMMEs face several challenges related to management, financing, and environmental issues (Brink et al., 2003).

9. Inaccessibility of the Finances

The availability of cash, the lifeblood of the business, has a significant impact on SMMEs' overall growth and development. However, acceptable access to financial capital continues to be a substantial challenge for small business operators all over the world, according to various studies (see Tengeh, 2013; Agwa-Ejon &

Mbohwa, 2015; Chimucheka & Mandipaka, 2015; Mukwarami & Tengeh, 2017). Some authors, like Mutyenyoka and Madzivhandila (2014), believe that financial aid groups like Khula Enterprise Finance and the South African Microfinance Apex Fund (SAMAF), which are intended to give financial assistance to small businesses, are not fully operational.

10. Lack of Suitable Technology

The impact of technology access on the growth of SMMEs is well documented in the literature, and its facilitation has received particular emphasis on sharing company information and having access to both domestic and international markets. Targeted attacks on foreign-owned SMMEs are also on the rise in South Africa, particularly in the townships where the majority of small companies, like spaza stores, are foreign-owned. The frequency of xenophobic-related incidents has a major negative influence on the development of SMMEs in townships and rural areas. A growing number of studies (see Asoba & Tengeh, 2016; Tengeh, 2016) have suggested that xenophobia may act as a hindrance to the development of SMMEs in South Africa. The study highlighted the negative consequences of xenophobia and competition on immigrant-owned businesses in South African local communities.

11. Limited Access to International Markets and Competition

Owing to globalization, the world's SMMEs now have a wide range of options because to globalization. Studies have revealed that SMME operators are having trouble accessing global marketplaces, which has caused their business operations to fail (Abor & Quartey, 2010). Sometimes, SMMEs' access to global markets is complicated by the ignorance of their existence (Fatoki & Garwe, 2010). In marketplaces where the playing field is level, the influence of the highly competitive business climate is thought to be minimal, although this is never the case in reality.

They are the key players in every market who monitor the rate of innovation, industry pricing, and other factors, and they frequently pose a threat to smaller or less powerful companies. Some research has emphasized the negative effects of competition on the growth of SMMEs. Competition is one of the biggest problems SMME operators face, according to Urban and Naidoo (2012), especially in developing nations where small enterprises find it difficult to withstand the pressure from larger competitors. Concurring, Mukwarami and Tengeh (2017) advanced that immigrant-owned enterprises in the spaza industry pose a serious threat to local South Africans.

12. Concluding Remarks

In conclusion, it is generally agreed that helping SMMEs may have the desired result, and local governments are better positioned to carry this through. To collect data from several databases of SMMEs operating inside the municipality and develop conclusions on the difficulties experienced by SMME operators in South African local municipalities, a desktop research approach was used. According to the research, the biggest barriers to the expansion of SMMEs in BLM include a lack of managerial skills, a high crime rate, a lack of access to international markets, and a lack of financial resources. Similarly, it has been suggested that problems like xenophobia and competition have a detrimental effect on the development of SMMEs. In contrast to other research, the study found that the absence of technological infrastructure posed only a minor barrier to the development of SMMEs.

13. Recommendation

Adopt policies that are inclusive and broad-based, policymakers and financial institutions may work together to address the crisis of limited access to financing. Such a project might call for initiatives to promote financial literacy among SMMEs. The training facilities are required to give entrepreneurs managerial abilities. It is recommended that the local government must give priority to crime prevention. The government must create, customize and implement relevant LED rules is one method to guarantee that local communities profit from pro-SMME efforts.

References

Abor, J., & Quartey, P. (2010). Issues in SME Development in Ghana and South Africa. *International Research Journal of Finance and Economics, 39*(6), 215–228.

Agwa-Ejon, J., & Mbohwa, C. (2015). Financial Challenges Faced by SMMES in Gauteng South Africa. *International Associatio for Management of Technology, IAMOT Conference Proceedings*, pp. 520–534.

Asoba, S. N. & Tengeh, R. K. (2016). Analysis of Start-Up Challenges of African Immigrant-Owned Businesses in Selected Craft Markets in Cape Town. *Environmental Economics, 7*(2), 97–105.

Brierley, S. (2021). Combining Patronage and Merit in Public Sector Recruitment. *The Journal of Politics, 83*(1), 182–197.

Brink, A., Cant, M., & Ligthelm, A. (2003). Problems Experienced by Small Businesses in South Africa. *16th Annual Conference of Small Enterprises Association of Australian andNew Zealand*, University of Ballarat, Ballarat, Australia, 28 September–1 October.

Bruwer. (2012). The Entrepreneurial Mind Set Profile of South African Small Medium and Micro Enterprises (SMMEs) in the Cape Metropole. *African Journal of Business Management, 6*(15), 5383–5388.

Cass, R. (2012). *Interdependent and Conflicting Objectives in South African SMME Policies: Competitiveness vs. Employment Creation.* School of Mechanical, Industrial and Aeronautical Engineering, University of the Witwatersrand, South Africa.

Chimucheka, T. (2015). The Contribution of Entrepreneurship Education in Improving Entrepreneurial Skills and Knowledge of SMME Owners and Managers. *Journal of Economics*, *6*(2), 149–155.

Chimucheka, T., & Mandipaka, F. (2015). Challenges Faced by Small, Medium and Microenterprises in the Nkonkbe Municipality. *International Business & Economic Journal*, *14*(2), 309–315.

Department of Cooperate Governance and Traditional Affairs (DCOGTA). (2015). *Annual Report 2014/15.*

Department of Trade and Industry. (2014). *Industrial Policy Action Plan: 2013/ 14–2015/16*. Pretoria.

Durokifa, A., Uwizeyimana, D., & Enaifoghe, A. (2022). Politics and Administration: Creating a Balance for Effective Service Delivery in Selected African Countries. *African Journal of Development Studies*, *12*(1), 333–352.

Edwards, L., & Rankin, N. (2015). *Labour Market Policies, Firm Dynamics and ExportPerformance in South Africa.* OECD Economics Department Working Papers, Paris: OECD Publishing.

Enaifoghe, A. O. (2022). Challenges of Municipal Service Delivery And Instruments For Enhancing South African Local Government Administration. *African Journal of Development Studies, 12*(3), 105–124

Enaifoghe, A. (2023). The Role of Ethical Behavior and Public Value Creation in the Local Government System in South Africa. *International Journal of Social Science Research and Review*, *6*(1), 471–483.

Enaifoghe, A., & Ramsuraj, T. (2023). The Function of Entrepreneurship and Small and Medium Enterprises in Promoting Local Economic Development in South Africa. *African Journal of Inter/Multidisciplinary Studies* (AJIMS), 5, 2023.

Enaifoghe, A. O., & Vezi-Magigaba, F. N. (2022). Rethinking The Sustainability of Local Economic Development: Entrepreneurship In South Africa. *Expert Journal of Business and Management, 10*(2), 77–90.

Enaifoghe, A., & Vezi-Magigaba, M. F. (2023). Conceptualizing the Role of Entrepreneurship and SME in Fostering South Africa's Local Economic Development. *International Journal of Research in Business and Social Science* (2147–4478), 12(4), 96–105.

European Commission. (2005). *SME Definition User Guide and Model Declaration*. Enterprise and Industry Publications.

Fatoki, O., & Garwe, D. (2010). Obstacles to the Growth of new SMEs in South Africa: A Principal Component Analysis Approach. *African Journal of Business Management, 4*(5), 729–738.

Krönke, M., Mattes, R., & Naidoo, V. (2022). *Mapping State Capacity in Africa: Professionalism and Reach*. Working Paper No. 190. Afrobarometer.

Lekhanya, M. L. (2015). Public Outlook on Small and Medium Enterprises as a Strategic Tool Foreconomic Growth and Job Creation in South Africa. *Journal of Governance and Regulation, 4*(4), 412–418.

Mahembe, E. (2011). *Literature Review on Small and Medium Enterprises' Access to Credit and Support in South Africa*. Underhill Corporate Solutions (UCS), Pretoria, South Africa.

Meyer, D. F. (2014). Local Economic Development (LED), Challenges and Solutions: The Case of the Northern Free State Region, South Africa. *Mediterranean Journal of Social Sciences, 5*(16), 624–643.

Mukumba, T. (2014). Overcoming SMEs Challenges Through Critical Success Factors: A Case of SMEs in the Western Cape Province, South Africa. *Economic and Business Review*, 16(1), 19–38.

Mukwarami, J., & Tengeh, R. K. (2017). Sustaining Native Entrepreneurship in South Africatownships: The Startup Agenda. *Acta Universitatis Danubius (Economica), 13*(4), 332–345.

Mukwarami, S., Mukwarami, J., & Tengeh, R. K. (2020). Local Economic Development and Small Business Failure: The Case of a Local Municipality in South Africa. *International Journal of Business and Globalisation, 25*(4), 489–502.

Mukwarami, S., Nyirenda, G., & Fakoya, M. B. (2017). The Governance of Corporate Social Responsibility and Return on Assets in the South Africa Mining Firms. *African Journal ofPublic Affairs, 9*(5), 36–153.

Mutyenyoka, E. M., & Madzivhandila, T. S. (2014). Employment Creation Through Small, Mediumand Micro Enterprises (SMMEs) in South

Africa: Challenges, Progress and Sustainability. *Mediterranean Journal of Social Sciences, 5*(25), 65–72.

National Planning Commission. (2011). *National Development Plan 2030: Executive Summary.* [online] https://www.gov.za/sites/default/files/Executive%20Summary-NDP%202030%20-%20Our%20future%20-%20make%20it%20work.pdf (Accessed 12 November 2017).

Nyawo, J., & Mubangizi, B. C. (2015). Art and Craft in Local Economic Development: Tourism Possibilities in Mtubatuba Local Municipality. *African Journal of Hospitality, Tourism and Leisure*, *4*(2), 1–15.

Ocloo, C. E., Akaba, S., & Worwui-Brown, D. K. (2014). Globalization and Competitiveness: Challenges of Small and Medium Enterprises (SMEs) in Accra, Ghana. *International Journal of Business and Social Science, 5*(4), 1–10.

Organisation for Economic Co-operation and Development (OECD). (2015). *OECD Economic Surveys: South Africa.* Paris: OECD Publishing.

Ramadani, V., Dana, L., Ratten, V., & Tahiri, S. (2015). The Context of Islamic Entrepreneurship and Business: Concept, Principles and Perspectives. *International Journal of Business and Globalisation, 15*(3), 244–261.

Scheers, L. (2011). SMEs' Marketing Skills Challenges in South Africa. *African Journal of Business Management, 5*(13), 5048–5056.

Small Enterprise Development Agency. (2016). *The Small, Medium and Micro Enterprise Sector of South Africa.* Research Note 1 [online] http://www.seda.org.za/Publications/Publications/The%20Small,%20Medium%20and%20Micro%20Enterprise%20Sector%20of%20South%20Africa%20Commissioned%20by%20Seda.pdf (Accessed 20 January 2017).

Soni, S. (2005). *The Challenges Facing Small Businesses: A Global Perspective.*

South Africa Institute of Chartered Accountants (SAICA). (2015).

Statistics South Africa. (2015). *Quarterly Labour Force Survey*, Quarter 2. Pretoria.

Tengeh, R. K. (2013). Advancing the Case for the Support and Promotion of African Immigrant-Owned Businesses in South Africa. *Mediterranean Journal of Social Sciences*, *4*(2), 347–359.

Tengeh, R. K. (2016). Entrepreneurial Resilience: The Case of Somali Grocery Shop Owners in a South African Township. *Problems and Perspectives in Management, 14*(4), 203–211.

Tengeh, R. K., & Mukwarami, J. (2017). The Growth Challenges of Native-Owned Spaza Shops in Selected Townships in South Africa. *International Journal of Applied Business and Economic Research*, *15*(22), 61–74.

Urban, B., & Naidoo, R. (2012). Business Sustainability: Empirical Evidence on SME Operational Skills in South Africa. *Journal of Small Business and Enterprise Development, 19*(1), 146–163.

World Bank. (2007). *South Africa: Enhancing the Effectiveness of Government in Promoting Micro, Small and Medium Enterprises*. Washington, DC: World Bank.

Tarlan Ahmadov, Wolfgang Gerstlberger and Viktoria Bondegård

Exploring Motivators, Enablers, and Barriers to Circular Economy Practices Implementation in Swedish Small and Medium-sized Enterprises (SMEs)

1. Introduction

Companies are operating in a complex environment that is constantly changing due to rapid technological growth and unforeseen challenges (Murray et al., 2017). To deal with these challenges, firms must reconsider their current strategies and practices (Bocken et al., 2016; Merli et al., 2018). The current patterns of production and consumption are unsustainable, which means that planetary resources are being depleted, and the ability of future generations to meet their needs is being weakened. It is therefore important for companies to adopt sustainable practices across various fields.

The Circular Economy (CE) is considered a new sustainable paradigm that aims to create a regenerative system with minimal resource input and waste, emissions, and energy leakage through the slowing, closing, and narrowing of material and energy loops. This is accomplished through strategies such as long-lasting design, maintenance, repair, reuse, remanufacturing, refurbishing, and recycling (Geissdoerfer et al., 2017).

Despite the benefits of CE, companies may find it challenging to implement CE strategies, particularly small and medium-sized enterprises (SMEs). Some companies fail during the implementation process, as reported by de Angelis (2021), and SMEs face unique challenges when trying to engage in the CE (Mura et al., 2020). The transition towards a CE requires significant changes in the way organizations operate, manage their resources, and collaborate with other stakeholders.

Despite the numerous studies conducted on CE and transition from different perspectives and levels, the research area is still relatively underdeveloped (Centobelli et al., 2020; Salvador et al., 2020; Santa-Maria et al., 2021). Much of the research on CE is still in its exploratory stage and is based on theoretical review and conceptualization, lacking empirical validation. Recently, SMEs' growing awareness of the importance of CE and the urgent need to shift from traditional linear economic models to more sustainable models has been noted. Studying the motivators, enablers, and barriers to CE practices implementation in SMEs is a significant as understanding these factors can help policymakers develop effective strategies to support SMEs in their transition to a circular economy.

This leads to the research problem of this study being that there is a lack of knowledge regarding source of motivation to CE practices implementation, and challenges Swedish SMEs face during their change process towards CE. Therefore, this study aims to acquire a comprehensive understanding and gain insight into the barriers and enablers faced by the SMEs during the implementation of CE practices. On this line, the study will aim to answer the below research question:

> What are the main sources of motivation, most common barriers, and enablers for implementation of circular economy practices by SMEs in Sweden?

The findings from this research could help identify main source of motivation, potential barriers, and enablers for implementing CE practices within SMEs, which will help the development of targeted policies, strategies, and interventions aimed at increasing the adoption of circular economy practices in SMEs and ultimately promoting sustainable economic growth in Sweden.

The chapter is organised as: Section 2 provides the background to the literature review that provide the existing research on the topic, Section 3 describes the methodology that the study employed, Section 4 presents the results of the study, and Section 5 provide the discussion and conclusion that interprets and explains the findings and their implications.

2. Literature Review

The notion of CE has gained increasing attention over the years at numerous levels, including politics, organizations, and science (Reike et al., 2018). According to Witjes and Lozano (2016), it is defined as a zero-waste regeneration system based on the concept that rubbish created within a company, is recycled, and reused by another company, with a viable economic path for tackling current environmental and socioeconomic concerns and fostering a more sustainable society. It is also noted by the European Commission (2019), the importance of becoming more circular, because it provides an economy with the capabilities to address climate change and biodiversity loss on several levels while simultaneously satisfying social needs. To distinguish between the linear economy and CE paradigms, which are characterized by the take-make-waste and regenerative resource models respectively, Figure 1 is presented to provide an illustrative comparison between the two systems.

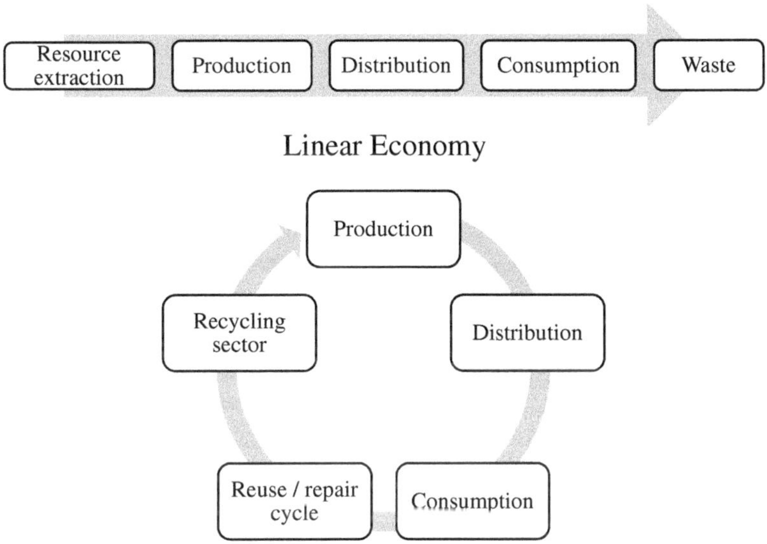

Figure 1. Linear vs. circular economy (Fura B., 2020).

SMEs are becoming more and more conscious of the advantages of reducing waste and enhancing resource efficiency, including material cost savings, competitive advantages, and market expansion (OECD, 2018). According to reports, SMEs have a high environmental footprint, contributing 60–70% of industrial pollution in Europe, particularly in the manufacturing sector (OECD, 2018). Manufacturing organizations, have high emissions and difficulties handling their material in a sustainable way, so they have a severe impact on the environment according to Bjørnbet et al. (2021) which needs to improve.

In Sweden, all ministers in the government have responsibility for the implementation of the Sustainable Developments Goals, and the government has appointed an Agenda 2030 delegation to draw up a national action plan (Regeringen och Regeringskansliet, 2023). The plan involves political commitment, policy integration, intergenerational timeframe, policy effects, coordination, local involvement, stakeholder participation and monitoring and reporting. Sweden however has a long history of attempting to increase circular material flows in society through recycling.

However, despite the previous facts about the positive progress, Sweden is more linear than it looks, and its material footprint is the third highest among EU nations, with 24.8 tonnes annually per person, according to a Circularity Gap assessment from 2022, which makes this another reason for future research in the different guidelines the government implements and how it is understood by the Swedish SMEs.

3. Methodology

The present study adopts an exploratory research design that is specifically aimed at understanding the adoption of CE within SMEs. As suggested by Swedberg (2020), an exploratory study is an ideal choice when there is limited knowledge in a given research area, which is precisely the case in this study. Hence, this design was deemed appropriate for addressing the research gaps and objectives of the current study. Through this research, the author intends to fill in the gaps that exist in the current literature and gain insights into the main motivators, enablers and barriers of SMEs regarding the adoption of CE practices, as well as identifying the challenges and opportunities associated with it in Sweden and semi-structured interviews, in particular, were found to be effective (Bryman, 2016).

Moreover, the study adopted an inductive approach for analyzing the collected data. This approach allowed the author to identify patterns and themes that emerged from the data and enabled to make sense of the findings (Braun & Clarke, 2019). By systematically identifying patterns and themes in the data, this approach can generate new insights and ideas that can inform future research and practice.

For data collection, the study utilizes the primary data collection method, which involved conducting semi-structured interviews with representatives from each SMEs. All interviews were recorded using the video communication platform Zoom, which allowed for efficient and accurate transcription of the data obtained (Braun & Clarke, 2019). The authors have carried out a total of 12 semi-structured interviews, which were conducted online using the Zoom communication platform. A list of all the interviewees can be found in Table 1

Table 1. Interview overview

Company	Position	Industry	Time	Date	Company size	Year Founded
A	Head of logistics	Agricultural	29:54	05.01.2023	Small	1980
B	Site manager	Machines, cable accessories, electric motors, generators and transformers and ventilation	35:66	05.01.2023	Small	1974
C	Sustainability manager	Manufacture of motor vehicles, engines, and turbines	37:05	09.01.2023	Medium	1957
D	Product Manager	Manufacture of pipes, wires, plastic	35:36	20.01.2023	Small	1986
E	Sustainability manager	Manufacture of heat pumps, water heaters, solar cells, electric boilers	49:13	25.01.2023	Medium	1989
F	Director of Technology	Manufacture of other metals	43:49	26.01.2023	Small	1940
G	Sustainability manager	Manufacturing of lifting and goods handling devices	27:58	27.01.2023	Medium	1959
H	Head of sustainability	Manufacture of steel barrels	33:05	27.01.2023	Small	1907
I	Head of logistics	Manufacturing of plastic parts	25:41	30.01.2023	Medium	1941
J	Head of logistics	Manufacturing of rubber goods, accessories for motor vehicles and engines	28:18	30.01.2023	Medium	1963
K	Head of logistics	Manufacturing of different metal	24:61	02.02.2023	Medium	1995
L	Head of logistics	Manufacture of trucks and other heavy motor vehicles	29:43	02.02.2023	Medium	1917

Source: Authors owns

4. Findings

This section is divided into three parts, starting with the presenting the main motivations behind the CE implementation, followed by barriers and enablers that SMEs in Sweden face.

4.1. Motivation behind CE Implementation

Twelve companies were asked why the circular economy matters to them. Their responses indicate that they are increasingly aware of the impact of their activities on the environment, and they are motivated by factors such as legal requirements, customer demands, and the desire to have a positive impact on future generations. Many of the companies are taking action to implement circular economy principles, such as reusing energy, developing better insulation, and working with sustainable materials. Some companies see circular economy as a way to increase profit, while others emphasize the need to eliminate unnecessary plastic items and ensure that the plastics, they do use are reusable, recyclable, or compostable.

Several companies also emphasized the importance of being seen as a "decent" or "nice" company (Company C) and of participating in creating a sustainable future (Company F). One company mentioned that public opinion can greatly influence their impact on the environment (Company G). Another company acknowledged that they need to be more intelligent in their resource use and lack knowledge regarding circularity (Company F). Several companies mentioned outside pressure as a driving force for sustainability efforts, such as customer demands (Company B, H), government regulations (Company D, I), and the need to control emissions and waste (Company J). One company noted that linear manufacturing is becoming a thing of the past and that recycling is highly valued (Company J).

Some interviewees note that legal requirements and stakeholder pressures are important factors in driving their organizations to adopt more sustainable practices. For instance, interviewee E states that legal requirements will partially affect their organization's approach to sustainability, while interviewee G argues that laws are forcing their organization to use more recycled raw materials and reduce their carbon footprint. Other interviewees suggest that internal factors, such as the personal values of top leaders, are also important drivers of sustainable practices. Interviewee B, for example, notes that their organization began to focus on sustainability after top leaders became interested in the topic. Similarly, interviewee G reports that individuals within their organization pushed for sustainability and helped to create a culture that values environmental responsibility.

Other interviewees suggest that the need to survive and remain competitive is a key driver of sustainable practices. For instance, interviewee H argues that their organization pursues sustainability because "we will not survive if we do nothing." This sentiment is echoed by interviewee L, who notes that sustainable practices are becoming increasingly relevant for their competitors as well. Interviewee D also suggests that considerations of customer demand and the company's image are important factors driving their organization to adopt more sustainable practices. The identified sources of motivations are shown in Figure 2 below.

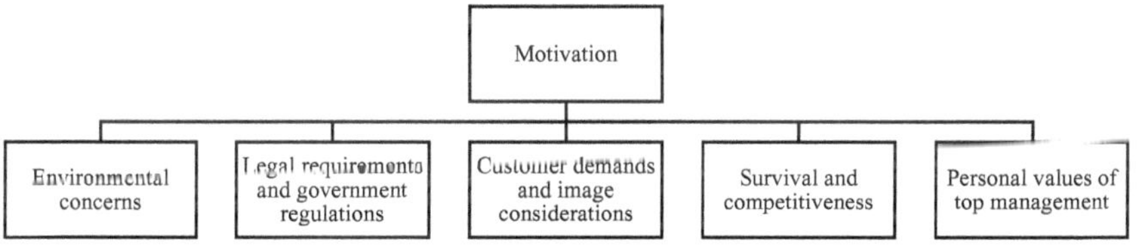

Figure 2. Source of motivations for driving organizational change towards CE practices.

4.2. Barriers for Implementation of CE Practices

The interview provided a series of responses from different individuals regarding the obstacles they face in implementing CE practices within their businesses. The responses reveal a range of internal and external barriers, including financial constraints, lack of support from parent companies, difficulties in finding suppliers who can provide sustainable materials, outdated equipment, regulatory requirements, and the need for more knowledge and technical improvements. The responses highlight the challenges of balancing economic considerations with environmental concerns and the importance of finding solutions that are both financially viable and environmentally sustainable. While exploring in depth the challenges faced by companies during their implementation of CE practices, the challenges can be divided into two broad sections: internal and external. According to Sarja et. al. (2021) internal barriers include lack of awareness, knowledge, and skills among staff, limited resources, and resistance to change. External barriers include limited access to reliable and relevant evidence, lack of support from policymakers and stakeholders, and conflicting interests. The study findings aligned with the literature.

4.2.1. Internal Barriers

The responses from the various companies show that there are differing views and experiences when it comes to implementing CE practices. Some companies feel that they lack the necessary resources or knowledge to make significant changes, while others believe that education and more openness to new ideas are needed. Communication and organizational issues were also cited as potential obstacles, as well as financial concerns and a lack of clear direction from leadership. However, there are also companies that have a strong culture of understanding and openness towards sustainability, and some have already made changes to their business plans to incorporate sustainability practices. Overall, it appears that there is a range of experiences and approaches to sustainability in different companies, with some facing more challenges than others in implementing changes (Figure 3).

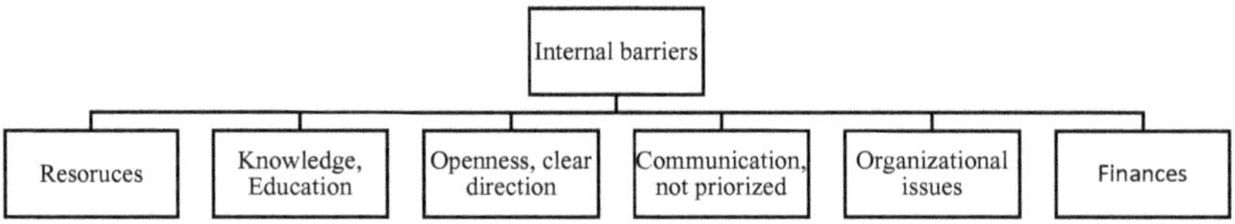

Figure 3. Internal barriers towards implementation of CE practices.

4.2.2. External Barriers

External barriers to CE implementation refer to obstacles that exist outside of a company or organization and prevent them from effectively implementing CE principles. These barriers can include economic, regulatory, social, cultural, and technological factors that hinder the adoption of circular practices and impede progress towards a CE. The findings of the interview data provide a diverse context (Figure 4). While some companies have been able to check the sustainability of their suppliers by researching them before entering into contracts, others find it hard to check and end contracts with unsustainable suppliers.

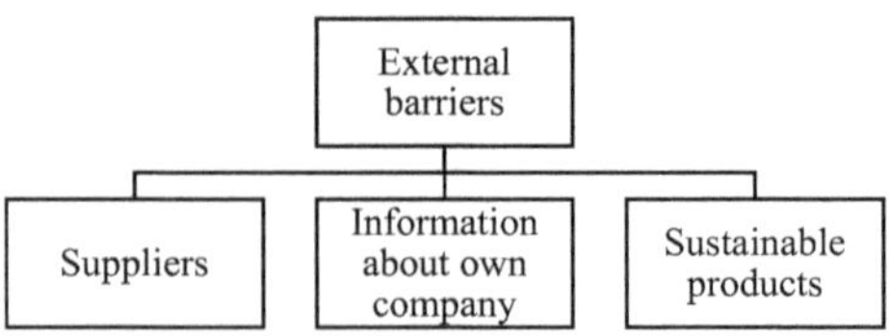

Figure 4. External barriers towards implementation of CE practices.

There is a growing awareness of the need for circular suppliers, but most companies do not have enough information about their own company to make it fully circular. Although some companies discuss circularity with their suppliers, they are still heavily dependent on them, and it is difficult to put pressure on them. Some suppliers are more sustainable than others, and it is important that the entire supply chain is interested in circular solutions. The main challenges faced by companies in this area are the limited availability of some sustainable products, the lack of data from suppliers, and the high prices and lower quality of some sustainable products. While some companies have a project with a supplier that has gone far, others are still waiting for more requirements to come to make it easier for them to handle some suppliers that should think more about the environment.

4.3. Drivers of Change towards CE

The interview data analysis revealed that the transition towards a CE is driven by a range of factors, including the changing preferences of customers, government policies, investor demand, and collaborations among stakeholders (Figure 5). Customers play a critical role in driving change towards circular economy practices, as they increasingly demand products and services that are sustainable and environmentally responsible. This demand for sustainability is further amplified by government policies that incentivize and regulate businesses towards circular practices, such as extended producer responsibility and product design regulations. Investors also play a key role, as they increasingly prioritize companies that adopt circular economy practices, leading to increased funding and investment in such initiatives.

Collaborations among stakeholders are also important drivers of change towards a circular economy. Such collaborations bring together different perspectives and expertise to develop innovative solutions for circular practices. Collaboration among companies can also lead to economies of scale, reducing costs and improving the adoption of circular practices.

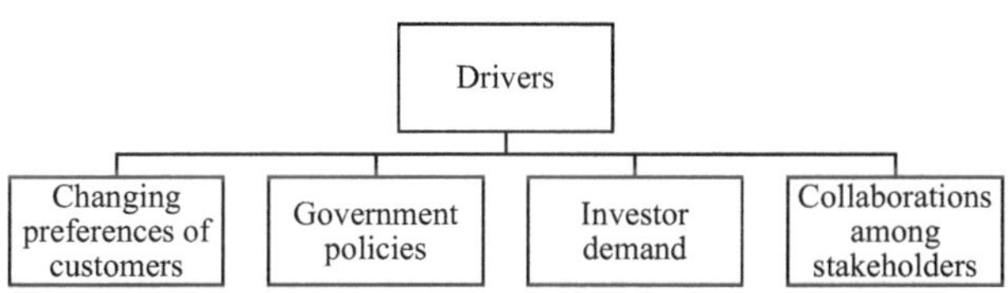

Figure 5. Drivers for implementation of CE practices.

5. Discussion and Conclusion

According to the findings of the interviews, the motivation, the challenges and enablers of SMEs involved in implementing circular practices varies. However, the outcomes vary depending on the firm and its unique production process. SMEs responses show that they are becoming more conscious of the environmental effect of their actions, and they are driven by motivations like as legal requirements, consumer expectations, and a desire to have a beneficial impact on future generations. The study's implementation findings can be explained by SMEs' perceptions of their involvement in moving to circular processes.

The study's findings in Swedish SMEs indicate that more work has to be done to replace old linear business methods and move them to CE. To be effective, the move from traditional to circular business operations should be based on a thorough understanding of CE principles. Inadequate knowledge appears to be a frequent issue among SMEs, as numerous research has demonstrated. Fonseca et al. (2018), for example, observed a broad lack of understanding of the CE's legal, fiscal, technological, and organizational components among Portuguese enterprises. Furthermore, Dissanayake and Weerasinghe (2021) noted a lack of workforce education on corporate sustainability as well as a lack of knowledge of the social and environmental implications of the company's behavior.

In general, it could be concluded that the barriers and enabalers mentioned in the literature also apply to a number of the SMEs in the sample. For example, a lack of finances, especially, is seen as a key barrier for smaller companies (Paolillo et al., 2021; Sánchez Garcia & Diez Sanz, 2018) SMEs in the sample mentioned this barrier, but as both something positive and negative that financial aspects are a hindering factor, but others see it as an opportunity to attract customers and employees. Another barrier mentioned in the study analysis is the lack of knowledge in SMEs. There is a question about how to implement CE, either due to the unfamiliarity of the concept of CE which is can be common accrding to Ormazabal et al. (2018) or due to the non-existent exchange of information among companies which is mentioned by Gregory et al. (2020) concluded that the transition to CE depends on the recognition by stakeholders that no single actor can address the core issue alone, so if there is an issue with vauge understanding when it comes from government, this should be addressed.

Based on the conclusion of the study, it is recommended that SMEs and policy makers take several actions to promote the implementation of circular economy practices in Swedish SMEs. Firstly, SMEs need to increase their knowledge and understanding of circular economy principles and practices to overcome the lack of knowledge barrier. This could be achieved through providing training and education to SMEs on CE practices, legal and fiscal aspects, and environmental and social implications of their behavior. Secondly, SMEs require financial support to overcome the barrier of limited resources, and policymakers need to provide financial incentives and grants for SMEs to adopt CE practices. Thirdly, collaboration and information sharing among companies need to be encouraged to address the barrier of non-existent exchange of information among companies. Finally, policymakers need to recognize that the transition to a circular economy requires a joint effort from all stakeholders and they need to create an enabling environment by implementing supportive policies and regulations.

Overall, the research provides valuable insights into the transition of SMEs to circular economy practices and highlights the need for a collaborative approach that involves stakeholders from various sectors. The contributions the research can inform policymakers, SME decision-makers, and researchers to develop evidence-based initiatives and strategies that can help overcome the barriers and enable a successful transition to circular economy practices.

References

Bjørnbet, M., Skjølsvik, T., & Klæboe, R. (2021). Health Effects of Low-Carbon Transitions: A Systematic Review of Health Impacts of Deep Decarbonization Pathways. *Environmental Research Letters*, *16*(4), 043008.

Bocken, N., Allwood, J. M., Willey, A. R., & King, J. M. (2016). Development of a Circular Economy Metric to Assess Product Circularity. *Journal of Cleaner Production*, *112*, 3780–3793.

Braun, V., & Clarke, V. (2019). Reflecting on Reflexive Thematic Analysis. *Qualitative Research in Sport, Exercise and Health*, *11*(4), 589–597.

Bryman, A. (2016). *Social Research Methods* (5th ed.). Oxford University Press.

Centobelli, P., Cerchione, R., Esposito, E., & Raffa, M. (2020). Circularity in Business Models: A Systematic Literature Review and Future Research Agenda. *Journal of Cleaner Production*, *271*, 122708.

de Angelis, R. (2021). Circular Economy Implementation in SMEs: An Evidence-Based Review. *Journal of Cleaner Production*, *288*, 125553.

Dissanayake, D. M. S. B., & Weerasinghe, T. D. (2021). Impact of Corporate Sustainability on Firm Performance: Evidence from an Emerging Economy. *Corporate Social Responsibility and Environmental Management*, *28*(1), 92–104.

European Commission. (2019). Communication from the Commission to the European Parliament, the Council, the European Economic and Social Committee and the Committee of the Regions: The European Green Deal. *COM(2019) 640 Final.* https://eur-lex.europa.eu/legal-content/EN/TXT/PDF/?uri=CELEX:52019DC0640&from=EN

Fonseca, L. M., Cabral, M., Pires, A., & Carvalho, H. (2018). Barriers and Drivers for the Implementation of Circular Economy Practices in Portuguese Organizations. *Journal of Cleaner Production*, *202*, 849–857.

Fura, B. (2020). Sustainable Circular Economy and Waste Management in the Fashion Industry. *Energies*, *13*(23), 6401.

Geissdoerfer, M., Savaget, P., Bocken, N. M. P., & Hultink, E. J. (2017). The Circular Economy–A New Sustainability Paradigm?. *Journal of Cleaner Production*, *143*, 757–768.

Gregory, A.J. et al. (2020). 'Stakeholder identification and engagement in problem structuring interventions', European Journal of Operational Research, 283(1), pp. 321–340. doi:10.1016/j.ejor.2019.10.044.

Merli, R., Preziosi, M., & Acampora, A. (2018). Business Models for the Circular Economy: An Exploratory Analysis. *Journal of Cleaner Production*, *190*, 201–215.

Mura, M., Farneti, F., & Rinaldi, C. (2020). Circular Economy Implementation in Small and Medium-Sized Enterprises: Barriers and Opportunities. *Sustainability*, *12*(16), 6488.

Murray, A., Skene, K., & Haynes, K. (2017). The Circular Economy: An Interdisciplinary Exploration of the Concept and Application in a Global Context. *Journal of Business Ethics*, 140(3), 369–380.

OECD. (2018). *Environmental Policy Toolkit for SME Greening in EU Eastern Partnership Countries*. Paris: OECD Green Growth Studies, OECD Publishing.

Ormazabal, M., Ruiz, V., & Garay, U. (2018). Circular Economy Business Models: Theoretical and Empirical Approaches. *Journal of Cleaner Production*, *175*, 481–495.

Paolillo, A., Castaldo, S., Lamberti, E., & Parente, R. (2021). The Circular Economy in SMEs: Drivers, Barriers, and Opportunities. *Sustainability*, *13*(3), 1253. https://doi.org/10.3390/su13031253

Regeringen och Regeringskansliet. (2023, January 31). Cirkulär ekonomi – strategi för omställningen i Sverige. *Regeringskansliet*. Retrieved April 4, 2023, from https://www.regeringen.se/rapporter/2023/01/strategi-for-cirkular-ekonomi/#:~:text=Den%20nationella%20strategin%20f%C3%B6r%20cirkul%C3%A4r,samt%20giftfria%20och%20cirkul%C3%A4ra%20materialkretslopp.

Reike, D., Vermeulen, W. J., & Witjes, S. (2018). The Circular Economy: New or Refurbished as CE 3.0? – Exploring Controversies in the Conceptualization of the Circular Economy through a Focus on History and Resource Value Retention Options. *Resources, Conservation and Recycling, 135*, 246–264.

Salvador, R., Patalakh, M., & Lopes, I. (2020). Circular Economy: Literature Review and Directions for Future Research. *Revista de Gestão, 27*(2), 157–174.

Sánchez García, J., & Díez Sanz, F. J. (2018). Barriers and Opportunities for a Circular Economy Implementation in SMEs: A Case Study. *Journal of Cleaner Production, 194*, 290–301.

Santa-Maria, M. J., Rodríguez-García, M., & López-Sánchez, J. I. (2021). Firm-Level Drivers of Circular Economy: Evidence from the European Union. *Journal of Cleaner Production, 292*, 126022.

Sarja, M., Onkila, T. & Mäkelä, M. (2021). A systematic literature review of the transition to the circular economy in business organizations: Obstacles, catalysts and ambivalences. Journal of Cleaner Production, 286, 125492.

Swedberg, R. (2020). Before Theory Comes Theorizing or How to Make Social Science More Interesting. *Sociologica, 14*(3), 17–25.

Witjes, S., & Lozano, R. (2016). Towards a More Circular Economy: Proposing a Framework Linking Sustainable Public Procurement and Sustainable Business Models. *Resources, Conservation and Recycling, 112*, 37–44.

Tanvir Alam Shahi Md. and Somosi Sarolta

Increasing Renewable Energy Auctions for the Accessibility of Low-Cost Clean Energy and Its Local Socio-Economic Impacts

1. Introduction

The access to energy is no longer a binary marvel – it is the quality energy access high up on the energy ladder (Csereklyei et al., 2017; Burke, 2013) and not the mere quantity that is related to the economic development. In many places, renewable energy (RE) technologies have proven valuable and sometimes vital. They play a significant role in sustaining current social change and economic growth and have recently been instrumental in pushing the energy access boundaries around the world. The global scenario is changing rapidly, increasing with the share of RE in the energy mix. According to the IEA monthly electricity statistics report from the end of 2020, global RE production was 3,269.1 terawatt-hours (TWh) in 2020, 7.5 % higher than in 2019. The share of renewable electricity in the mix was 31.6 % in 2020, up from 28.6 % in 2019. Wind and solar production were mainly responsible for the increase in renewables, up by 95.8 TWh or 11.6 % and 73.0 TWh or 20.2 % respectively in 2020 compared to 2019.

The growing emphasis on environmental issues increases public and private awareness and growing support of the topic. There is increasing pressure on the industry to meet such needs. Fossil fuel (FF)-based power generation could also lose its earlier role in the energy mix due to price reductions in constantly increasing power generation from RE. This can be partially explained by the theory of learning curves. Although FF-based power generation may gain price benefits from higher efficiency or smart technologies, the RE market is moving at a much faster pace. Wright (1936) provided a framework for forecasting cost declines due to cumulative production. Moore (1965) referring to the transistor market development – predicted it would double every two years because of time. Others later explained the cost reductions by economies of scale (Goddard, 1982) or combined the abovementioned factors with each other (Swanson, 2011[1];

1 Swanson (2011) also formulated a "law" especially for the clean energy market. He projected a 20 % drop in the price of solar PV modules for every doubling of cumulated shipped volume.

Sinclair et al., 2000). Clean technology cost reductions arise from fundamental physics and lower input material costs from scale as well as lower labor costs through manufacturing automation and lower waste driven by higher efficiency. All these cost reductions appear naturally due to manufacturing scale and vertical integration rather than performance improvements. Thus, the advances in clean technology are a function of experience and production, closely related to "learning by doing."

Besides the learning curve-indicated technological progress, the new channels of support for RE generation have also contributed to the drastic fall in RE prices, thus improving the accessibility of low cost clean energy for wider consumer groups in the society. However, finance and sustainability are the most important design criteria for investing in RE. Studies show that significant results can arise from all support channels (Izgec et al., 2017), especially if designed carefully (del Río et al., 2021), while others also emphasise that support schemes may differ in their effect, depending on their design (Lilliestam et al., 2021). The features of cost-effectiveness, enabling real price discovery regarding the project and resulting in a lower support level mean that many countries worldwide are shifting from feed-in tariffs to a competitive auction process (Kreiss et al., 2017). Because, auctions provide an effective means of distribution for governments and a market-based approach that addresses several objectives such as promoting renewable energy, reducing tariffs, attracting foreign investment, improving reliability, regulating CO2 emissions, and supporting economic development (Hochberg & Poudineh, 2018).

For local industrial development, RE auction scheme may be seen as an opportunity and for this policy makers need to focus on the localization of production activities (Hansen et al., 2020; Bayer et al., 2018; Hochsteller & Kostka, 2015). For the Argentinian RE projects that source more than 60 % of the equipment and electro-mechanic components locally were eligible to receive tax credits equal to 20 % of the amount of equipment purchased locally (Menzis et al., 2019). Hansen et al. (2020) treated local content requirement (LCR)[2] as a focal tool in RE auction schemes motivating local industrial development by specifying the use of locally produced content. Mentioning the Brazilian case, they mention that if the domestic steel industry is well-developed that can contribute a congenial atmosphere as a steel supplier for producing steel turbine

2 LCR defines as the percentage of the total project cost secured locally through both equipment and services along with locally produced components, civil engineering work and consultancy fee (IRENA 2013; Hansen et al. 2020).

tower. del Rio (2017) mentions that for making LCR effective, it might be needed a minimum level of domestic manufacturing capability and the auctioneer should overview the local technological market. For manufacturing equipment of RE technologies on the relevant future market size, capacity-based volume auction is highly preferable and it can encourage innovation and supply chain improvement (del Rio, 2017; del Rio et al., 2016).

Not the end here, projects awarded in Morocco have been reporting the benefits achieved due to inclusion of socio-economic development goals as qualification requirement. Morocco's "Noor-Ouarzazate" RE project consisted of four phases. Phase-I indeed sourced 30–35 % of the project cost in local components and services. Throughout the four phases, 70 % i.e., 6,430 Moroccans were employed and a third of the jobs were sourced locally from the region of Ouarzazate. Yet again, Renewable Energy Independent Power Producer Procurement Program (REIPPPP) in South Africa consisted of seven rounds that attracted 14.64 billion USD by March 2019. When it comes to local content, 3.27 billion USD were spent locally out of total spending of 90.3 billion USD. In terms of job creation, the REIPPPP has created a total of 40,134 job-years for South African citizens. The procurement was surpassed with local equity shareholding across all around reaching 52 %. The REIPPPP contributes to Broad Based Black Economic Empowerment (BBBEE) and the creation of Black industrialists and Black South Africans means own on average 33 % of the projects (IRENA, 2019). Further, LCR has a contributory role in NIMBY syndrome/Nimbyism. Nimby, is a characterization of opposition by residents to proposed developments in their local area, as well as support for strict land use regulations. It carries the connotation that such residents are only opposing the development because it is close to them and that they would tolerate or support it if it were built farther away. The residents are often called Nimbys, and their viewpoint is called Nimbyism. In this connection, del Rio (2019) aurged for the local community support. Botta (2019) argues that for reducing/abolishing the NIMBY[3] syndrome, there is an obligation to offer a fixed percentage of project shares to local residents. This step not only mitigates the risk but also ensures financial gains to promote RE and expands support. Drawing a suggestion, AURES II (2021) states an obligation to provide a strategic plan with estimation on the impact of the installation on the local employment and industrial value chain. This LCR feature in the auction designing has a positive impact of the

3 https://www.rechargenews.com/transition/the-six-paradoxes-slowing-down-the-energy-transition/2-1-732488

society. The impacts of the learning curve and the various support channels work together and strengthen each other, enabling lower prices electricity to be the prime motivation for the further espousal of auction schemes globally for gaining wider positive socio-economic returns.

2. Methodology

It has been piloted systematic literature review focusing three aims: first, to find out the potentiality of auction; second, to identify the design features of the auction and third, to find out the gains of the auction following some country-specific empirical evidences. For examining how auction is used in relation to cost-effective renewable energy deployment, it has been steered the systematic literature review that comprised a reproducible search and applied explicit criteria for the inclusion and exclusion of studies (Sovacool et al., 2018). Based on the view of the Petticrew and Roberts (2006), a semi-structured approach was conducted.

Along with that the authors intended to investigate the levelized cost of energy (LCOE) from solar and wind sources for a country where competitive auction is not being implemented yet. The LCOE is being used to analyse global price trends that quantifies the average cost of producing a unit of electricity in a given power plant and represents the average minimum price at which electricity needs to be sold to break even (Reichelstein & Sahoo, 2015) as the lower production cost ensures lower supply cost for the end-users. In this situation, the authors selected two solar and one on-shore wind power plants of Bangladesh those are recently implemented/implementation stage under utility-scale (IPP model) as a study area. After that there followed per unit cost comparison with some countries where auction process are practicing. Due to the unavailability of data for Bangladesh in the international reliable sources, the base data has been collected from the companies through the authors' personal communication[4]. Data for other countries were collected from the International Energy Agency (IEA-NEA, 2020) database. It is needed to mention that the power projects in Bangladesh (both conventional and renewable energy) are still awarded on an unsolicited basis, such as through Power Purchase Agreements (PPAs) or Requests for Quotations (RFQs), and tariffs are determined through direct negotiation between the Bangladesh Power Development Board (BPDB) and Independent Power Producers (IPPs).

4 Md. Bellal Hossain, email to author, 30 December 2020.

To calculate the LCOE, the initial investment, i.e. the total average cost of building and operating the power plant over its entire life is divided by the total electricity production of the plant over its entire life (see Equation 1).

$$(1)\ \text{LCOE} = \frac{\text{Initial Investment} + \sum_{t=1}^{n} \frac{\text{O \& M Expenditure}_t}{(1+\text{CoC})^t}}{\sum_{t=1}^{n} \frac{\text{Electricity Generated}_t}{(1+\text{CoC})^t}}$$

Here, Initial Investment = the initial cost or capital cost/mega-watt (MW) (CAPEX) at t = 0

O & M Expenditure_t = inflation adjusted operation & maintenance cost/MW and each year (OPEX)
Electricity Generated_t = electricity generated in mega-watt-hours (MWh) per MW each year corresponding to the annual full-load hour (FLH)
n = the life time of the plant
t = year
CoC = the discount rate privately

3. Implications

Compared to some countries, the LCOE found higher in Bangladesh and the country has not been implemented auction scheme yet. Thus, the capital costs are higher here; for example, the total capital cost to establish a 7.4 MW solar PV is 44.45 USD/MWh, whereas a total capital cost of 31.91 USD/MWh was required in India to establish a 35 MW plant (Table 1). Another notable segment is discount rate, with a discount rate of 12 % each for the two solar and one on-shore wind plants for Bangladesh, which is higher than the current global trend. Discount rate (CoC) influences the LCOE significantly, because if the rate is high, then the LCOE will be enhanced and vice versa. For instance, if the CoC were 6 %, then the LCOE for India's 35 MW solar PV would be 32.92 USD/MWh, i.e. just a reduction of 3.68 USD/MWh for a 1 % reduction of CoC (IEA-NEA, 2020). The same scenarios (for both total capital and CoC) are depicted in the on-shore wind energy case (Table 2).

Table 1. LCOE for utility-scale solar PV

Country	Plant size (MW)	Construction costs (USD/ MWh)	Refurbishment costs (USD/ MWh)	Decommissioning costs (USD/ MWh)	Total capital costs (USD/ MWh)	Discount rate	LCOE (USD/ MWh)
France	25	30.17	0	0.25	**30.42**	0.07	**33.94**
India	35	31.65	0	0.26	**31.91**	0.07	**35.60**
USA	100	38.55	0	0.32	**38.87**	0.07	**44.25**
Brazil	25	39.17	0	0.33	**39.5**	0.07	**46.02**
Canada	20	55.39	0	0.46	**55.85**	0.07	**62.47**
Bangladesh*	7.4	42.33	0	2.12	**44.45**	0.12	**45.41**
	50 (IPP model)	59.61	0	5.96	**65.57**	0.12	**70.62**

Source: IEA-NEA (2020).

* Base data for Bangladesh were collected through authors' personal communication.

Table 2. LCOE for utility-scale on-shore wind

Country	Plant Size (MW)	Construction costs (USD/ MWh)	Refurbishment costs (USD/ MWh)	Decommissioning costs (USD/ MWh)	Total capital costs (USD/ MWh)	Discount rate	LCOE (USD/ MWh)
Brazil	30	27.38	0	0.23	**27.61**	0.07	**33.59**
India	65	31.92	0	0.27	**32.19**	0.07	**35.91**
Netherlands	50	25.42	0.3	0.21	**25.93**	0.07	**41.16**
Finland	30	37.62	0	0.31	**37.93**	0.07	**44.87**
Italy	10	37.65	0	0.31	**37.96**	0.07	**52.87**
	20	49.17	0	0.41	**49.58**	0.07	**59.52**
France	50	38.04	0	0.32	**38.36**	0.07	**56.09**
Bangladesh*	55 (IPP Model)	45.92	0	0	**45.92**	0.12	**54.19**

Source: IEA-NEA (2020).

* Base data for Bangladesh were collected through authors' personal communication.

But from 2010 to 2019, the global average contracted price for solar energy dropped by 78 % (IRENA, 2019). Similarly, the wind price also fell; however, compared to solar, the reduction rate did not reach the same level and the weighted average price of wind dropped only by 33 %. In 2020, the total per kilowatt (kW) installed cost was 883 USD for solar photovoltaic, 3185 USD for off-shore wind and 1355 USD for on-shore wind.[5] The reduction in technology costs in this time resulted in global RE experts and decision makers firmly accepting the auction scheme as a medium to shape the market price of renewables in their precise framework and circumvent inventors' windfall earnings. Not only the technologically induced price reductions of RE sources but also the support system affects the final set of average prices. There is evidence for the impact of fiscal incentives for RE investments on the 16–33 % decrease of LCOE even in a developing country like Colombia (Castillo-Ramírez et al., 2017). The following figure (Figure 1) illustrates the trends of average total installed costs (USD/kW) and the levelized costs of energy (LCOE, in 2019 USD/kWh) witnessed in the last decade from 2010 to 2019.

The IEA (2019) stated that the use of competitive auctions has accelerated cost reductions for some renewable technologies, notably solar PV, on-shore wind and off-shore wind. However, these prices cannot be followed consistently, as each country and technology have different resource potentials, financing conditions and a different set of auction designs. IEA data show that from 2017 to 2020, the average auction prices for solar PV and wind were both higher for Europe than in other regions/countries worldwide. Figure 2 shows that the prices at solar and wind auctions have decreased significantly in the last decade.

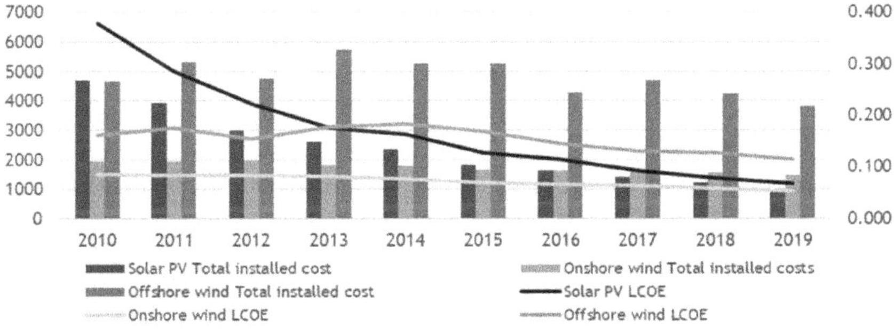

Figure 1. Global weighted average of total installed cost (in 2019 USD/kW) and LCOE (in 2019 USD/kWh) of selected RE (2010–2019).

Source: Authors' construction based on IRENA official data[6].

5 https://www.irena.org/Data/View-data-by-topic/Costs/Global-Trends

6 https://www.irena.org/Statistics/View-Data-by-Topic/Costs/Global-LCOE-and-Auction-values

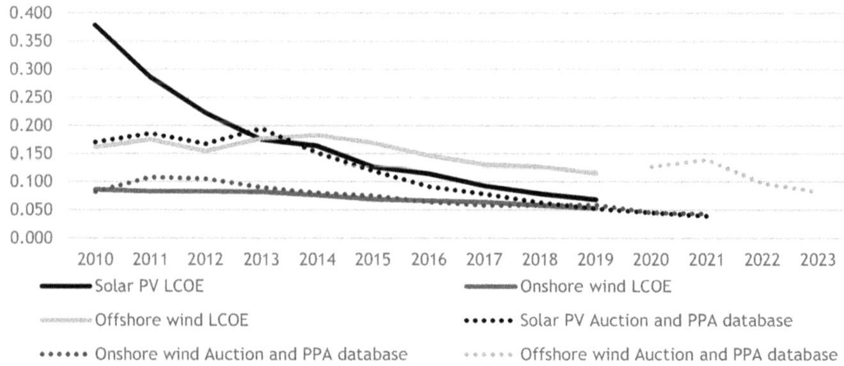

Figure 2. Global weighted average of LCOE and PPA/auction prices (in 2019 USD/kWh).

Source: Authors' construction based on IRENA official data[7].

The auction and PPA database indicates the cost of electricity from solar photovoltaic decline to USD 0.039/kWh in 2021, 43 % lower than the global weighted-average cost in 2019 whereas on-shore wind decline to USD 0.043/kWh in 2021, 19 % lower than the global weighted-average LCOE in 2019 and off-shore wind decline to USD 0.082/kWh in 2023, 29 % lower than the global weighted-average LCOE in 2019.[8] Further, there was a notable price decrease for on-shore wind in Brazil from 28.96 USD/MWh in December 2017 to 18.58 USD/MWh in April 2018. For solar PV, 17 GW capacity was solely owed by India at an average price of 42.3 USD/MWh and the Philippines received bids for a 50 MW capacity at a low cost of 43.9 USD/MWh (IRENA, 2019).

It should be acknowledged that comparisons between LCOEs and auction prices remain an important challenge. However, limited information is available on contract-winning projects, which makes it difficult to state whether these tender-determined prices will become benchmarks for future costs of RE generation. This can be a future study as well. Again, way forward for reducing CoC is another room for the policymakers for the next advance study.

7 LCOEs usually reflect higher values. According to the IEA, among others, the three main reasons are: auction prices may not always represent full costs, aggressive bidding of certain players and current auction prices only reflect a small portion of the market.

8 https://www.irena.org/Data/View-data-by-topic/Costs/Global-Trends

The deployment of high volume renewable energy is being driven by a combination of factors, including the socio-economic benefits of RE, the decreasing costs of RE technologies, concerns about pollution and climate change, goals for accelerating RE deployment, advances in RE technology, the actions of corporations and investors to reduce their carbon footprint, and public support for RE (IRENA – GCGET, 2019). These trends are leading to an increased integration of clean energy into the economy, as demonstrated by its contribution to a country's GDP.

4. Conclusions and Policy Recommendations

Many countries have failed to adequately prepare for the adoption of alternative energy sources. Consequently, when the topic of "alternative energy sources" is raised, poorer and developing nations often present unjustifiable excuses for not implementing them. The concept of an immediate or temporary solution is not applicable to the energy sector. To achieve desired goals and attain societal and economic benefits, it is crucial for countries to incorporate low-cost, sustainable, and renewable energy sources into their long-term development plans. Developed nations have adopted such long-term energy planning strategies. However, many poorer and developing countries, such as Bangladesh, suffer from incorrect and inconsistent energy policies, coupled with mismanagement in this sector.

To ensure the progress of any sector, including renewable energy, it is crucial to have a clearly defined vision and well-structured strategies. Meeting renewable energy targets requires a detailed plan, budget, timeline, and a careful balance between application and productivity. By implementing these requirements and customizing technology-neutral, location-specific volume auctions, along with tools for socio-economic development and qualification criteria, it becomes feasible to generate various advantages for societies and economies with untapped renewable energy potential that have yet to adopt auction schemes.

Kunze and Becker (2015) and Hall and Klitgaard (2012) introduced the concept of energy technological politics. They argue that the use of centralized energy sources like fossil fuels leads to the concentration of economic and political power. This theory serves as the basis for the energy democracy movement, which advocates for the adoption of renewable energy sources to promote decentralized power and politics. The movement contends that renewable energy sources, being more widely dispersed, contribute to decentralization and enhance democracy, in contrast to centralized energy sources that weaken democratic systems. The relationship between energy and politics is often described as a balance between centralization and decentralization. Fossil fuels, as centralized sources, result in concentrated political power and weakened democracy, while decentralized sources such as solar and wind energy foster distributed political power and stronger democracy. These theoretical connections underscore the importance of energy choices in shaping political systems. Therefore, a successful transition to clean energy necessitates political support at the systemic level as well as backing from local communities. This not only leads to economically sustainable outcomes but also drives the future development of renewable energy. Consequently, decisions made at the central level play a critical role, and sustainable energy policies, including short, medium, and long-term strategies, should guide these decisions. In other words, well-defined legal regulations are crucial for the production of clean energy.

To attract more investors to renewable energy generation, policymakers are reducing subsidies for fossil fuels. During this transition, it is important to encourage consumers to adopt energy-efficient practices and conserve energy. According to Szabo (2022), natural gas can serve as a transitional fuel because of its relatively cleaner characteristics compared to coal, liquefied natural gas (LNG), and high-speed furnace oil (HFO). Additionally, it is crucial to diversify energy sources as a means of ensuring energy security and promoting a sustainable future. Countries must prioritize their energy security and avoid relying solely on one source to meet their growing demand, thus necessitating the diversification of energy sources.

An inclusive approach to the future of the energy sector necessitates the involvement of leaders from prominent nations in developing a framework that is in line with the evolving energy landscape. Organizations such as the International Energy Agency (IEA), Organization of Petroleum Exporting Countries (OPEC) and commodity exchanges have played a significant role in shaping the hydrocarbon industry. However, the shift towards renewable energy calls for the establishment of new institutions, political agreements, and frameworks that take into account the perspectives of diverse stakeholders from both the public and private sectors. Neglecting this aspect could potentially result in geopolitical conflicts, with some parties emerging as winners while others as losers.

Lastly, the utilization of auctions to support renewable energy is justified by two primary reasons. Firstly, they facilitate the allocation of support based on competitive determination, accurately reflecting the actual costs of the chosen projects. Secondly, they promote a fair and competitive method of managing the deployment volume of renewable energy, steering clear of preferential treatment based on timing and effectively controlling support budgets. These arguments can be persuasive to policymakers grappling with increasing support obligations that can burden consumers and taxpayers. Nevertheless, substantial empirical evidence indicates that the advantages of auction schemes surpass these arguments across various aspects.

Ethics Statements

The authors collected date from the published sources and taking consent from the concern companies where there are no violations of ethics. In this work, there was no involvement of human/animal subjects.

Acknowledgments

This research did not receive any specific grant from funding agencies in the public, commercial, or not-for-profit sectors.

Declaration of Interests

❑ The authors declare that they have no known competing financial interests or personal relationships that could have appeared to influence the work reported in this paper.

References

AURES II. (2021). Auctions for the Support of Renewable Energy in Spain: Results and Lesson Learnt. *Auctions for Renewable Energy Support* II, Karlsruhe.

Bayer, B., Bertholt, L., & Freitas, B. (2018). The Brazilian Experience with Auctions for Wind Power: An Assessment of Project Delays and Potential Mitigation Measures. *Energy Policy, 122*, 97–117.

Botta, E. (2019). An Experimental Approach to Climate Finance: The Impact of Auction Design and Policy Uncertainty on Renewable Energy Equity Cost in Europe. *Energy Policy, 133*, 1–13.

Burke, P. J. (2013). The NationalLevel Energy Ladder and Its Carbon Implications. *Environment and Development Economics, 18*(4), 484–503.

Castillo-Ramirez, A., Mejia-Giraldo, D., & Molina-Castro, J. D. (2017). Fiscal Incentives Impact for RETs Investments in Colombia. *Energy Source, Part B: Economics, Planning, and Policy, 12*(9), 759–764.

Csereklyei, Zs., Thurner, P.W., Langer, J., & Küchenhoff, H. (2017). Energy Paths in the European Union: A Model-Based Clustering Approach. *Energy Economics, 65*, 442–457.

Goddard, C. (1982). Debunking the Learning Curve. *IEEE Transactions on Components, Hybrids, and Manufacturing Technology*, *5*, 328–335.

Hall, C. A. S., & Klitgaard, K. A. (2012). *Energy and Wealth of Nations*. New York: Springer.

Hansen, U.E., Nygaard, I., Morris, M., & Robbins, B. (2020). The Effects of Local Content Requirements in Auction Schemes for Renewable Energy in Developing Countries: A Literature Review. *Renewable and Sustainable Energy Reviews, 127*, 1–12.

Hochberg, M., & Poudineh, R. (2018). Renewable Auction Design in Theory and Practice: Lessons from the Experience of Brazil and Mexico. *The Oxford Institute of Energy Studies, EL*(28), 1–62.

Hochsteller, K., & Kostka, G. (2015). Wind and Solar Power in Brazil and China: Interests, State Business Relations and Policy Outcomes. *Global Environment Politics, 15*, 74–94.

IEA. (2019). *Have the Prices from Competitive auctions Become the "new normal" Prices for Renewables*? Paris: International Energy Agency.

IEA. (2020). *Monthly OECD Electricity Statistics*. Paris: International Energy Agency.

IEA-NEA. (2020). *Project Costs of Generating Electricity*. Paris: International Energy Agency-Nuclear Energy Agency.

IRENA. (2013). *Renewable Energy Auctions in Developing Countries*. Abu Dhabi: International Renewable Energy Agency.

IRENA. (2019). *Renewable Energy Auctions-Status and Trends: Beyond Price*. Abu Dhabi: International Renewable Energy Agency.

IRENA—GCGET. (2019). *A New World: The Geopolitics of the Energy Transformation*. Abu Dhabi: International Renewable Energy Agency – Global Commission on the Geopolitics of Energy Transformation.

Izgeç, M. M., Tamer, E., Adnan, S., & Ömürgönülşen, M. (2017). Financial Sustainability Analysis of Renewable Energy Plant Applications. *Energy Sources Part B: Economics, Planning, and Policy*, *12*(10), 895–902.

Kreiss, J., Ehnhart, K. M., & Haufe, M. C. (2017). Appropriate Design of Auctions for Renewable Energy Support—Prequalifications and Penalties. *Energy Policy*, *101*, 512–520.

Kunze, C., & Becker, S. (2015). Collective Ownership in Renewable Energy and Opportunities for Sustainable Degrowth. *Sustainability Science, 10*, 425–437.

Lilliestam, J., Ollier, L., Labordena, M., Pfenninger, S., & Thonig, R. (2021). The Near- to Mid-Term Outlook for Concentrating Solar Power: Mostly Cloudy, Chance of Sun. *Energy Sources, Part B: Economics, Planning, and Policy*, *16*(1), 23–41.

Menzies, C., Marquardt, M., & Spieler, N. (2019). *Auctions for the Support of Renewable Energy in Argentina: Main Results and Lessons Learnt*. AURES II Project Report No. D2.1-AR.

Moore, G. E. (1965). Cramming More Components Onto Integrated Circuits. Intel.Com. *Electronics Magazine*, *38*(8). https://newsroom.intel.com/wp-content/uploads/sites/11/2018/05/moores-law-electronics.pdf (Accessed 2 April 2021).

Pitticrew, M., & Roberts, H. (2006). *Systematic Reviews of Social Sciences: A Practical Guide*. Victoria: Blackwell Publishing. https://doi.org/10.1002/978047075 4887.

Reichelstein, S., & Sahoo, A. (2015). Time of Day Pricing and the Levelized Cost of Intermittent Power Generation. *Energy Economics*, *48*, 97–108.

del Rio, P. (2017). Designing Auctions for Renewable Electricity Support-Best Practices from Around the World. *Energy for Sustainable Development*, *41*, 1–13.

del Rio, P. (2019). *Auctions for the support of renewable energy in Mexico: Main results and lessons learnt*. AURES II project report no. D2.1-MX.

del Rio, P., Fitch-Roy, O., & Woodman, B. (2016). *Identification of Alternative Options*. AURES Project Repot No. 6.1.

del Río, P., Papadopoulou, A., & Calvet, N. (2021). Dispatchable RES and Flexibility in High RES Penetration Scenarios: Solutions for Further Deployment. *Energy Sources, Part B: Economics, Planning, and Policy*, 16(1), 1–3.

Sinclair, G., Klepper, S., & Cohen, W. (2000). What's Experience Got to Do with It? Sources of Cost Reduction in a Large Specialty Chemicals Producer. *Management Science*, *46*(1), 28–45.

Sovacool, B.K., Axsen, J., & Sorrell, S. (2018). Promoting Novelty, Rigor, and Style in Energy Social Science: Towards Codes of Practice for Appropriate Methods and Research Design. *Energy Research and Social Science*, *45*, 12–42.

Swanson, R. (2011). *The Silicon Photovoltaic Roadmap*. The Stanford Energy Seminar. https://www.youtube.com/watch?v=_MbG1-JgtXg&ab_channel=Stanford (Accessed 2 April 2021).

Szabo, J. (2022). Energy Transition or Transformation? Power and Politics in the European Natural Gas Industry's Transformismo. *Energy Research and Social Science*, *69*, 1–14.

Wright, T. P. (1936). Factors Affecting the Cost of Airplanes. *Journal of Aeronautical Science*, *3*(4), 122–128.

Alicja Jajko-Siwek

Are Richer Pensioners also Healthier? Self-Rated Health and Pension Adequacy: Evidence from Poland

1. Introduction

"Noble health, no one will know what you taste like until you're gone," says the Polish poet, Jan Kochanowski. These words are extremely relevant in the face of the unprecedented pandemic threat that Polish society was facing. The health situation in Poland has been an inspiration to examine the health condition of Polish pensioners, especially in the context of the adequacy of their pension benefits. The question arose as to whether people who receive adequate pension benefits enjoy better health than those with inadequate benefits, or in other words, whether pension adequacy is a guarantee of good health, where adequacy is understood as the ability to maintain, to a reasonable degree, a previous standard of living after retirement (EC, 2012). This study aims to determine how the adequacy of pension benefits is related to the self-rated health of retired people.

The authors of the most comprehensive study related to the problems of aging and old age in Poland, that is, the study by PolSenior (Mossakowska et. al., 2012), suggest that the overall assessment of the health situation of the elderly should take into account several aspects of old age, both subjective and objective. Following this suggestion, features from both of these areas were incorporated into our study.

The primary variable used to define the health status of pensioners was self-rated health. According to Kulik et al. (2011), it is estimated that only approximately 10–20 % of elderly individuals show features of successful aging. Since their health depends to a great extent on receiving appropriate medical care, the study included variables describing the availability of medical visits and hospital care. This issue was repeatedly raised in the PolSenior study. Hence, the variables included in the study are the number of visits to the doctor and hospital stays during the previous year. As indicated by Kulik et al. (2011), the health condition of elderly individuals is that they simultaneously suffer from many chronic diseases, the main cause of their impaired functioning.

The psychological aspect of health was taken into account by introducing a variable describing the propensity to depression. Puto et. al. (2019) and his colleagues indicate gender and age as the main factors contributing to the deterioration of the psychosocial condition of pensioners. Women and the elderly are more prone to depression. Furthermore, proper nutrition, which results in appropriate body weight, has been recognized as a preventive factor for good health. This feature is best described by the BMI index (Mossakowska et. al., 2012).

The financial situation of each pensioner is largely determined by their pension benefit level. As Błędowski (2012) believes, pension benefits become the main, and most often the only, source of income in old age. In our study we illustrate the link between the financial situation of pensioners and their self-rated health by referring health-related factors to the adequacy of pensions. Moreover, the study includes the relationship between the health situation of the surveyed pensioners and their gender, age, and education. In particular, it indicates the gender and age of pensioners as the main reasons for the health problems of elderly individuals (Puto et al., 2019). A summary of all variables used in our study for the classification of pensioners is presented in Table 1.

Table 1. Variables used in the study

No.	Variable	Name	Designation in SHARELIFE	Scale
1	Gender	Gender	Gender	1, 2
2	Age of respondent	Age	Age	0–102
3	Level of education, ISCED 97 coding	Education	isced1997_r	0–6
4	State of health – subjective assessment	Health	Sphus	1–5
5	Seen/talked to a medical doctor in last 12 months	Doctor	hc002_mod	0–20
6	In hospital in last 12 months	Hospital	hc012_	1, 5
7	Number of chronic diseases	Disease	chronic mod	0–7
8	EURO depression scale	Depression	Eurod	0–12
9	Body mass index	BMI	Bmi2	0–4
10	Adequacy of pension benefit	Pension	-	0, 1

Source: Author's own calculations based on SHARELIFE data.

2. Methods

2.1. Data

Data were collected from the Survey of Health, Aging and Retirement in Europe (SHARE) – specifically, the "SHARE: 50+ in Europe" SHARELIFE edition The data come from round 7 of the study, carried out in 28 European Union countries (Börsch-Supan, 2019). The procedure for extracting the data necessary for the analysis was as follows: first, respondents from Poland were selected. Then, the sample was limited to retired people and to people who reported both their last salary before retirement and the value of their first pension, where it was possible to estimate the salary replacement rate (RR) as the measure of pension adequacy. The use of replacement rate had several advantages, such as the availability of data for its calculation, speed of calculation, and ease of interpretation (Borella & Fornero, 2009; Chybalski, 2016; EU, 2018; OECD, 2019). The study sample was then divided into people receiving adequate and inadequate pension benefits, which allowed us to generate the qualitative variable "Pension". As the criterion of adequacy, based on the level adopted in the literature (Palmer, 1989, 1994; Czepulis-Rutkowska, 2000), a replacement rate at the 70 % level was assumed. In the last step, the sample size was verified for those people who answered questions about their physical and mental health.

The analyzed sample consists of 533 people, 287 of whom (53.85 %) received adequate pension benefits. The proportion of people with adequate and inadequate benefits was fairly even for women and men: an adequate benefit was provided to 51.72 % of women and 56.38 % of men.

2.2. Measurement Models

"Pension" plays the role of the dependent variable in the first part of the study, describing the level of the pension benefit in the form of an adequate or inadequate replacement rate. In the second part of the study, carried out separately for pensioners with adequate and inadequate benefits, "Health" was considered the dependent variable.

Decision trees constitute the research method used in the study. Due to the qualitative nature of the variables, classification trees were constructed (Breiman et al., 1984; Gatnar, 2001; Jajko-Siwek, 2020). In the first stage of the study, the classification branched out into two classes of the variable "Pension" – adequate and inadequate pension. In the second stage, there were five classes for the "Health" variable: excellent, very good, good, fair, and poor.

The Classification and Regression Tree (CART) method with the Gini index as a division measure was used as the tree-building algorithm. Tenfold cross-validation was used for validation purposes. With the use of the CART method, it was also possible to rank the variables applied in the classification. To compare the significance of variables, their importance was normalized, obtaining relative significance measures expressed in ranking points. The most important variable received 1 point in the ranking, and the lowest potential significance was 0 points. The accuracy of the tree was measured by the percentage of properly classified objects. Calculations were performed using TIBCO StatisticaTM 13 (TIBCO Software Inc., Palo Alto, USA).

3. Results

3.1. Descriptive Statistics

The average "Age" of pensioners from the sample was 70.80 years (Table 2). The youngest pensioner was 52 years old, and the oldest was 94 years old. Pensioners receiving inadequate pensions are generally older than those with an adequate pension, but this difference is not statistically significant.

Table 2. Descriptive statistics for quantitative variables

Variable	Pension	N	Average	Std. dev.
Age	Total	533	70.80	7.12
Doctor			7.54	7.89
Disease			1.53	1.43
Depression			3.02	1.76
Age	Adequate	287	70.41	7.22
Doctor			7.10	7.53
Disease			1.49	1.32
Depression			3.02	1.87
Age	Inadequate	246	71.27	6.99
Doctor			8.04	8.28
Disease			1.58	1.56
Depression			3.02	1.64

Source: Author's own calculations based on SHARELIFE data.

The "Education" of people in retirement was measured on the isced1997_r scale, which distinguishes 7 levels of education: no education, primary, lower secondary, secondary, postsecondary, bachelor's, and master's degrees. Forty percent of people in the sample had adequate pensions and at least secondary education. People with inadequate pensions and at least secondary education constituted 35 % of the sample. The pensioners from both groups being studied most often had secondary education. There were no uneducated people and no graduates in the studied population.

The key variable describing the self-rated health of pensioners was called "Health" (sphus – self-perceived health, US scale). People receiving adequate pension benefits described their health as good, very good, or excellent more often (25.3 %) than those receiving inadequate pensions (18.8 %). According to studies by the Central Statistical Office of Poland, good self-rated health is very strongly dependent on the age of the respondents (GUS, 2014). In our study 35% of 60 to 69-year-olds rate themselves in this way. In the group of 70-year-olds, only 21 % can boast of good health. Unfortunately, among 80-year-olds, this group constitutes only 12 %.

Another variable regarding the health of pensioners, called "Doctor", refers to the number of visits to the doctor in the last twelve months. For both the adequate and inadequate groups, on average, the number of medical visits amounted to approximately 7–8 a year, but with very high variability, averaging 8 visits (Table 2).

The variable indicating pensioners' access to medical services was their hospital stays during the past year. This variable was called "Hospital". The need to use hospital care was higher in the group of retired people with adequate benefits (20 %) than in the group with inadequate benefits (16 %).

The occurrence of chronic diseases is typical of old age. The diseases include hypertension, cancer, Parkinson's disease, elevated cholesterol levels, diabetes, cataracts, stomach ulcers, and previous heart attacks and strokes. The variable describing the number of chronic diseases was called "Diseases". The results for this variable indicate that, on average, the examined people had 1.53 diseases (Table 2), with the differentiation at the level of plus or minus 1.43 diseases. In the adequate pension group, the number of diseases was lower (1.49) than in the inadequate pension group (1.58). However, this difference was not statistically significant. A maximum of 7 chronic diseases were recorded simultaneously in one person.

The mental aspect of health was taken into account in the study by a variable describing the self-rated tendency to depression. The variable, called "Depression", ranged from 0 to 12 points, with 0 referring to the lack of a tendency and 12 describing a high predictor of depression. The average level of depression self-assessment, at approximately 3 points in both groups of pensioners, was accompanied by a right-sided distribution asymmetry of the propensity to depression. This means that most of the respondents indicated a lower level of propensity than the average level would suggest (Table 2).

Finally, health prevention was taken into account in the study through the BMI index in the form of four levels of weight: underweight, normal weight, overweight, and obesity. The "BMI" variable reflects the eating style of pensioners. Since proper eating habits are important for the elderly in maintaining their health, this factor was also included in the study. Elderly people undergo many intense changes in the circulatory, nervous, digestive, and skeletal systems. These changes should, in turn, be reflected in changes in their diet, thanks to which their body can function properly, which minimizes the risk of civilization diseases such as obesity or hypertension (Jurczak et. al., 2011). As Table 3 indicates, pensioners in both the adequate and inadequate groups were mostly overweight or obese – approximately 69 % of them. Only one out of four pensioners had a normal weight.

Table 3. BMI of pensioners

Pension	BMI			
	underweight	**normal**	**overweight**	**obesity**
Adequate	0.3	24.4	44.6	30.7
Inadequate	0.4	25.6	43.5	30.5
Total	0.4	25.0	44.1	30.6

Source: Author's own calculations based on SHARELIFE data.

4. Classification Trees

The first variable analyzed was "Pension", which included both pensioners receiving adequate pensions and pensioners receiving inadequate pensions. The results of the classification are presented in Figure 1. The accuracy of the tree is around 59 %.

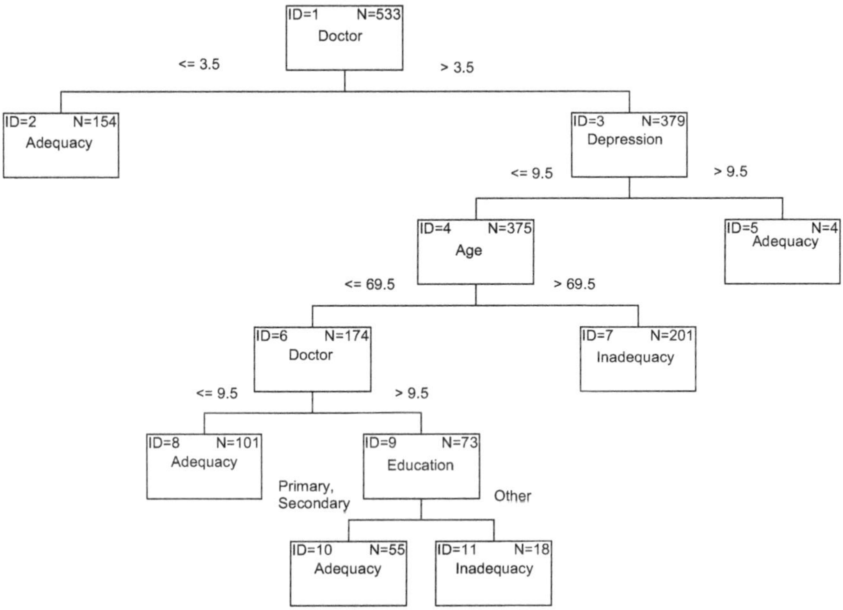

Figure 1. Decision tree for estimating adequate and inadequate pensions.
Source: Author's own calculations based on SHARELIFE data.

People who have adequate pension benefits rarely see a doctor – a maximum of three times a year. If they go to the doctor more often, they are also highly prone to depression. Adequate pensions are also provided to "younger" pensioners, *i.e.*, people under the age of 70, with a low or average tendency to depression, who visit a doctor frequently (up to nine times a year) or often (more than nine times a year). Most often, they have primary or secondary education.

At the same time, relatively young people, those under the age of 70, with a low or medium tendency to depression, often going to the doctor, and having higher than secondary education, did not receive an adequate pension benefit. An inadequate pension also applies to people over the age of 69, visiting a doctor four to nine times a year, with a low or average tendency to depression.

Figure 2 shows that the level of education comes first in the ranking of importance. It is followed by the number of doctor visits during one year and the pensioner age. Interestingly, the gender variable is only fourth from the bottom of the ranking, which means that the health status of women and men in terms of pension adequacy is quite similar.

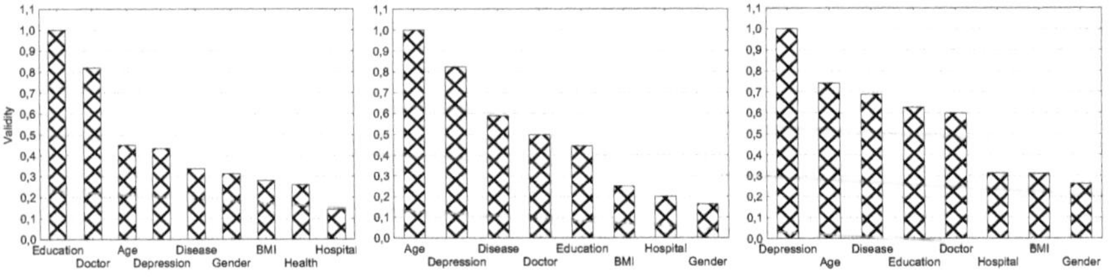

Figure 2. Ranking of variables for pension adequacy (a) self-perceived health and adequate pensions (b) self-perceived health and inadequate pensions (c).

Source: Author's own calculations based on SHARELIFE data.

In the second step, how pensioners receiving adequate and inadequate pensions perceive their health was examined. "Health" was the classifying variable in this case for the pensioners' health self-assessment. The decision tree presented in Figure 3 shows the health of pensioners with adequate benefits. This group represents people who believe that they have poor, fair, or good health. Due to a very small size (2.8 % of the sample), classes containing people with very good and excellent health conditions were not distinguished. The accuracy of the tree is around 47 %.

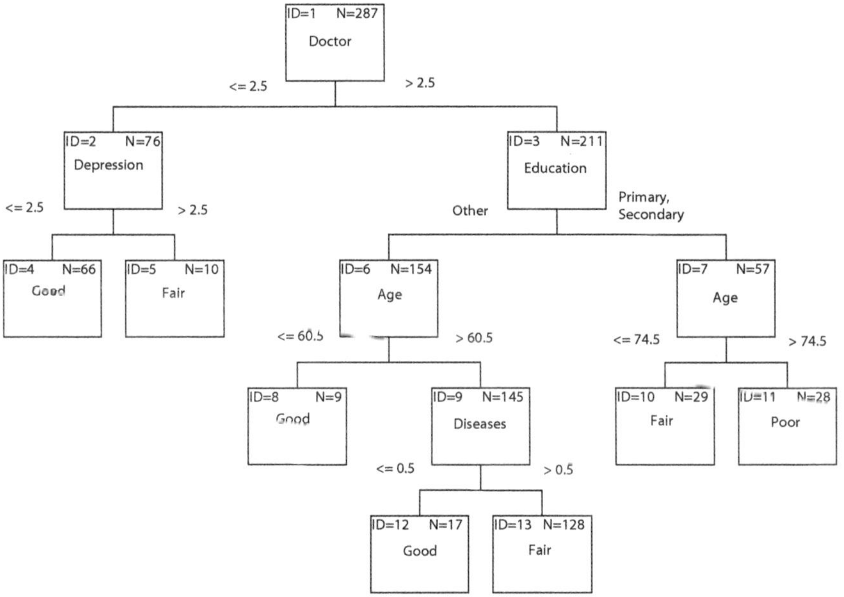

Figure 3. Decision tree for estimating self-perceived health – people with adequate pensions.

Source: Author's own calculations based on SHARELIFE data.

Good health was declared by people who rarely visit the doctor – a maximum of twice a year – as well as people who go to the doctor more often but have an education higher than secondary and are no more than 60 years of age. In the case of people aged 60 and older, good health was declared only by people who do not have chronic diseases.

People who assess their health as fair rarely see a doctor, *i.e.*, a maximum of twice a year, but indicate a tendency to depression, or go to the doctor more often than twice a year, have at least a postsecondary education, are aged over 60, and declare the presence of chronic diseases. The third group of people with fair health had medical appointments more than twice a year, primary or secondary education, and were not more than 74 years old.

People who declared poor health often visit a doctor, have primary or secondary education and were aged over 74.

Thus, age, tendency to have depression, and the number of chronic diseases constitute the variables differentiating the population of people who receive adequate pensions in terms of their health condition (Figure 2). The number of visits to the doctor and education are the other two important factors here. Therefore, it can be concluded that the assessment of health results mainly from the severity of disease symptoms, *i.e.*, the number of chronic diseases and a tendency toward depression -- which are strongly correlated with the age of the respondents. The number of visits to the doctor was inevitably linked with emerging disease problems. Gender, on the other hand, is the least significant variable in the study, which means that both women and men assess their health conditions similarly. The surveyed population is also quite homogeneous in their health status assessments relating to hospital stays and BMI.

The characteristics of people receiving inadequate pensions relating to self-assessment of their health condition are presented in Figure 4.

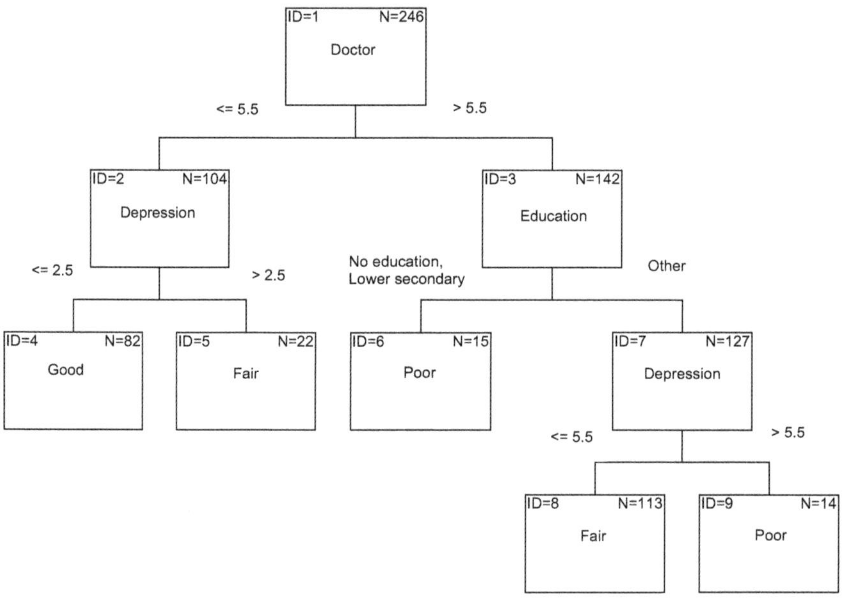

Figure 4. Decision tree for estimating self-perceived health – people with inadequate pensions.

Source: Author's own calculations based on SHARELIFE data.

The same as in the group with adequate benefits, people who believe that they have poor, fair, or good health can be represented in this group. It was not possible to observe classes containing people with very good and excellent health (only 1.5 % of the population). The accuracy of the tree is around 60 %.

Good health is declared only by people who visit the doctor not more than twice a year.

People who see a doctor often – three to five times a year or even more often – but have at least postsecondary education, and have some tendency to depression, report fair health.

Poor health is declared by people who frequently visit a doctor and have no education or have only primary education, as well as by the people who visit a doctor more than five times a year, have at least secondary education, and have an above-average tendency to depression.

The first three variables that differentiate the population of people receiving inadequate pensions in terms of their health condition are identical to those of people receiving adequate pensions, and they include the tendency to depression, age, and the number of chronic diseases (Figure 2). The variables that follow these also remain in a similar order. Therefore, it seems that the criteria for people with adequate and inadequate benefits when assessing their health condition are similar. Regardless of the monetary value of their benefits, pensioners assess their health by relying on the same factors, mostly, their diseases.

5. Conclusions

In previous studies, persons with low socioeconomic status generally have poorer self-rated health than persons with high socioeconomic status (Kawachi et al., 1999; Lantz et al., 2001; Yngwe et al., 2001; Knesebeck et al., 2003). Our findings show that the self-rated health condition is independent of the adequacy of pension benefits. Good self-rated health is not due to an adequate pension. People with adequate and inadequate pension benefits perceive their health similarly. The financial situation is not a fundamental factor in health perception among elderly individuals.

Similar conclusions came from Molarius and others (Molarius et al., 2007), whose findings support the view that one's financial condition is independent of his or her poor self-rated health. The researchers' findings suggest that the relationship between occupational status and poor self-rated health is mediated. As a multidimensional concept, self-rated health status is related not only to objective measures of health but also to various other factors, such as age, gender, education, marital status, and personal traits (Aro & Hasan, 1987; Sundquist & Johansson, 1997; Barsky et al., 1992).

It can therefore be concluded that the key factor in self-rated health is the severity of physical and mental disease symptoms. Additionally, the availability of principal medical services is highly ranked by pensioners, as the frequency of visits to the doctor is directly related to health problems. The age of pensioners also strongly influences how they see their health condition. Moving on to other characteristics of retired people's health, it can be observed that men and women perceive their health similarly, as the ranking of variables shows. The same goes for people who are slim and obese and people with or without hospital care. Other researchers have also emphasized that obesity and being underweight were independently related to poor self-rated health (Molarius et al., 2007).

The present study supports the notion that self-rated health is primarily related to diseases, both physical and mental, and the age of pensioners. In the context of the adequacy of pension benefits, three categories of people can therefore be distinguished:

- healthy people – rarely visiting a doctor;
- people suffering from depression – with a high tendency to depression and therefore, frequent medical appointments;

"average" people – that is, "younger" pensioners, with primary or secondary education, with an average or higher frequency of visiting a doctor, and with an average tendency to depression.

For people with inadequate benefits, there are two groups:

- average "younger" people – people with relatively high education, with an average frequency of visiting a doctor and a moderate tendency to depression.
- average "older" people – people who visit a doctor with an average frequency and have a moderate tendency to depression.

Summing up the results obtained, it is justified to formulate the conclusion that retired people rate their health better the younger they are, the fewer chronic diseases they have, the lower the tendency to depression they display, and that they disregard pension benefits' adequacy.

The key points from the research are as follows:

- Good self-rated health is independent of pension adequacy.
- The relative material situation is not a key factor in self-rated health.
- Self-rated health is related to physical and mental health conditions.
- The age of pensioners influences self-rated health.
- Men and women rated their health similarly.

References

Aro, S., & Hasan, J. (1987). Occupational Class, Psychosocial Stress and Morbidity. *Annals of Clinical Research, 19,* 62–68.

Barsky, A. J., Cleary, P. D., & Klerman, G. L. (1992). Determinants of Perceived Health Status of Medical Outpatients. *Social Science and Medicine, 34,* 1147–54.

Błedowski, P. (2012). *Raport na temat sytuacji osób starszych w Polsce.* Instytut Pracy i Spraw Socjalnych.

Borella, M., & Fornero E. (2009). *Adequacy of Pension Systems in Europe: An Analysis Based on Comprehensive Replacement Rates.* ENEPRI Research Reports No. 68.

Börsch-Supan, A. (2019). *Survey of Health, Ageing and Retirement in Europe (SHARE), Wave 7. 2019.* Release version: 7.0.0. SHARE-ERIC. Data set. https://doi.org/10.6103/SHARE.w7.700.

Breiman, L., Friedman, J. H., Olshen, R. A., & Stone, C. J. (1984). *Classification and Regression Trees.* Wadsworth & Brooks/Cole Advanced Books & Software.

Chybalski, F. (2016). The Multidimensional Efficiency of Pension Systems: Definition and Measurement in Cross-Country Studies. *Social Indicators Research, 128*(1), 15–34.

Czepulis-Rutkowska, Z. (2000). *Systemy emerytalne a poziom zabezpieczenia materialnego emerytów.* Instytut Pracy i Spraw Socjalnych.

EC. (2012). *Pension Adequacy in the European Union 2010–2050.* European Commission. Retrieved October 13, 2022 from https://ec.europa.eu/social/BlobServlet?docId=7805&langId=en

EU. (2018). *The 2018 Pension Adequacy Report: Current and Future Income Adequacy in Old Age in the EU.* European Union.

Gatnar, E. (2001). *Nieparametryczna metoda dyskryminacji i regresji.* PWN.

GUS. (2014). *Stan zdrowia ludności Polski w 2014 r.* GUS. Retrieved October 13, 2022 from https://stat.gov.pl/obszary-tematyczne/zdrowie/zdrowie/stan-zdrowia-ludnosci-polski-w-2014-r-,6,6.html

Jajko-Siwek, A. (2020). The Impact of the Flexibilization of Employment Histories on the Pension Adequacy in Poland. *Sustainability, 12*(19), 8260. https://doi.org/10.3390/su12198260

Jurczak, I., Barylski, M., & Irzmański, R. (2011). Znaczenie diety u osób w wieku podeszłym – ważny aspekt prewencji zdrowia czy nieistotna codzienność? *Geriatria, 5,* 127–133.

Kawachi, I., Kennedy, B. P., & Glass, R. (1999). Social Capital and Self-Rated Health: A Contextual Analysis. *American Journal of Public Health, 89,* 1187–93.

Knesebeck, O., Luschen, G., Cockerham, W. C., & Siegrist, J. (2003). Socioeconomic Status and Health among the Aged in the United States and Germany: A Comparative Cross-Sectional Study. *Social Science and Medicine, 57*, 1643–52.

Kulik, T. B., Janiszewska, M., Pirog, E., Pacian, A., Stefanowicz, A., & Żołnierczuk-Kieliszek D, Pacian J. (2011). Sytuacja zdrowotna osób starszych w Polsce i innych krajach europejskich. *Medycyna Ogólna i Nauki o Zdrowiu, 17,* 90–95.

Lantz, P. M., Lynch, J. W., House, J. S., et al. (2001). Socioeconomic Disparities in Health Change in a Longitudinal Study of US Adults: The Role of Health-Risk Behaviours. *Social Science and Medicine, 53,* 29–40.

Molarius, A., Berglund, K., Eriksson, C., Lambe, M., Nordström, E., Eriksson, H.G., & Feldman, I. (2007). Socioeconomic Conditions, Lifestyle Factors, and Self-Rated Health among Men and Women in Sweden. *European Journal of Public Health, 17*(2), 125–133. https://doi.org/10.1093/eurpub/ckl070

Mossakowska, M., Więcek, A., & Błędowski, P. (2012). *Aspekty medyczne, psychologiczne, socjologiczne i ekonomiczne starzenia się ludzi w Polsce. PolSenior*. Termedia.

OECD. (2019). *Pensions at a Glance 2019: OECD and G20 Indicators*. https://doi.org/10.1787/b6d3dcfc-en.

Palmer, B. A. (1989). Tax Reform and Retirement Income Replacement Ratios. *The Journal of Risk and Insurance, 56*(4), 702–725. http://dx.doi.org/10.2307/253454

Palmer, B. A. (1994). Retirement Income Replacement Ratios: An Update. *Benefits Quarterly, 10*(2), 59–75.

Puto, G., Repka, I., Ścisło, L., Walewska, E., Skrzypoń, D., Kawalec-Kajstura, E., Dąbczyńska, M., & Zurzycka, P. (2019). Psychosocial Problems Affecting the Elderly, *Medical Studies, 35*(3), 224–229.

Sundquist, J., & Johansson, S. E. (1997). Self-Reported Poor Health and Low Educational Level Predictors for Mortality: A Population-Based Follow Up Study of 39156 People in Sweden. *Journal Epidemiol Community Health,51,* 35–40.

Yngwe, M. A., Diderichsen, F., & Whitehead, M., et al. (2001). The Role of Income Differences in Explaining Social Inequalities in Self-Rated Health in Sweden and Britain. *Journal of Epidemiology Community Health, 55,* 556–61.

Kerstin Knees

Early Childhood Education in the Kindergarten Landscape of North-Rhine-Westfalia, Germany

1. Introduction

In 2023, Germany will have approximately 84 million inhabitants. This peak is related to rising birth rates and increasing migration, especially in cities and metropolitan areas, where the number of inhabitants and the proportion of migrants in the population is steadily increasing. The most populous federal state is North Rhine-Westphalia with approximately 18.6 million inhabitants. Approximately 6 million people here have a migration background and learn German as a second language. The kindergarten landscape is undergoing increasing change in NRW. Older facilities closed groups and fixed structures are gradually being converted into open, modern buildings with various functional spaces. Participation permeates the pedagogy, the attitude as well as the rooms, walls are dismantled, rooms are connected with each other, fixed group structures are dissolved. Closed educational concepts in the day-care centers are being opened up, borders and regulations are being adapted to this. Everything in the day care centers aims at the free development of the child. The implementation of participation is about the realization of children's rights, that children are strengthened in their self-concept, that they are involved in decisions and learn to communicate their own needs. On 19 November 2019, the Federal State of North Rhine-Westphalia decided to invest a further 5.5 billion euros in education and promotion in the elementary sector as part of the structural program of the Federal Republic of Germany. The language support for children in the facilities, which until then had been supported with €70 million, was increased to €100 million. In the process, it was decided that €1.2 billion would be invested in early childhood education in NRW (Betz , 2019). In addition, day care for children and support for families through, for example, off-peak care, is to be supported and parents are to be exempted from the monthly kindergarten fees in the penultimate and last kindergarten year of a child. In this way, the educational offer in the elementary sector is to be made accessible to more families. This is what the politicians want. However, in May 2023 there will be a shortage of 378,000 kindergarten places in Germany. Cities like Aachen in North Rhine-Westphalia regularly have to close their day-care centers for two days because they simply do not have the staff to look after the children five days a week. (welt.de, 2023). According to a recent study by the Bertelsmann Foundation, more than half of all daycare groups in Germany are too large. In March, the staffing ratio for 1.7 million children was no longer appropriate for children.

In 2001, the Pisa shock came overnight in Germany and the discussion began about when the educational process should begin for children. It was agreed relatively quickly that education does not begin at school, but in the years before. Germany is in the middle of the international field when it comes to the distribution of educational equality. While 79 out of every 100 children of academics make it to university, in Germany only 27 out of every 100 children from non-academic families do so. Children who grow up at home from an early age through reading aloud, playing, cognitive challenges and a strong emotional bond with parents who explain the world to them and who introduce the child culturally into society have better prospects for success in school and work. For decades, schools were given sole responsibility for educational injustice. If a child failed, it was the school's fault. A study by sociologist Jan Skopek from Trinity College in Dublin investigated when exactly the differences arise. His result is that glaring effects of origin are already evident in three-year-olds before they start school. Three-year-olds who receive support and attention at home, regardless of whether they come from immigrant families or not, have a strong understanding of numbers and shapes and develop an elaborate use of language like their peers from educationally disadvantaged families. This is because achievement- and learning-oriented parents specifically promote their children's language development and provide a cognitively stimulating environment.

School does not make this worse, but it does not narrow the differences anymore either (Brügelmann, 2002).

Therefore experts like educational researcher Brügelmann advocate not only starting much earlier, but also much more comprehensively than before.

In the elementary sector, concepts have been increasingly implemented in recent years that further promote, for example, science education, early mathematical support, movement, or language education. In addition to the educational requirements in the early childhood sector, parental work is also of crucial importance. Cooperation with parents or other caregivers in day care centers is one of the essential prerequisites of the new early childhood education. This is not only reflected in the scientific discourse (Viernickel, 2006), but is also reflected in Germany in the normative requirements of the Social Code and in the educational and orientation plans of the 16 federal states for day care centers, in North Rhine-Westphalia it is the "Bildungsgrundsätze NRW". The cooperation between parents and pedagogical staff is very important because they are jointly responsible for the well-being of the child in different areas of life. One requirement in the programs is that parents "be informed and appropriately involved before decisions are made in essential matters of education, upbringing and care". (§ 27 paragraph 1-page 1HKJGB). Another requirement is that children in day-care centers are to be involved in decisions affecting their lives in the facility, as stated not only in the resolution of the Standing Conference of the Ministers of Education and Cultural Affairs of 2004 in the joint framework of the Länder for early education in day-care facilities. This form of participation is called "participation". According to Sturzenhecker (2005), participation means growing into democratic structures in which the child is increasingly involved in participation and decision-making processes. However, not only parents are involved, but parents are also allowed to openly express their wishes, ideas and demands. In this context, day care centers have the mandate to be complementary to families. This means that the content and structure of their services must be geared to the situation, wishes and needs of families. And in order to be able to address the needs of the families and to guarantee individual support for the child, the exchange with parents is an indispensable prerequisite. The professionals play a leading role in this, as they have a great influence on the process of cooperation – they shape the framework conditions, interact with the parents and thus include the information from the family in their daily work. The term "educational partnership" describes the need for parents and pedagogical staff to exchange ideas in the interest of the children and to promote the child's development in partnership. This means that both of the children's important reference systems cooperate closely, exchange views, weigh their attitudes and support each other in the interest of the children. (Textor, 2006).

2. Methodology

Within the framework of the study, 20 kindergarten teachers at the end of their third year of training from 20 different institutions were interviewed. This survey was in qualitative research design and included 13 questions per interview. None of the facilities is located in a socially deprived area or in the immediate vicinity of a large city. All are located in rural, village areas. The facilities are run by different organizations and differ in their conception: open, partially open or closed concepts. The aim was to find out what challenges the trainee educators face at the end of their last year of training. In doing so, their view of their everyday life in their future profession was asked. They were asked about the catchment area or the clientele of the institution, about group sizes, about the educational partnership with parents, about the proportion of children with a migration background, about language or communication difficulties and about special challenges in everyday life as well as the number of staff. This survey is aimed exclusively at the perspective of the prospective professionals. The interviews were open, axial and selectively coded.

Code model:

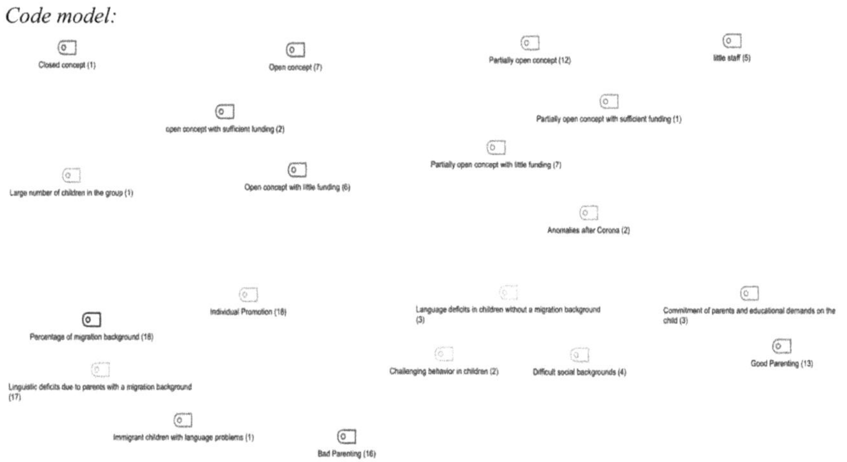

Figure 1. Results of 20 interviews.

3. Results

All kindergarten teachers unanimously concluded that the quality of their work and the day-to-day structures in the kindergarten strongly depend on the staffing ratio. All the trainee kindergarten teachers interviewed stated that they have been short of staff for some time, at least since Corona, and to a large extent. If too many educators are ill and absent, the work with the children suffers considerably. This means that individual support or individual work with a single child is no longer possible. Group sizes in the various concepts are then greatly increased and only in the afternoon or at off-peak times is it possible to deal with a child individually for a short time. Some report that they do not interact with a child alone because other children immediately join them when they see a teacher talking to a child; others report a maximum of 3 minutes for a single child. The results of educators from partly open and open concepts are congruent. In particular, any support needs cannot be addressed in everyday life. It does not matter whether the professionals work in a closed, partially open or open concept. If there are not enough staff, areas are closed or the time for bringing the children to school is shortened or restricted on a daily basis.

The interviews also made it clear that the different facilities mostly have very similar forms of cooperation with parents and the same challenges associated with this. At the beginning, when parents decide on a particular facility and during the settling-in phase, the rules of the day care center are explained to the parents, the annual schedule, the tasks, the development and observation documentation are explained and the participation of the parents in the sense of an "educational partnership" is made clear. When a child settles into a day care center, it is important to design customized offers for the parents and their children, but given the great diversity of life situations, the individual parents and thus the heterogeneity of parenthood, it can generally be assumed that there is no such thing as "the parents". And professionalism on the part of the institution is characterized by the fact that the respective interactions and the offers should be adapted to the specific target group. Once the parents and the child have arrived at the facility after the settling-in period, the parents' presence time at the facility is significantly reduced.

Most often, the educators then facilitate or plan door-to-door talks, individual parent talks or development talks, celebrations or regular parent evenings, in which they exchange information with the parents about the child or processes in the day care center.

In all 20 facilities, the educators report on all spectrums of social classes among the parents: from educationally deprived classes, parents who do not speak any German and have no interest in any interaction, to highly privileged academic families; almost all types of parents are represented everywhere. This means a great challenge for the educational staff in all 20 facilities, because the needs of the parents are also very different. In order to create an optimal living and developmental environment for the child, continuous cooperation with the parents, at least based on door-to-door talks and regular developmental discussions, based on systematic observation and documentation of the child, is of great importance. However, this does not take place across the board. Some facilities offer this only to a limited extent; one facility stated that it does not currently offer any participatory parental work. In addition to the door-to-door talks and minute development talks, innovative possibilities such as "WhatsApp groups" or certain Kita apps are used in some day-care centers to exchange information, but then often not by all parents, which makes the exchange or cooperation more difficult for many parents, especially the immigrant families often do not have the language skills or the possibilities to network with the other parents and the professionals. Only some of the interviewed facilities work with digital media as a means of communication. For non-German-speaking parents, letters to parents are translated or attempts are made to convey the concerns with the English language or with signs. How low threshold offers must be in order to reach all parents remains open in the survey. Thus, it is precisely those parents who often need to be reached who are not reached. This means that participation for all parents is not given, and the professionals hardly ever enter an exchange about the child. Individual professionals stated that these parents do not understand or implement even the simplest facts or that they avoid the exchange.

The day-care centers all have pedagogical focuses and certifications according to which they orient their pedagogical work. Due to the high staff shortage, however, there is often no time to devote to this promotion in the educational areas. Thus, a certified movement kindergarten often cannot offer more sports programs than other day care centers because there is simply not enough staff to supervise the children in the gymnasiums or in the outdoor area. As a result, the promotion of all educational areas suffers. Thus, the educational mission of the day-care centers loses its effect and turns into "keeping children safe".

4. Discussion

What needs to be looked at is the supervision ratio of each individual nursery schoolteacher. North Rhine-Westphalia has a childcare ratio in the U3 sector of one specialist looks after 3.7 children; in the Ü3 sector she looks after an average of 8.6 children. In practice, however, they look after at least 5 or more children in the U3 sector and sometimes up to 25 children in the Ü3 sector. This is because the childcare ratio, which is only a guideline, does not include sick days, holidays, training days for colleagues and, finally, unfilled positions.

One aspect that has increased since 2015 is the growing number of refugee children and children with a migration background in the facilities, i.e., children who do not speak German at all or only partially and thus need more time and attention to understand things. The language barrier ensures that the children are unable to communicate verbally with the educators and express their feelings, thoughts, experiences or needs. But also playing with the other children can become a problem if rules of the game, procedures or needs of others are not understood and thus cannot be implemented, which leads to frustration and in the worst case to aggression.

There are too few staff everywhere and too much sick leave to cope well with the day-to-day work. Children with special needs or language problems then make the daily work even more difficult. The prospective educators interviewed all work in rural areas, so they are not as affected by this problem as the professionals in large cities, precarious locations, and social hotspots. There, the proportion of migrants is often over 70 % and much more, and the staff shortage is high.

Some of the educators interviewed report that immigrant parents also often have problems understanding. Even if there are not so many parents in rural areas, the few parents who cannot be reached linguistically make it difficult to work with the parents and with the parents themselves.

Insufficient cooperation between pairs of parents or parents and the institution can hinder the development of a supportive and cooperative environment for the child. Parents not understanding or not wanting to attend parent-teacher conferences, development meetings or celebrations can mean that parents are not sufficiently informed about the child's development in the social space of the day care center and do not receive the resources or support they need to optimally support their child. The irregular or absent participation of parents will lead to them missing important information and being less involved in the educational process of their children, this can grow into educational or behavioral deficits as the pedagogical staff is not able to offer adequate support and encouragement (Leu, 2014).

The basic idea of participation, which has led to the opening of daycare concepts from closed concepts to partially open and open concepts, demands the involvement of children, parents and educators in decision-making processes and the shaping of everyday life in the kindergarten. The legal anchoring of strengthening the rights of the child by allowing him or her to have a say means an improvement in the child's participation and educational opportunities. If there is good communication between all actors, participation can be successful. However, there are aspects that make participation difficult in everyday life, for example time and resource requirements. Participation requires time so that resources can be implemented effectively. It requires additional communication, planning and organization and time to ensure that all stakeholders are heard, and their perspectives are considered. Consideration must be given to the complexity of decision-making when many people are involved in decision-making processes. It can be difficult to reach consensus or agreement, especially when different interests and opinions clash. This can lead to slower decision-making and limited flexibility in adapting to changing needs. Children may be overburdened if they are involved in too many decision-making processes.

They need to be able to understand the information provided by adults, make appropriate decisions, and weigh up possible consequences. However, this implies having sufficient language skills, which cannot be expected per se from children with a migration background. A final aspect is that parents and children have a different point of view than educators when it comes to pedagogical actions and topics in the day care center, which can lead to different ideas about how certain things should be implemented.

5. Conclusion

After analyzing the interviews and literature, it can be concluded that the lack of staff in the day care centers and communication problems at all levels are significant challenges. The staff shortage is a nationwide problem and is not limited to certain regions.

The present analysis makes it clear that language development is a central aspect of early childhood education and thus has a direct impact on the further course of education as well as the social integration of children. Language deficits can lead to long-term consequences such as limited educational opportunities and social disadvantage. An adequate childcare ratio, an appropriate key between educators and children is crucial to ensure adequate care, individual support, and assistance. The current shortage of staff, however, means that educators often reach their limits and cannot devote the necessary time and attention to each child. The consequences do not remain in the day care center with the affected children but have a long-term impact on society as a whole. Because these children carry these deficits such as lack of social behavior, untrained fine or gross motor skills, and the ability to concentrate into their school careers.

It is important to recognize that the problems mentioned and the immense staff shortage in day care centers are a complex problem that cannot be easily solved. A comprehensive solution strategy requires a combination of measures at different levels; at the political level, sufficient financial resources should be allocated to the education and care infrastructure. In practice, the childcare ratio needs to be reconsidered in order to ensure adequate staffing. At the same time, it is of great importance to invest in the education and training of pedagogical staff in order to further develop their intercultural and inclusion competences. Parental work needs to be considered to what extent parents can be involved; people from other countries need to be made aware that education for their children in Germany is essential so that they can live an independent life later.

References

Betz, T. (2019). *Kinder zwischen Chancen und Barrieren.* Forschungsbericht 2. Zum Verhältnis von Schule und Familie aus der Sicht von Kindern: Ihre Perspektiven, ihre Positionen. https://doi.org/10.25656/01:20581

BMFSFJ. Abgerufen am 14.05.2023 von: https://www.bmfsfj.de/bmfsfj/aktuelles/presse/pressemitteilungen/nordrhein-westfalen-und-der-bund-unterzeichnen-gute-kita-vertrag-ueber-rund-1-2-milliarden-euro-141188. (o. J.).

Brügelmann, H. (2002). Heterogenität, Integration, Differenzierung: Empirische Befunde-pädagogische Prinzipien. In: Heinzel, F., Prengel, A. (Htrsg.), Jahrbuch Grundschulforschung, Bd.6, Opladen: Leske + Budrich.

Leu, H. R. (2014). *Non-formales und informelles Lernen – unverzichtbare Elemente frühpädagogischer Professionalisierung.* Eine Analyse vor dem Hintergrund des Deutschen Qualifikationsrahmens. Weiterbildungsinitiative Frühpädagogische Fachkräfte, WiFF-Expertisen (Bd.40).

Sturzenhecker, B. (2005). Begründungen und Qualitätsstandards von Partizipation-auch für Ganztagsschule. *Heft* 2/2005, 30–34

Textor, M. (2006). Elternarbeit mit Migrant/innen. In Textor, M.R., Bostelmann, A.(Hrsg.), *Kindergartenpädagogik Online-Handbuch.*

Viernickel, S. (2006). Qualitätskriterien und Standards im Bereich der frühkindlichen Bildung und Betreuung. *Studienbuch… zum Bildungs- und Sozialmanagement, 14.* IBUS.

Welt.de. Abgerufen am 14.05. 2023 von https://www.welt.de/politik/deutschland/article245204520/Kitaplaetze-Bundesweit-fehlen-laut-Bundesfamilienministerium-378-000.html. (o. J.).

Nejla Peka

Early Marriage: One of the Most Serious Violations of Children's Rights

1. Introduction

The purpose of this exploratory study is to investigate about the challenges in legal framework and the role that legislative measures play in promoting and protecting Children's Rights from the male administration of the power by public authorities[1] and especially for promoting and protecting children rights[2].

The study employs a mixed methodology, comprising a review of the legislation, institutional framework and of the relevant literature in the field of social cohesion, health, education and child protection concerning the early marriages, especially towards girls.

The findings of this paper are supported in prior research in analyzing a lot of documents, strategies, prepared by international institutions, NHRI's, NGO-s and other government institutions. The in-depth analysis of the qualitative data revealed a basic understanding of promoting and protecting children rights in my country.

Early marriages, as a typical phenomenon of developing societies, constitute a sharp social problem, which affects those countries, where the respect and protection of human rights leaves much to be desired, where discrimination and social exclusion for vulnerable categories are evident and severely affect their quality of life.

In various international acts, such as international and regional conventions on human rights[3], protocols, early marriage is defined as a phenomenon that mostly affects children and constitutes a violation of human rights, mainly the rights of girls and women, causing great damage in terms of health, healthy living, education and protection from violence. Being married forces girls into

1 Law no.8454/1999, "On organization and functioning of the People's Advocate Institution in Republic of Albania".

2 Law no.155/2014, in explicitly way is provision the established of a new Commissioner for Promoting and Protecting Children Rights. (Article 10), Official Gazette no.195, pap.10897.

3 Convention on Consent for Marriage, Minimum Age for Marriage and Registration of Marriages; The CEDAW Convention, as well as the UN CRC.

physical and emotional relationships at a very young, early age, for which, from an age point of view, they are not ready.

The 2030 ASD and the 17 SDGs, adopted by the UNGA, constitute a new impetus in global efforts to achieve sustainable development and aim to address the challenges global issues such as poverty, inequality and climate change, as well as improve access to health and education, build strong institutions and partnerships[4].

Married children are considered incapable of giving full consent, since a child does not have the legal capacity to act[5]. In this sense, child marriages must be considered absolutely, as a violation of human rights and, especially of children's rights.

As we mentioned above, the Albanian legislation provides for marriages under the age of 18 for special cases, with a court decision, thus leaving the judiciary to appreciate and interpret in this case, when a case will be qualified as a "special case". Judges, even in this legal ambiguity, have the opportunity to ban early marriages in their decision-making, taking into account their definition and interpretation in international conventions.

The quantitative *data* of child marriages in Albania are low, but they are encountered as a practice, mainly in the Roma Community, as well as in some isolated rural areas. Thus, according to INSTAT data[6], the marriage of girls under the age of 18 remains a worrying phenomenon[7].

2. Literature Review, Definition of the Concept "early marriage"

As a phenomenon, it has been addressed in contexts such as: ethnic-based social exclusion, discrimination, poverty, child labor and their exploitation for trafficking purposes. It is worth emphasizing the fact that marriages involving children are not registered, so there is no accurate statistical data on this phenomenon. The damage that this phenomenon causes in the psycho-social, physical, moral and healthy development of children is associated with great

4 Objective no.5 of the UN ASD aims to eliminate all harmful practices, such as early and forced child marriages.

5 See the provisions in the Civil Code of the RoA.

6 During 2019, the Albanian courts allowed the marriage of 20 minor girls under 18 years old, while in 2018, this number was 24.

7 http://www.instat.gov.al/media/1143/burrat_dhe_grat__ne_shqiperi_2017_libri.pdf

costs in terms of the wellbeing of childhood, education, healthy living and limits their opportunities for normal development.

However, whether economic or cultural, the damage that these marriages cause not only emotionally, spiritually and mentally, but also physically, to young girls and the opportunities they have for a future cannot be justified differently.

Child marriage is a gender-based phenomenon that affects girls and boys in different ways[8]. Married child girls are also affected by domestic violence and sexual abuse within unequal relationships[9]. The situation is completely opposite for boys of the same age group[10].

If we refer to the definition given for early marriages according to social sciences, child marriage is the official or unofficial union of two people, when at least one of them is under 18 years old. By virtue of being children, "child spouses" are considered incapable of giving full consent. That being said, in legal terms, child marriages are considered a violation of human rights and, in particular, the rights of the child.

Through this book chapter is aimed to achieve a more comprehensive understanding regarding early child marriage definition and concepts not only in legislation, but also in strategic documents or recommendations provided by international organizations.

Except some special reports provided by the Office of the UNHCHR and NHRI's such as Ombudsman or Commissioner for Protection and Promote Children's Rights.[11]

Meanwhile, during the research on this phenomenon vacuum in Albanian literature concerning the elaboration of the early marriage was identified. There are international authors such as Syanemyr (2020) who provides a review on the effects in reducing child marriage and the importance of education and economic opportunities offer young women as acceptable alternatives to early marriage (par.9).

---

8 The number of boys in early marriage worldwide is significantly lower than that of girls.

9 In the INSTAT publication "Men and women in Albania", there are 10 married girls under the age of 18 for every 1000 marriages. In total, the "under 19" age group accounts for 17.4 % of all marriages.

10 INSTAT informed that "*...there are no marriages for boys before the age of 18, and the percentage of married boys aged 18–19 is negligible...*".

11 The recommendation of the CPPCR in the People's Advocate Institution addressed to the state authorities, www.avokatipopullit.gov.al

Nabila, Roswiyani and Satyad (2021) in their paper discuss about the factors affecting early marriage decisions in a specific study case such as Indonesia. Their findings discovered that early marriage generally occurs because of family ties, gender inequality, poverty and economic survival strategies, control over sexuality and protecting family honors, tradition and culture, and insecurity. One of the factors identified as a key issue which is similar in Albania case too, relates to control over sexuality and protecting family honor (p. 1400).

Child marriage in Albania is a complex issue impacted by several risk factors such as poverty, exploitation and marginalization. It's necessary to provide a better legislation harmonization between laws that define the protection of CR and the best interest of the child with other laws that foresee the relationship between parents and children (Family Code) and state authorities guaranteeing children's rights.

Meanwhile, children married (especially girls) at an early age need special protection, through the strategies design, action plans and the undertaking of concrete actions, which aim to provide them with access to education, life skills, health and opportunities to be participants actively in society. In this case, in determining the "best interest of the child"[12] (2013, CRC/C/GC/14), all his legal rights, as well as any individual circumstances, must be taken into account.

Considering the above mentioning the development hypothesis centers around the concern the vacuum existing in Albania legislation regarding this phenomenon.

3. Hypothesis

A vacuum exists in legislation regulation (Family Code of Albania) and lack of harmonization regarding laws defining the concept of early marriage before 18 years old considering that this age is the limit age that CRC and the Albanian legislation (law no.18/2017) has considered appropriate for marriage.

Hypothesis explanation: in the Family Code of Albania an age limit for marriage (18 years old) is provided, recognizing the court discretion, by specifying important reasons, when marriages can be allowed before this age. What is lacking is exactly the definition of the minimal age boundary when the early marriage is allowed by the court.

---

12 General Comment No. 14 "On the right of the child to have his/her best interests taken as a primary consideration, 2013, CRC / C / GC / 14.

4. Research Methodology

This study is based on a qualitative methodology entrenching primary resources in international legal framework regulating early child marriages and original data from field expertise. The consultation with the international legal framework and recommendations of the international organizational, served as a basis to understand policy overview of this phenomenon. For this reason, a comparison is provided between international and national legislation in the related field.

The study case below elaborates on a story of two minors, part of Fier municipality, Roma Community, which is described as an intensive systematic investigation to generalize over similar problems this community is facing.

The concern that this case raised gave the incentive of the People's Advocate Institution to extend administrative investigation toward local responsible institutions in charge with child protection. After the examination of the case, a legislative recommendation was issued identifying state authorities, responsible to take measures for amendment of legislation and also drafting strategic and action plans to minimize this phenomenon.

5. Study Case

In exercising the duty of Commissioner of the Protection and Promotion of the Children's Rights in Albania, starting from the protection of the best interest of the child, several cases have been handled *"ex-officio"* for this issue. Specifically, such a case was the marriage of two minors (13 and 16 years old), members of the Roma Community in Fier municipality, in a difficult and a complex situation, and became parents of a baby. The mayor of Fier informed that the case of the 13-year-old minor was handled by them. On the part of the CPU (Child Protection Unit), the minor mother was supported, with psychological and legal assistance, help with food packages, and they also helped with the process of registering the child based on the civil status law. This case is now being treated and monitored by the CPU in Fier municipality. The case, despite the treatment and support of the local structures for the two minors who became parents, strengthen out the importance of the awareness of the whole society that the empowerment and economic support of families in need, mostly helps to prevent this phenomenon.

6. The International Legal Framework

The minimum age for marriage should be 18 years for both girls and boys. When they get married, they take on important responsibilities. Therefore, marriage should not be permitted before they have attained full maturity and capacity to act (CRO, 2015). According to the WHO, when minors, especially girls, marry and have children, their health can be negatively affected and their education hindered. As a result, their economic autonomy is limited[13].

The CRC does not expressly prohibit child marriage, but has linked it, among others, to the right to free expression, protection from violence and abuse, protection from harmful traditional practices. A child is defined "*...as any human being under the age of 18 years, unless, under the law applicable to the child, the age of majority is reached earlier...*". Despite the lack of reference in the CRC, the UNCRC has determined that "*...the minimum age for marriage should be for girls as well as for boys, the age of 18 years...*". The provisions of this convention are permeated by the principle of the highest interest of the child, so this principle also prevails in the institution of marriage.

Likewise, in addition to this principle, the CRC foresees in some of its articles the protection of the rights of children at risk from marriage[14]. It can be considered as a form of discrimination based on gender, since mostly girls are affected by this phenomenon. The UNCRC has recommended that the phenomenon of child marriage should be approached through the principle of the best interest of the child, also seeking the protection of the rights to free expression, freedom from violence and abuse, as well as from harmful traditional practices.

GR no.31, of the CEDAW, as well as GC no.18, of the Committee of RC, on harmful practices have determined that "*...child marriage, it is any marriage where at least one of the parties is under the age of 18...*". Also, according to this recommendation, child marriage is considered to be a form of forced marriage, given that one and/or both parties have not expressed full, free and informed consent.

GR no.21, of the CEDAW Committee, also determines that the right of a woman to choose her husband and to marry freely is essential for her life, for her dignity and equality as a human being.

The CEDAW Convention guarantees the responsibility of the state to ensure these rights, which are fundamentally rights of human being. CEDAW's provisions on child marriage provide that men and women have the same right to marry, have the same right to freely choose a spouse and marry only of their own free will and full consent, as well as the engagement and marriage of a child will have no legal effect[15].

---

13 CEDAW Committee, par.36, General Recommendations 21.

14 Article 2, 13, 24 and 28 of CRC.

15 Article 16 (1).

We can say that the two conventions (CRC&CEDAW) in the context of equality, complement each other, concluding that early marriages violate the right of girls for gender equality. Whereas, the CRC, although it does not specifically prohibit the marriage of children, it clearly defines the age of 18 as the legal age for marriage. CEDAW considers child marriage void *ab initio*.

The Parliamentary Assembly of the CoE has asked the national parliaments of the member countries of the CoE to adapt their legislation, in order to increase the minimum legal age of marriage for women and men to 18 years[16]. Meanwhile, the European Parliament in 2019, clearly recommends the prohibition of these marriages. The resolution of the EP requires the EU member states, as well as the countries with which they cooperate, to prohibit by law child marriages, early marriages and forced marriages.

The UNGA has adopted a significant number of resolutions on early and forced child marriage[17].

Therefore, the UN "urges" member states to adopt and strictly implement legislation to ensure that marriage is entered into only with the free and full consent of the spouses and to adopt and strictly implement laws regarding the minimum age legal consent and the minimum age for marriage, as well as to raise the minimum age for marriage, when necessary[18].

The WHO in 2011 approved its guidelines[19], where among the six recommendations given, one of them is dedicated precisely to prevention of marriages under the age of 18.

Likewise, this guide also contains the areas where efforts should be focused, such as: interventions to improve legislation and state policies for the protection of children from early marriages, etc.

Actions to end child, early and forced marriages have increased at international, regional and national levels[20]. The connection with the implementation and monitoring of the SDGs (objective 5.3) is evident.

16 Resolution 1468 (2005) "On forced marriages and child marriages".

17 Resolutions 69/156 (2014); 71/175 (2016) &3/73 (2018).

18 www.un.org/esa/population/cpd, 2012.

19 "Preventing early pregnancy and poor reproductive outcomes among adolescents in developing countries" https://www.who.int/maternal_child_adolescent/documents/preventing_early_pregnancy/en/

20 36. 27.9.2013 "Strengthening efforts to prevent and eliminate child, early and forced marriage: challenges, achievements, best practices and implementation gaps", https://ap.ohchr.org/documents/dpage_e.aspx?si=A/HRC/RES/24/23

7. National Legal Framework in the Field

Early marriages constitute an infringement and violation of children's rights, including the right to equality based on sex and age, to education and development, to marry and create a family, to lived, to have a possible standard of well-being. It is very important for a country to include clear concepts in its domestic legislation that specifically define the minimum age for marriage. This, also in function of fulfilling the commitments undertaken through the ratification of several international conventions on human rights, for the harmonization of national legislation with international standards (GREVIO, 2017).

Our Constitution provides that "*...everyone has the right to marry and have a family...*", as well as "*...marriage and family enjoy the special protection of the state...*"[21]. Children, young people, pregnant women and new mothers have the right to special protection from the state[22].

The Family Code[23] has sanctioned by defining, that "*...Parents, the competent bodies and the courts, should have the highest interest of the child as their primary consideration...*"[24]. According to this law, the minimum legal age for marriage in Albania is 18 years. Essential importance is given to giving consent for marriage[25].

Similarly, the FC prohibits marriage under age[26]. Meanwhile, in this law, it is determined that the court can allow marriages under age, if there are some reasons, which are considered important by it[27]. Specifically, in Article 7 (2), in most cases, the courts have supported their legal reasoning to allow marriages under the age of 18.

Apart from the age limit for marriage, Albanian legislation does not define any measures to prevent child marriages.

8. Finding and Discussions

In our country, this phenomenon appears intertwined with the problem of non-registration in the civil status of children, who are in a difficult situation and without economic support, mainly from members of the Roma Community or

21 Article 53.
22 Article 54.
23 Law no.9062/2003.
24 Article 2 of the Law.
25 Article 8 of the Civil Code.
26 Article 7/1, law no. 9062/2003.
27 Article 7/2.

who live in deep rural areas. The responsible state institutions for the protection and guarantee of human rights, must dedicate special attention to the situation of the Roma and Egyptian Community, through taking the necessary measures to ensure and meet their basic living needs. The daily reality has made us reflect deeply and understand that the Roma (also the Egyptians) today are a vulnerable group and at risk, like some other social categories in the country.

Today, an increased attention and institutional commitment is needed, to respond to the basic living needs of these communities, concretized with measures that have a direct impact and that ensure an acceptable standard of living. Providing additional financial assistance, basic living means, guaranteeing the provision of basic social services and access to these services for these communities, are some of the recommendations to support these communities. No one should be left behind in any unusual situation, providing in any case interaction, support and social solidarity.

9. Conclusion

Child protection is a component of each of the MDG. A protective environment, encompassing all areas of social life, where laws, services and practices reduce the risks children face, can prevent many forms of violence, exploitation and abuse against children from occurring.

Nevertheless, while the Family Code sets an age limit for marriage (18 years old) and recognizes the court discretion, for important reasons, to allow marriage before this age, it is unclear and does not determine how far this boundary can entrench and in the same time limit itself. The legislation on the rights and protection of the child provides that "*… the realization and protection of children's rights is based on respect for dignity, honor and personality of the child, thus guaranteeing sustainable physical, mental, moral, spiritual and social development…*"[28]. Realization of this principle in practice by the responsible state authorities means providing protection for children from any form of violence, offering them protection.

This is due to the fact that child marriage is one of the most serious violations of children's rights and a serious form of their abuse.

Currently, it is recognized that early and forced marriage with minors are harmful practices in violation of HR.

---

28 Article 6/2, law no.18/2017.

Therefore, considering the above mentioned, the Commissioner of CR in the People's Advocate Institution of Albania, after investigating and treating the study case, raised the need to evaluate the changes in Family Code, amending it with the goal to preventing child marriages, based on the protection of their best interests[29].

Also, it is necessary to repeal article 7 (2) of this law which recognizes the right of the courts to approve marriages under the age of 18 and the reconceptualization of a provision, which defines the minimum age, below which exceptions are not allowed from the legal age to marry, an obligation, originating from the UN CRC.

The responsible state authorities, must include in their strategic documents for Children's Rights (UNICEF, 2014), the awareness and sensitization of society and actors in the field, NGO-s and individuals, regarding the consequences of the occurrence of child marriages, so that the problem is addressed in an integrated and comprehensive manner.

Efforts to end child marriage should aim at coordinated and budgeted actions reflected in efficient policies at the multi-sectorial level in education, health, defense and other sectors.

Recommendations on the case of Albania

- It is imperative to strengthen the criteria for allowing early marriages and their monitoring by local structures.
- The repeating cycle of poverty should be prevented by marriages occurring at an early age.
- Legal reasoning in all judicial and administrative processes, as well as their decisions, must be based on the principle in the best interest of the child.
- It is necessary for state institutions to take measures for monitoring local level for essential problems such as the education and employment of married girls under the age of 18.
- The situation urges for the authorities to review the legislation in force in order to establish appropriate additional safeguards.

References

Constitution of RoA.

Civil Code of RoA.

29 The recommendation of the CPPCR addressed to the state authorities, www.avokatipopullit.gov.al

CEDAW and the Committee for Children's Rights CRC. (2014). *Joint General Recommendation No.31 of the CEDAW Committee/General Comment No.18 of the CRC on Harmful Practices*, November 14.

CEDAW Committee, Paragraph 36, General Recommendations 21.

CRC/C/ALB/CO/2-4. (2012). *Concluding Observations for Albania Following the Periodic Report on the CRC.*

Children's Rights Observatory. (CRO). (2015). *Early Marriages in Albania.* "Natyra" Press.

Field Expertise/Personal Experience – The Recommendation of the Commissioner for the Protection and Promotion of Children's Rights in the People's Advocate Institution Addressed to the State Authorities. www.avokatipopullit.gov.al

GREVIO. (2017). *Report on Legislative Measures in Implementation of the CoE CEDAW Convention.*

General Comment No.14. *On the Right of the Child to Have His/Her Best Interests Taken as a Primary Consideration, 2013*, CRC / C / GC / 14.

General Comment No.4 of the UN Committee on the RC (2003). *Adolescent Health and Development in the Context of the CRC*, CRC/GC/2003/4.

INSTAT Publication. *Men and Women in Albania.*

Law No.8454/1999. *On Organization and Functioning of the Ombudsman in the Republic of Albania.*

Law No. 9062/2003. *Family Code.*

Law No.18/2017. *On the Rights and Protection of the Child.*

Nabila, R., Roswiyani, R., & Satyadi, H. (2021). A Literature Review of Factors Influencing Early Marriage Decisions in Indonesia, Advances in Social Science. *Education and Humanities Research, 655*, 1392–1402

Report of the Office of the UN High Commissioner for HR 2014. *Preventing and Eliminating Early and Forced Child Marriages*, A/HRC/26/22

Resolution 1468. (2005). *On Forced Marriages and Child Marriages.*

Syanemyr, J. (2020). *Literature Review on Effects of Interventions to Reduce the Prevalence of Child Marriage*. Bergen: Chr. Michelsen Institute (CMI Report R 2020:02) https://www.cmi.no/publications/7358-literature-review-on-effects-of-interventions-to-reduce-the-prevalence-of-child-marriage

UNICEF. (2014). *Protecting Children from Violence, Rape and Abuse – Early Marriage.*

Dora Naletina, Ivana Štulec and Mia Dragica Milković

Volatility of Maritime Freight Rates in Pandemic: Case Study of Transcontinental Sourcing

1. Introduction

Today's world is extremely well connected and heavily dependent on maritime trade. The maritime market is the result of global production and as such, is subject to cyclical changes, recessions and expansions (Jerebić & Pavlin, 2018). Maritime transport is sensitive to external factors, such as changes in international trade, the political situation, current financial trends, the level of technological development, changes in legislation, etc. (Agbaba, 2020). In recent years, the stability of supply chains has been threatened under the influence of various pressures, and the pandemic caused by the COVID-19 virus and Russia's invasion of Ukraine have further shaken the entire world market (Rožić et al., 2022).

Considering that more than 80 % of the global trade is delivered by ship (UNCTAD, 2022b), the disruptions caused by pandemic and war caused disruptions in the maritime market like no other crisis before. The maritime market is exposed to a high level of volatility and changes in demand that fluctuate over a certain period (Agbaba, 2020). The recovery of the entire world economy is threatened by such high volatility of freight rates in container maritime transport, which is additionally reflected in the disruption of the stability of supply chains (Naletina, 2021). Earlier crisis times already influenced the need to research this problem, so Alizadeh and Nomikos (2011) pointed out that the relationship between cargo volume (demand for transportation) and freight rates is asymmetrical. Therefore, when the market is faced with disturbances in demand, volatility is significantly higher than in situations of stability. The biggest consequences caused by the volatility of freight rates are ultimately borne by consumers. The increase in freight rates has already had an impact on the price growth of consumer goods that reach the market for their final consumption by sea (Rožić et al., 2022). Taking into account all of the above, as well as the fact that freight rates are among the most volatile asset classes (Lam et al., 2021), the focus of this paper is precisely on the volatility of freight rates during the COVID-19 pandemic. A case study was conducted on a Croatian company that sources goods from China to determine how pandemic and rising freight rates affected its strategic positioning. Following research questions can be defined:

- How pandemic impacted business operations of a company that sources transcontinental?
- How rising freight rates affected its supply chain?
- How company responded to market changes, regarding its strategy and operations?

2. Maritime Market in the Pandemic Era

Maritime logistics is currently responsible for almost 90 % of international cargo transport. Maritime transport is the preferred method of transporting international shipments thanks to the locations of important ports and excellent connections with other land transport means (Fratila et al., 2021). Maritime transport offers great flexibility and versatility, adapting to any type of cargo and transport needs (Alderton, 2010). The demand for maritime transport services is primarily influenced by trends in the world economy: trends in production, the level of purchasing power and income per household (Domijan-Arneri, 2014). Thus, the maritime market is characterized by very high volatility, unpredictability and volatility, and is therefore unable to respond to changes in the market in a timely manner because it cannot physically increase or decrease its offer.

2.1. Container Shipping in the Pandemic Era

At the beginning of the pandemic, it was predicted that maritime trade, including container shipping, would experience a sharp decline. However, the new way of life and numerous isolation measures have led to new patterns of shopping, i.e. the flourishing of e-commerce and thus to changes in consumption. The above has led to an increased demand for the import of ready-made consumer products, a large part of which is transported in shipping containers. In anticipation of new waves of the pandemic, stocks are built up and procured in advance, which only contributed to a further increase in container trade flows. Surprisingly, the increase in demand was greater than expected, and it was not met with sufficient capacity, and empty containers for transporting goods became unavailable. Given that most market participants were not prepared for this volatility in demand, supply chains faced not only a shortage of containers, but also a shortage of equipment, truck drivers and dock labor (Naletina, 2021). As a result, traffic jams started to form, and the turnaround time was significantly longer.

Several reasons are crucial for the shortage of containers themselves. Primarily, the trade imbalance, changes in trade patterns and the disruptions resulting from the pandemic have led to a shift in the "geography" of containerization. A large amount of empty containers remained stranded in ports across Europe and the US, instead of returning to East Asia in the first half of the year. When "blank sailing" was introduced, the mismatch between supply and demand for containers further worsened (UNCTAD, 2021). Consequently, it is concluded that the retention time of containers increased, and empty containers could not be returned to the system when they were most needed.

2.2. The Role of Shipping Alliances in the Pandemic Era

The COVID-19 pandemic forced global maritime market to develop certain types of joint strategies. There would be nothing wrong in the carrier capacity management strategies, if there was no coordinated way in which they are implemented among the members of various alliances that are largely exempt from antitrust regulation. There has been a pronounced concentration, as well as vertical integration along the supply chain. The process of horizontal integration through alliances has evolved to the current state, where the top ten shipping companies, grouped in three alliances, control more than 90 % of oceanic container traffic (Cullinane & Haralambides, 2021).

When the pandemic began to affect global trade in March 2020, the alliances decided to move quickly to reduce excess capacity and prevent a sharp drop in freight rates. Together, they cancelled more than 400 sailings, thus removing 10 % of the nominal capacity of twenty-foot equivalent units (TEU) from active service (Cullinane & Haralambides, 2021). As demand slowly returned from dormancy, freight rates rose again, and alliances activated idle ships. It is important to emphasize that all of the above is happening at a time when global oil demand is low, resulting in significantly cheaper fuel costs for carriers than at the beginning of the year, when the aforementioned IMO 2020 regulation came into force, allowing carriers to maximize their profits in on a scale that would once have been unimaginable.

2.3. Freight Rates on the Maritime Market in the Pandemic Era

Transportation prices are a major component of trade costs. The restriction of movement forced many shipping companies to send ships on routes, while at the same time they had a lot of free capacity (Naletina, 2021). The container shortage can be more easily understood as the depletion of container supplies due to the many inefficiencies associated with the pandemic. Namely, the ships often they had to wait a long time for unloading, which led to significantly slower turnaround time in the ports.

The sharp rise in freight rates has faced many companies with transportation costs that almost erode any profit margin on lower-value goods. Higher freight costs are disrupting global supply chains and affecting companies' production decisions. The level of disruption depends on the volume of shipping and whether said company's margins tolerate higher shipping costs. The price gap widened even further, causing smaller shippers to be squeezed out of international trade by unbearably higher shipping costs. Even the largest shippers, who have enough purchasing power to enter into long-term contracts with shipping lines, are not immune to current volatility. The impact of the increase in freight rates in container shipping causes variations in prices that affect entire economies and various goods and are not characteristic only of less developed or developing countries (UNCTAD, 2021).

Such market developments led to the culmination of freight rates that reached their historical peak by the end of 2020 and the beginning of 2021. Figure 1 shows chronological movement of Shangai freight index for containers in the period following 2008 world crisis up to pandemic.

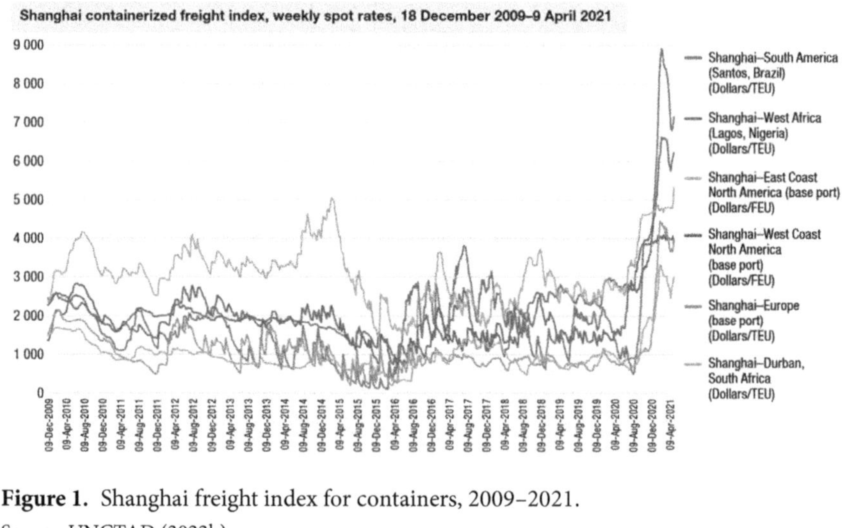

Figure 1. Shanghai freight index for containers, 2009–2021.
Source: UNCTAD (2022b).

The smallest relative increase in the freight rate was recorded in the Asia-East Coast North American route of 63 %, while the increase in freight from China to South America was an unprecedented 443 % higher than the median for that route (UNCTAD, 2021). Longer routes, including the China-South America and China-West Africa routes, require multiple ships for a weekly supply, which implies that a large number of containers remain trapped on the said ships. Freight rates on shorter routes marked by two or three weeks of supplies tend to be highly variable and volatile, since subtracting or adding even one supply has a significant effect on the number of remaining supplies.

2.4. Seaport Positioning Strategies in Times of Crisis

The competitive struggle of ports to take over the accommodation of global supply chains has led to functional changes in seaports, which are becoming the centres of the new, globalized world. In this regard, the functional and spatial grouping of activities takes place in the wider domain of the seaport, with an aim to, directly or indirectly, enable flawless and sustainable transport, and to maintain transformation and numerous information processes within global supply chains (Notteboom & Haralambides, 2020).

The ports had to undergo the process of adapting to the new conditions. Port and transport networks were caught unprepared for such a rapid transition in demand, and as a result, supply chains suffered from shortages of equipment, truck drivers and dockside labor, primarily due to quarantine and restrictions on personal mobility caused by the pandemic (Cullinane & Haralambides, 2021). Lower levels of economic activity combined with broader ongoing structural trends in the world economy, have forced port actors, planning authorities and supply chain managers to re-examine and update development and investment plans related to seaports (Alamoush et al., 2022). Recognizing the role, the maritime sector has in revitalising global trade, 20 members of the Port Authorities Roundtable from Asia, Europe, the Middle East and North America decided in April 2020 to commit to ensuring that ports in their ownership remain open during the pandemic. The aforementioned declaration, initiated by Singapore, calls on port authorities to collaborate and thus create best practices to ensure that port operations can remain unhindered (Faqiang & Abliakimova, 2020).

For an adequate response to disruptions in the supply chain, it is essential to establish capacity flexibility in container ports. Among the tactical responses of terminal operators to disruptions in maritime supply chains were proactive and adaptive strategies. Proactive measures included actions taken by the company to engage in new maritime supply chains and even to participate in the establishment of new maritime chains (Mańkowska et al., 2020). On the other hand, adjustment measures covered the actions taken by port terminals, as a direct consequence of the pandemic, in the form of changes in the existing maritime supply chains. Thus, the majority of container terminals, in the presented circumstances of less or non-existent demand and suspended business activities, showed significant adaptive capabilities. Namely, they were looking for new customers, ships and cargoes and started introducing rationalization strategies, i.e. increased cost control. Automation and digitization played a key role in organizational changes. Due to all of the above, the impact of COVID-19 on container ports was shorter and on a much smaller scale than initially expected. The scope of engagement and tactical decisions undertaken by terminals and port operators during the pandemic depended on the type of terminal, i.e. whether it is a universal or specialized terminal, and its main function within the supply chain.

The response to the pandemic is structured in the form of emergency measures related to port operations, management and communication, protection measures related to business and financial returns, measures to support customers, stakeholders and the community, and measures to restart port operations (Faqiang & Abliakimova, 2020). The main strategic goal of the port during the pandemic was to maintain operations and establish work arrangements and protocols to protect the health and safety of key port workers (UNCTAD, 2022a).

3. Case Study

A study of the volatility of freight rates was carried out on the case of the Croatian company Pneumatik Ltd. (*cro.* Pneumatik d.o.o.) that is an importer and distributor of premium brands of tires, engaging both in wholesale and retail. The company was founded in 1996 and currently employs more than 90 employees and manages more than 100,000 stock keeping units. Study was conducted from May to July 2022. A mixed study approach was applied, combining analysis of secondary data (company internal documents) and exploratory research through in-depth interviews with company employees in charge of procurement. Two in-depth interviews were conducted in the company headquarters, with the procurement manager, who had been employed in the company for 6 years, and the junior director, who had been employed in the company for 11 years.

The pandemic has made the procurement process very difficult for the company. Due to isolation and numerous other health measures, it was difficult to coordinate the work of the company with global partners. Communication was difficult and took place exclusively via e-mail. The biggest challenge and shock to the company was lack of all types of pneumatics, a problem faced globally. Under normal business conditions, after sending the order to the factory, the goods were delivered within 2–3 days. During the pandemic, almost 50 % of the requested goods were not available because production was stopped. The goods that were produced, had a delivery time of up to a month, sometimes even more. Therefore, the company encountered difficulties in making its own deliveries to third parties. The biggest problem was the cooperation with state-owned companies, which have signed forward contracts with defined specifications. On that regard it is worth noting that not a single container with all terrain tires arrived in Europe during the whole year of 2021.

The procurement process encountered numerous changes. After the once simple 'just in time' procurement with short delivery times, the company had to start planning procurement in advance, resulting in preparations for the winter season beginning already in March. In addition, obligations towards third parties began to be fulfilled with various alternatives, and thus cooperation was achieved with new partners and factories. The company turned to ensuring safety stocks of the best-selling goods, while still trying to maintain the less demanded goods on the principle of JIT procurement. Such goods began to be procured on the very requests of the customers, but with an extended delivery period, about which the customer is informed in a timely manner. As a result, many buyers, whether in wholesale or retail, started to manage their procurement process in advance. E.g. retail customers contacted the company for special orders even 2 months in advance.

During the pandemic, freight rates increased from EUR 1,590 to EUR 18,235 for the transport of one container. As shown in Figure 2, in 2019, freight rates stagnated, and the changes were insignificant. In 2020, when a pandemic broke out, freight rates started to rise. In the first half of 2020, the freight paid amounted to EUR 1,650. In the second half of 2020, the freight already amounted to EUR 6,100 resulting in a price increase of 270 % in 2020 alone. Bay the end of 2021 the freight amounted to EUR 18,235 reaching thus unprofitable highs. From 2019 to 2021 the price of container transport increased by overwhelming 1046 % luring the company to reconsider its procuring from China. With pandemic slowly reaching its end, prices began to stabilize. In 2022 the cost of transportation of one container fell to EUR 10,100 which is still considerably high compared to pre-pandemic. It can be argued that pandemic aftermath will be felt long after it ends.

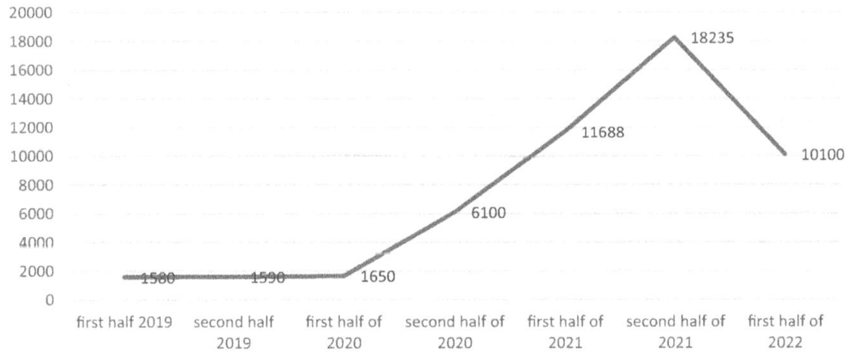

Figure 2. Freight rates in EUR, 2019–2022.
Source: Own research.

Price fluctuations in container maritime transport altered the company's perception regarding sourcing from China. Goods from China were mostly shipped by see and were sold at affordable prices, becoming thus extremely popular with customers who are not interested in premium tires. With the steep increase in freight rates, the selling price of the mentioned tires also increased, reaching the prices of premium brands. The sale fell proportionally, and there was a question of procurement accountability. In addition, container transport has extended the already long enough delivery period. As a results, the procurement from China decreased significantly, even though it was not abandoned all together.

Likewise, the pandemic had a significant impact on the sales prices of company's products. The price of certain products sourced from China, due to the increased purchase price, has increased by as much as 100 % from the former selling prices. The prices of other brands also increased significantly, and price fluctuations occurred a couple of times a month, so that the company was forced to completely change the price list of its own products on a monthly basis. Changing the prices of thousands of products every month was extremely difficult and tiring both for the director and for the employees who had to adjust them in the company's program. The error of the human factor in this challenging period was high. Displeasure of changing prices extended to customers as well. Figure 3 shows the development of purchasing price of a pneumatic produced in and sourced from China. Since period 2019–2022 is shown, before Croatia adopted the euro, prices are presented in Croatian kunas (1 EUR ≈ 7,5 HRK).

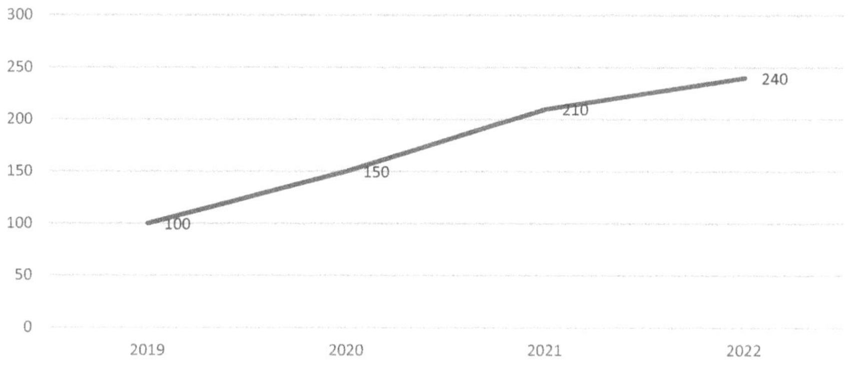

Figure 3. Purchasing price of a pneumatic produced in and sourced from China in HRK, 2019–2022.

Source: Own research.

Purchasing price encountered steep increase from 2019 to 2021 and proceeded to rise further in 2022, even though at a less steep rate. The company did not have much choice but to adjust their selling prices to the new procurement conditions. For certain products, they charged smaller margins in order to remain competitive on the market. Releasing the workforce was not an option, so the company tried to focus on reducing costs through other channels, transitioning to renewable energy sources, reducing delivery trips, or consolidating deliveries, and reducing working hours in certain branches. The company's crisis management system handled new challenges with praises. Not a single branch was closed, not a single salary was delayed or reduced, started construction development project was not suspended, existing customers were retained, and what is most important, not a single employee was fired. However, there is a noticeable drop in sales compared to pre-pandemic time. In order to strengthen its resilience, company plans to expand cooperation with other partners. What is concluded to be crucial for the survival of a company in crisis time is a professional and capable team, ready to take risks and that quickly responds to sudden market changes.

4. Conclusion

Disruptions caused by COVID-19 pandemic resulted in disruptions in the maritime market like no other crisis before. Shipping companies and companies that use shipping services were faced with great challenges. In addition to significant delays in deliveries, there was a previously unrecorded increase in freight rates in the market. The growth of freight rates is a global problem, given that the majority of goods are transported by sea. Although the maritime shipping industry has partially recovered from the pandemic, the negative impact of the pandemic on the industry is still not over, which is primarily reflected through the extreme volatility of freight rates on the maritime market.

In order to study effects for companies engaged in transcontinental sourcing, a case of Croatian company sourcing pneumatics from China was studied. Study was conducted as a secondary analysis of internal company documents and a primary study in form of in-depth interviews with high-ranked employees in charge of procurement. The goods that were transported in containers from China extended the already long enough delivery period, and the price of transporting one container reached the amount of almost EUR 19,000. Although in 2022 the amount of freight fell, it is still almost 10 times higher than it was in 2019. Thanks to the team of experts employed in the mentioned company, and their relatively quick reactions in completely new market conditions, the company managed to get through the pandemic without laying off workers and reducing wages.

The paper contributes to the development and enrichment of business strategies and managerial tactics in responding to changes in market conditions regarding supply chain interruptions and freight rates increase in maritime container shipping, with special emphasis being put on transcontinental sourcing.

References

Agbaba, R. (2020). Maritime Challenges in Crisis Times. *Pomorski zbornik, 59*(1), 51–60.

Alamoush, A. S., Ballini, F., & Ölçer, A. I. (2022). Ports, Maritime Transport, and Industry: The Immediate Impact of COVID-19 and the Way Forward. *Maritime Technology and Research*, *4*(1), 250092.

Alderton, P. M. (2010). *Reeds Sea Transport: Operation and Economics*. London: Bloomsbury Publishing.

Alizadeh, A. H., & Nomikos, N. K. (2011). Dynamics of the Term Structure and Volatility of Shipping Freight Rates. *Journal of Transport Economics and Policy*, *45*(1), 105–128.

Cullinane, K., & Haralambides, H. (2021). Global Trends in Maritime and Port Economics: The COVID-19 Pandemic and Beyond. *Maritime Economics & Logistics*, *23*, 369–380.

Domijan-Arneri, I. (2014). *Poslovanje u morskom brodarstvu*. Split: Pomorski fakultet Split.

Faqiang, L., & Abliakimova, E. (2020). Safe Ports: Law, Theory, Practice under Conditions of the COVID-19 Pandemic. *Lex Portus*, *24*, 7–34.

Fratila, A., Gavril, I. A., Nita, S. C., & Hrebenciuc, A. (2021). The Importance of Maritime Transport for Economic Growth in the European Union: A Panel Data Analysis. *Sustainability*, *13*, 7961.

Jerebić, V., & Pavlin, S. (2018). Global Economy Crisis and Its Impact on Operational Container Carrier's Strategy. *Promet-Traffic&Transportation*, *30*(2), 187–194.

Lam, J. S. L., Li, Q., & Pu, S. (2021). Volatility and Uncertainty in Container Shipping Market. In: *New Maritime Business: Uncertainty, Sustainability, Technology and Big Data* (pp. 11–32). Berlin: Springer International Publishing.

Mańkowska, M., Pluciński, M., Kotowska, I., & Filina-Dawidowicz, L. (2020). Seaports during the COVID-19 Pandemic: The Terminal Operators' Tactical Responses to Disruptions in Maritime Supply Chains. *Energies*, *14*(14), 4339.

Naletina, D. (2021). Volatilnost vozarina u kontejnerskom pomorskom prometu u doba pandemije COVID-19. *Poslovna izvrsnost*, *15*(2), 105–118.

Notteboom, T. E., & Haralambides, H. E. (2020). Port Management and Governance in a Post-COVID-19 Era: Quo Vadis?. *Maritime Economics and Logistics, 22*, 329–352.

Rožić, T., Naletina, D., & Zając, M. (2022). Volatile Freight Rates in Maritime Container Industry in Times of Crises. *Applied Sciences*, *12*(17), 8452.

UNCTAD. (2021). *COVID-19 and Maritime Transport: Impact and Responses.* Retrieved from: https://unctad.org/webflyer/covid-19-and-maritime-transport-impact-and-responses (March 26, 2022).

UNCTAD. (2022a). *Emerging Strategies for Ports During the Pandemic.* Retrieved from: https://unctad.org/webflyer/emerging-strategies-ports-during-pandemic (August 29, 2022).

UNCTAD. (2022b). *Review of Maritime Transport 2022. Navigating Stormy Waters*. New York: United Nations Publications.

Elira Luli

The Importance of Normative – Ethical Values in Civic Education: A Case Study of Albania's Pre-University System

1. Introduction

Education is one of the most essential individuals' journeys, not only for the quality of intellectual knowledge to gain during this path but also for the kind of learning experience the citizens should gain to empower and equip themselves with values and norms that promote civic and participatory engagement. Educational principles since classical times remained central to West educational institutions and values because, as society's necessity, the primary goal of education remains the modeling of responsible citizens with high moral values, intellectual background, and strong character. Today education remains the most crucial institution for cultivating and equipping society with the knowledge to address unlawful practices, negative phenomena, political and governance issues, the rule of law malversation, and the role and mission of institutions. Citizens` ability to analyze drives them to more engagement and interactivity with governance levels whenever there is a lack of transparency, accountability, or governance detachment from public goods.

Through general consent/ common sense among scholars and experts through different periods, it has been established that the ethical values embodied in public integrity are ***honesty, justice, trust, impartiality, equality, and non-discrimination/respect for others*** – all values of a universal nature, accepted as such by all societies. While civic education can also be obtained through other channels, such as family, media, and civil society, educational institutions are the most integral pillars to enshrine and share such values. "Most if not all societies recognize a need to educate youth to be "civic-minded"; that is, to think and care about the welfare of the community", "and not simply about their own individual well-being" (Crittenden & Levine, 2018).

"The task of realizing integrity in education, inquiry, and knowledge is to ensure that first "it implies an action on our mental nature, and the formation of a character" (Nillsen, 2005, p. 87), with an intertwined methodology of theory and practice.

The countries that faced extreme changes from the prolonged isolation and totalitarian regimes found themselves in socioeconomic, political, and cultural fragilities and fallibilities. They fell under systematic pressure caused by these deficits through these transition decades. In such circumstances, ethics and ethical education with a drive to upgrade into civic education were not seen as a priority in the pre-university system, not exclusively because of the lack of a dedicated school curriculum devoted to these subjects but merely because of the methodology used to instill these values in the younger generation properly. Meanwhile, in a long-term perspective, modeling society according to these values was of imperative importance for two reasons: 1. the society would learn to behave according to these principles; 2. Society then starts to act as a catalyzing force to fend off negative phenomena in case of their manifestation; 3. According to Jefferson, education becomes "the means for safeguarding individual rights, especially against the intrusions of the state (Crittenden & Levine, 2018).

Given the preceding explanation, the study aims to show a general overview of the significance that civic education as an integral part of ethical education has on transitioning societies in contemporary times, focusing mainly on the case of Albanian (pre-university system).

The main objective is to explore how applicable in practice these mechanisms are and how long-term practical they are for the civic education of generations.

Since the study elaborates on concepts such as ethical – civic education, integrity, ethics, civic values, norms, and discipline in the pre-university school system, an explanation of these concepts follows:

"***Ethics*** is a reflective system of values, principles, virtues, and ideals that shape our lives and determine the basis for the relationships that we form with others and ourselves." (Ethico, 2017, p. 7).

"***Values*** are important, deep-rooted, pervasive and lasting beliefs, attitudes, ideals, and attachments which are usually shared by the members of a given community and concern what is good or bad." (*ibid*, 2017, 7).

"***A norm*** is a rule that guides behavior among members of a society or group. Founding sociologist Émile Durkheim considered norms to be social facts: things which exist in society independent of individuals, and that shape our thoughts and behavior" (Cole, 2018).

"***Discipline***, etymologically speaking, is rooted in a learning situation; it conveys the notion of submission to rules or some kind of order." (Peter, 2015)

"***Ethical Education*** is a particular brand of education that focuses on teaching children to be virtuous and law-abiding citizens." (Khin, 2018, p. 19).

Civic Education "is the study of the theoretical, political, and practical aspects of citizenship and its rights and duties. (Alehegn 2020)" It "can be broadly defined as providing information and learning experiences to equip and empower citizens to participate in democratic processes."[1]

2. Literature Review

A series of authors have been identified through the literature review process, elaborating on the importance of these values in education. These authors distinguish from those who brought scientific expertise in education from an ethical perspective, especially during contemporary times. Contemporary authors see civic ethical education as crucial to cultivating good citizens who understand the issues a country faces and the duties and obligations in society. (Tafese & Desta, 2014). Alscher and McElvany (2022) highlight the persistence of significant research gaps regarding the identification of the most crucial teaching quality facets in civic education. At the same time, there are many contemporary authors, such as Leenders, Wiel & Eoud. (2008) who have researched moral education and how high school students and teachers deal with values, dialogue, and diversity. Peters (1966/2015) "provides a proper ethical foundation for education in a democratic society," while Khin (2018) elaborates on the importance of ethical values in education as ethical guidance because the urgency of the present times calls for it.

This research in the Albanian context aims to enrich the existing body of knowledge by shedding light on the specific dynamics, challenges, and opportunities inherent in promoting ethical values and civic education within Albania's socio-cultural and educational landscape.

2.1 Development of Hypothesis

In the case of Albania, civic ethical education in the pre-university school system has not been efficient enough to fulfill its mission during these transition years in building young citizens with integrity and helping them to instill a sense of responsibility, solidarity, and ethical behavior and in helping them to play a more active and participating role in their community/national level.

Hypothesis: If the comprehensive package of laws, regulations, instruments, and especially designed curricula for courses in ethical and civic education are effectively implemented, then it would lead to the successful instilling of integrity values and norms in young citizens.

---

1 Definition by Civic Education.
Jennifer Rietbergen-McCracken1.
https://www.civicus.org/documents/toolkits/PGX_B_Civic%20Education.pdf

3. Research Methodology

The analysis follows a qualitative methodology, collecting data based on primary sources (existing literature on civic-ethical education, the national legal framework for this field, reports, various articles, and original data collected from unstructured interviews with (anonymous) – subject-matter experts. The sample selection is a group of five experts composed of professionals/field experts who are knowledgeable and experienced in the field of education and, more specifically, civic-ethical education. The participants' list comprises as follows: (01)-Elementary teacher of the subject "Social Education"; (02)-High School teacher of the subject "Citizenship education"; (03)- Education Inspector in the Education Directory, Ministry of Education, Youth and Sports; (04) – Ex/ education inspector in the Education Directory, Ministry of Education, Youth and Sports; (05)- Citizenship Education Subject text drafter for High school curricula. As this study is exploratory by nature, the expert's opinion was imperative to fill the voids of what happens and is missing in the practical realm. The interviewees were assured of anonymity upon their request because they wanted to feel comfortable sharing sensitive or personal information and to speak openly without fear of retribution or judgment – reducing possible social desirability bias by being honest responses while their identity was concealed. The original data gathered through open questions from personal communication with experts in unstructured interviews yield an analysis of the findings in the second session of the study.

Variables:

V [*Independent Variable*]: Ineffective Implementation of Designed Courses in Curricula for Ethical and Civic Education and a Comprehensive Package of Laws, Regulations, and Instruments

V [*Dependent Variable*]: Instilling Integrity Values and Norms in Young Citizens

---

↘ **Research Question** ↙

Does ineffective implementation of designed curricula for courses in ethical and civic education and a comprehensive package of laws, regulations, instruments, impact the process of a successful instilling of integrity values and norms in young citizens?

In this formulation, the lack of effective implementation is the cause, while the failure to instill integrity values and norms in young citizens is the effect.

The hypothesis implies that if the comprehensive package of laws, regulations, instruments, and designed courses in curricula for ethical and civic education were effectively implemented, it would successfully instill integrity values and norms in young citizens.

To test this hypothesis, this study provides a general overview of the legal and structural framework of the mechanism in place expected to bring and forge civic educational acquisition and behavior and compares by discussing in the second section the effectiveness of the implementation of the comprehensive package, especially the designed curricula in pre-university educational settings and evaluate its impact and effectiveness on instilling integrity values and norms in young citizens.

4. Elaboration of Collected Data

4.1. The Existing Mechanisms/Instruments Applied in the Pre-University Educational Environment

Western education today places an enormous emphasis on the integrity of individuals as a value channeled in honesty, justice, and good intentions for better serving and contributing to society, the nation, and the labor market (private and public). Moreover, there is a common understanding "that education should be "democratic" as "no one in democracy would seriously dispute" (Peters, 2015) on that.

Albania has been structuring and approximating laws on education and policies and undertaking reforms in the frames of the EU accession process. Regarding integrity building in frames of ethical and civic education, there is a complete package of laws, regulations, and instruments. The question is about the approach in the practical realm toward these values with all the existing mechanisms in place. Since 32 years in Albania, "the transition and building of a new culture of liberal democracy has been and continues to be particularly difficult" (Nurellari, 2017), where the state as a continuation of the socialist tradition is still seen among Albanians as a true parent", "….while the individual, like the child, is innocent and irresponsible" (*ibid*). The opposite is noted in developed and countries that enjoy adequate levels of democracy. Such "countries or regions" have managed to obtain "…higher educational attainment" and "…enjoy lower crime rates, better health outcomes or improved performance across different socioeconomic measures" (Miles-Touya & Rossi: 2016). A "..strong and positive correlation between educational attainment and civic outcomes has supported the view that education is effective at promoting civic behavior" (*ibid*).

In the Albanian pre-university system, the legal framework, laws, by-laws, internal regulations, related curricula, or existing mechanisms are complete and to a certain extend – developed according to contemporary standards.

In elementary school, pupils are introduced to the basic principles and norms that convey "the main moral virtues – beneficial for the individual and for society" (Acer, 2017, p. 19) through relevant subjects designed for this purpose.

Referring to the existing instruments and mechanisms such as the Code of ethics, instructions for internal regulations, school bodies structured in commissions (ethics and discipline), and the Safety Officer constitute the chain links to guarantee the quality and expected standards in a pre-university system presumed to extend the relevant results in long-term. However, what does this package include?

The Code of Ethics is a unifying regulatory framework for all pre-university teachers containing important ethical principles for school academic staff behavior. It aims to create a "motivating environment for learning[2]. It also foresees duties for other educational institutions as well as the function of the Ethics Commission," which operates as an educational body according to (Article 33 of the Law on Pre-University Education (69/2012))". This commission examines cases of behavior "contradicting the basic" principles and "measures against the teacher are taken only following the legislation in force and by the relevant institutions."[3]

Apart from the "Code of Ethics" and the "Regulations for the operation of pre-university institutions in the Republic of Albania" with a "purpose to define mandatory rules for implementation by educational institutions and their employees in the pre-university education system in the Republic of Albania and the by-laws in force."[4], the Security Officer Institute has an important active role too.

The 'School Security Officer' is a new structure introduced in 2018 to increase security, surveillance, and prompt measures against negative phenomena such as violence, using or selling narcotics, and acting in cases of breaking the rules or lacking discipline. This figure has special importance because it polices all these

2 "The Teachers' Code of Ethics in the pre-university system (public and private) by Ministry of Education, Youth and Science, 2012.
https://arsimi.gov.al/wp-content/uploads/2018/02/dok-0033.pdf

3 *Ibid.*

4 https://arsimi.gov.al/wp-content/uploads/2020/01/Udher-Nr.-31-date-28.01.2020-Rregullore-per-IAP.pdf
Order nr.31, dt. 28.01.2020.

phenomena that can be disturbing and escalate into more aggravated forms or persistence. As "a guardian figure," "attached to the teaching staff and the parents' staff," the security officer is "a direct communication bridge" in the teacher-student-parent trinome and "a direct communication bridge with the Police for all those cases when there is a need to involve the Police."[5].

Additionally, in the schools of the pre-university system, there are commissions divided into the "Ethics and Behavior Commission" and "Discipline Commission." The commissions try to improve ethics and behavior in educational institutions if specific cases are deemed appropriate to intervene.

Meantime, the Order 31/202/IAP (Pre-University Institutions)[6], foresees disciplinary measures, the role of the psychologist, and the security officer. All these are structured or top institutes standing as guarantying pillars, respect for ethics in general, and measures for disciplinary violations. However, the object of the study is related to education, civic, and social formation, particularly the foundation of civic education and law education, without further elaborating on the measures in cases of violations or abusive phenomena.

The main concern presented in this case through this study is to explore how these subjects/courses fulfill their objectives to form responsible individuals who build knowledge on rule of law, social responsibility, civic norms, active participation and know their meanings in practice since at the early stage of life.

5. Findings Analysis

5.1. Building Integrity in Young Citizens. A Reality Immersed in Challenges

Individuals are most of the time in an internal struggle with the self due to the egoistic instinct that directs the self towards the desire to be powerful and dominant over others, exploiting and benefiting as much as possible by all means. Therefore, education is seen as a powerful instrument to instruct and guide citizens towards ethical limitations, moral behavior, and self-control that

5 Oficeri i Sigurise ne shkolla, projekti me i ri per rritjen e sigurise ne shkolla./ School Security Officer, the newest initiative to increasing school safety. https://www.kryeministria.al/newsroom/security-officers-schools-newest-programme-enhance-school-safety/

6 Order No.31/2020 on regulatory approval for the functioning of pre-university educational institutions in the Albanian Republic https://arsimi.gov.al/wp-content/uploads/2020/01/Udher-Nr.-31-date-28.01.2020-Rregullore-per-IAP.pdf

manages to contain egoism while maintaining balance with the rest of society. Even though an individual is a product of circumstances and the emancipation level of society, teachers have a missionary duty "to shape moral education in a school in practice" so that "the students" can "experience it every day" (Leenders, Veugelers & Ewoud 2008, 61).

Developed societies have now created a system of universal values and beliefs spread internationally. All countries that want to be part of the great international family must accept and standardize according to this system or model, contribute, and respect it.

After the 90s, Albanian society experienced a multi-dimensional transition. Due to the extreme change, citizens found it hard to recreate themselves in a society lacking democratic traditions. At the same time, the laws were inherited as an overly formalist tool, just as they had served the state party in an oppressive regime that lasted almost half a century. Later on, as part of the reforms, many laws were changed and adopted without understanding the current nature and understanding of society. Accordingly, the law that is not embedded in a mature political environment and a sound society's mindset and culture, and especially "if radically divorced from morality, ultimately becomes a contradiction in terms and makes a cruel mockery of assuredly then-unattainable justice" (Gregory, 2017, p. 175).

Given the challenges of a world changing rapidly within globalization, technological advancement, and efficient education (sound methodologies and instruments) for molding young citizens through civic and ethical education is crucial, especially at the initial stage of life.

In EU countries, there is a particular importance attached to the ethical dimension of teaching and learning beginning already in the preschool system through a methodology that advances and is continuously updated. According to "Teacher Manifesto for the 21st Century", "published by the Council of Europe in Strasbourg Ethico 2017, p. 15)

In the case of Albania, the subjects that enable the character formation of young citizens (as aforementioned) are "Civic/social Education" in the first grades in elementary and "Citizenship Education" in high school at a later phase during the teenage years. "The texts and narratives of the "Citizenship Education" subject are too theoretically descriptive. What needs to be changed in the vast volume of theory, knowledge, and concepts is the way theoretical elaborations are put into practice. Giving more priority to inclusive debates and discussions is crucial, using different topics and concepts (such as human dignity, equality, justice, the rule of law, and discrimination) and clarifying them in practice with exercises and simulation situations.[7] Teachers generally follow the relevant official programs and syllabuses. However, if the programs are enriched and updated with more practical methods, " then a teacher finds it more accessible during the discussions to introduce new ways of instilling knowledge and concepts."[8] Given that these subjects have a moralizing character, "even the students do not evaluate them as important and follow the lessons with a kind of annoyance."[9] Therefore, new methods must be found and introduced to stimulate their interest while learning these subjects.

"It is often noticed that these subjects slide from the proper importance" (*ibid*) since "teachers in the elementary school focus more on subjects such as language and mathematics because parents also have a greater demand on teachers for these subjects and expect their children to achieve higher results."[10] there. The same happens in high school because of a heavily loaded curriculum giving more importance to other subjects.

Some other reasons include "the lack of teaching competencies for the right age groups, the lack of professionals and professionalism, devotion and commitment."[11]. The latter is related to financial incentives and efficient field training and how morally, professionally, and financially stimulated teachers feel to make the subject/course more attractive and entertaining. "The quest after material values has destroyed the educational system in general. Meanwhile, technological and digital transformation is being misused. Instead of being in the function of children's learning, it has turned into a barrier for defining civic values."[12]

---

7 High School Teacher (02) of "Active Citizenship" (anonymous), "personal communication – informal/unstructured interview," dt. January 19, 2023.

8 Education inspector in the Directory of Education (Ministry of Education, Youth, and Sports (03) (anonymous), "personal communication – informal/unstructured interview," dt. January 14, 2023.

9 High school Teacher (02) of "Active Citizenship" (anonymous), "personal communication – informal/unstructured interview," dt. January 19, 2023

10 Elementary teacher (01) (anonymous), "personal communication – informal/unstructured interview," dt. January 22, 2023,

11 Ex/Education inspector (04) (anonymous), "personal communication – informal/unstructured interview", dt. January 21, 2023.

12 High school Teacher (02) of "Active Citizenship" (anonymous), "personal communication – informal/unstructured interview," dt. January 19, 2023.

"Teachers are not adequately trained in this subject. A lack of devotion in teaching is noted, and the continuous qualification of teachers has significant gaps."[13]

"Parents are always less engaged in their childrens' education due to other commitments in professional life or career, transforming the student-teacher-child trinome in most cases a fragile and inefficient relationship. Frequent cases are noted when the family makes the school responsible, and the school makes the family responsible.[14] Gaps are felt in the continuation of the learning process moving from one grade to the next or from one system to another higher one, not establishing a basis of sustainability in civic education quality. Often the texts are translated without any high quality; moreover, there are subjects of arts, innovation, creativity, as well as those of a social nature, but they are not promoted, and their applicability is weak."[15]. In most cases, schools lack the tools for practical work, and pupils cannot witness practical results *(ibid).* "Projects have been included in educational programs, but interactive education through games, discussions, or even sports is neglected."[16] The problem remains two-fold: it is about "knowledge production and knowledge comprehension: the gap between them continues to widen evermore" (Nillsen, 2005, p. 91)

Based on the current background of the society, existing difficulties and challenges, and a stubborn culture that has been inherited by suppressing and disregarding values – ethical education in the subjects of civic education and citizenship in the pre-university school system is of vital importance for the development of society, social-cultural change based on democratic and humanistic values and norms. A long-term strategy is compelling to constantly update the curriculums for these subjects according to the conditions and demands of transforming societies because "it is easier to build strong children than to repair broken man."[17] The learning environment requires the necessary methods and tools to make pupils and high school students "aware of a larger intellectual and human picture within which such attitudes" regarding negative phenomena "are seen to arise from a lack of awareness and from a state of mind

13 Citizenship subject text-drafter (05) (anonymous), "personal communication – informal/unstructured interview," dt. January 22, 2023.

14 Ex/Education inspector (04) (anonymous), "personal communication – informal/ unstructured interview," dt. January 21, 2023.

15 Elementary teacher (01) (anonymous), "personal communication – informal/ unstructured interview", dt. January 22, 2023.

16 (*ibid*) (02).

17 Quote by Frederick Douglas.

which unjustifiably separates one's own actions and attitudes from their potential wider consequences, including consequences for the self as well as others" (Nillsen, 2005, p. 8).

6. Conclusions

Teaching with integrity and cultivating ethical and civic education in young citizens has been an indispensable human endeavor to instill values in society through the learning process constantly.

The essence of the civic education curricula and methodology, regardless of the human and life evolutional path, has moved in parallel with such developments. Ethics and morals are closely linked with the law. As such, they can find no compatibility with those societies whose laws do not express the will of the majority – therefore, civic education is essential first to bring a general normative and comprehensive civic knowledge effectively and then expect successful applicability.

The methodology is vital to ingrain with practical methods and cases – hand in hand with theory – the ethical education, and these subjects/courses should be kept from the teacher's discretion for receiving the proper importance or not.

The elaboration of collected data from the interviewed experts shows that the lack of effective implementation of a comprehensive package of laws, regulations, instruments, and designed curricula for ethical and civic education in the pre-university system exists as reflected above. Such shortfalls result in a failure in practice to instill integrity values and norms in young citizens throughout all the transition period.

In the case of Albania, it is important that the teachers act as a unified troupe operating according to the same standards for a generation that develops and grows at a faster pace, where technology advances briskly and shifts the youth into realities or parallel worlds that are often suspicious and fake. The developments of post-modernity make the education of the new generation a challenging matter, especially in transitioning societies. For this reason, before the responsibility can be pointed in the institutions and how they should function according to liberal approaches and how a country is governed, the mentality of a passive and individualistic society must be changed firstly through education.

Recommendation on the case of Albania:

- Building coherence among teachers through continuous training and further qualifications is imperative to face the challenges of new, unpredicted contexts where new generations are grounded.

- Continuous evaluations are needed to measure the level of ethical behavior and especially how much familiar are pupils and teenagers in the classroom with ethical-related principles and negative phenomena. Programs and curricula need to be updated according to the data gathered for systematic improvement in the effectiveness of the school environment and student learning.
- Students need suitable environments and conditions in all the country's schools where laboratories and other environments are operable to enable different and various skills, where the highest priority addresses civic education.
- Education Strategies regarding ethical education are crucial to induce a change in general culture, and students walk safer into a civilized path through subtle knowledge and methodology.
- It is not a cliché that the student's success depends on the teacher's potential. Anyhow teaching should be transformed and heightened into a more prestigious profession by getting more stimulus financially and professionally.
- Textbooks in general, especially those related to ethical education, should be improved and refined (avoiding copy-paste models) from other countries. Albanian academia has plenty of academic potentials to dispose at the service of texts and curriculum improvements.
- The curricula should envision and properly define simulation, creative activities, projects, and even outdoor events, which better equip students with normative values and civic attitudes/behaviors.
- Of crucial importance is the realization of frequent collaborations and exchange programs between the Albanian and European countries' pedagogical staff to exchange the most successful and updated experiences and methodologies in place to instill civic norms and values in students.
- Also, the selection of teachers should be based on rigorous criteria. A person delivering effective teaching includes qualities that define, first of all, a citizen with a sound civic culture and integrity in the classroom.

References

Acer. (2017). *(Preçi, Zahaj, Bodinaku, Keta, Kosta) Etika në sistemin arsimor shqiptar*, Raport studimor. Mirgeeralb, p. 292. https://epale.ec.europa.eu/sites/default/files/raport-studimin-etika-ne-sistemin-arsimor-ne-shqiperi.pdf

Alscher, P., Ludewig, U., & McElvany, N. (2022). Civic Education, Teaching Quality and Students' Willingness to Participate in Political and Civic Life: Political Interest and Knowledge as Mediators. *J Youth Adolesc*, *51*(10), 1886–1900. https://doi.org/10.1007/s10964-022-01639-9. Epub 2022 June 1. PMID: 35648262; PMCID: PMC9363305.

Cole. (2018). *What Is a Norm? Why Does it Matter?, Thought.co, Social Science.* https://www.thoughtco.com/why-a-norm-matter-3026644

Crittenden, Jack, & Peter Levine. (2018). Civic Education. In Edward N. Zalta (ed.), *The Stanford Encyclopedia of Philosophy* (Fall 2018 Edition). URL = https://plato.stanford.edu/archives/fall2018/entries/civic-education/.

Ethiko. (2017). *Ethics and Values Education in Schools and Kindergartens.* Policy Paper, (Project has been funded ëith support from the European Commission, Erasmus+ programme and Slovene national agency for Erasmus+), p.175 https://ec.europa.eu/programmes/erasmus-plus/project-result-content/4f9f32c2-ad65-4a5f-9855-a296d9521923/Ethika_O4_Policy%20Paper_EN.pdf

Gregory. (2017). Teaching Moral Values in Public Schools, Article 4. *The Catholic Laëer, 31*(3), Part of the Catholic Studies Commons, and the Education Common. https://scholarship.la

Khin. (2019). The Important Role of Ethical Values in Education. *Mandalay University Research Journal, 9.*

Kodi i etikes se mesueseve ne arsimin parauniversitar public dhe privat./Code of ethics for teachers in public and private pre-university education. *Arsimi.gov.al.* https://arsimi.gov.al/wp-content/uploads/2018/02/dok-0033.pdf

Leenders., Veugelers, & Eëoud. (2008). *Moral Education and Citizenship Education at Pre-University Schools.* https://doi.org/10.1163/9789087906368_005.

Ligji Nr. 69/2012, *Për sistemin arsimor parauniversitar në republikën e shqipërisë i azhornuar dhe aktet nënligjore në zbatim të tij, Fletorja zyrtare e republikes se Shqiperise.*/ Law No. 69/2012, On the Pre-University Education System in the Republic of Albania (Updated) and the By-laws in Its Implementation, Official Bulletin of the Republic of Albania. https://arsimi.gov.al/wp-content/uploads/2019/02/Permbledhje-parauniversitari-8-Tetor-2020.pdf

Miles-Touya, D., & Rossi, M. (2016). Cultural Transmission of Civic Attitudes. *Springer Plus, 5*, 949. https://doi.org/10.1186/s40064-016-2616-4

Nillsen. (2005). The Concept of Integrity in Teaching and Learning. *Journal of University Teaching & Learning Practice, 2*(3), Article 9. https://files.eric.ed.gov/fulltext/EJ1059490.pdf

Nurellari, A. (2017). Liria e keqkuptuar si licencë dhe mungesa e përgjegjësisë personale në shoqërinë shqiptare/ Freedom Misunderstood as a License and Lack of Personal Responsibility in Albanian Society. *Journal: SBunker.* https://sbunker.net/teh/88580/liria-e-keqkuptuar-si-licence-dhe-mungesa-e-pergjegjesise-personale-ne-shoqerine-shqiptare/

Peters, R. S. (2015). *Ethics and Education* (Routledge Revivals). Routledge. (Book)

Tafese, S. G., & Desta, D. T. (2014). The Roles of Civics and Ethical Education in Shaping Attitude of the Students in Higher Education: The Case of Mekelle University. *Journal of Education and Practice*, 5(30). www.iiste.org, ISSN 2222-1735 (Paper) ISSN 2222-288X (Online). https://core.ac.uk/reader/234636450

Urdher 31/2020, Per miratimin e rregullores per funksionimin e institucioneve arsimore parauniversitare ne Republiken e Shqiperise/ Order 31/2020, For the Approval of the Regulation for the Operation of Pre-University Educational Institutions in the Republic of Albania. *arsimi.gov.al*. https://arsimi.gov.al/wp-content/uploads/2020/01/Udher-Nr.-31-date-28.01.2020-Rregullore-per-IAP.pdf

Hayati Yusof and Zulnurhaini Zolkaply

Community Relations in USA and Malaysia

1. Introduction

In general, the term **community** refers to a corporation's area of business influence. This includes the city, town or location in which the corporation conducts its business operations. Today the term community captures not only geographical area of doing business but also to apply to a range of groups who will be affected directly or indirectly by the corporation's actions (Lawrence et al., 2023). Other than the site or geographical community, there are several other types of community such as the fence line community, virtual communities, communities of interest and the employee community (Lawrence et al., 2023).

The relationship between the corporation and its community is one of mutual inter-dependence (Figure 1). Referring to Figure 1, both the corporations and the community need something from each other. A corporation depends on the community for education and training, to access facilities and participate in activities conducted by the recreational parks, museums, local clinics, enjoy public transportations, to obtain public safety services such as police and fire safety departments, etc. On the other hand, the community relies on the corporations for job creation and training provision, pay taxes, support local education, arts and cultural initiatives, hire and assist people with disabilities and support public safety and economic developments (Lawrence et al., 2023).

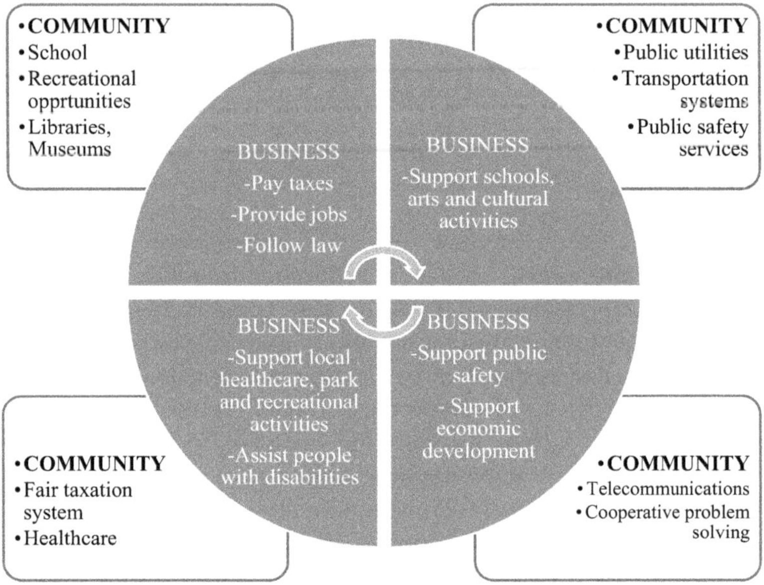

Figure 1. The mutual inter-relationship between corporations and its community.
Source: Lawrence, A., Weber, J., Hill, V. D & Wasieleski, D.M. (2023). *Business and Society*. New York: McGraw-Hill Publishing.

Also known as **corporate giving**, corporate philanthropy is the "voluntary and unconditional cash and/or other asset donations contributed by private firms for public purposes" (Lawrence et al., 2023, p. 403). In the USA, tax incentives have encouraged corporate giving for educational, charitable, scientific and religious purposes. Its tax rules allowed corporations to deduct all giving from their taxable income provided that the giving does not exceed 10% of their before tax income (Lawrence et al., 2023).

The recent popular trend is to align the corporate giving with the corporation's business goals and objectives strategically so that it will benefit both the donors and the recipients (the community). This is known as strategic philanthropy. **Strategic philanthropy** refers to "corporate philanthropy that is linked directly or indirectly towards business goals and objectives". (Lawrence et al., 2023, p. 409). While strategic philanthropy may help to generate higher demands for goods and services or generate more trained workers, sometimes they can backfire if stakeholders find it too self-serving or self-purpose. For instance, employees may find the distinction between normal working time and volunteering time blurry. As a result, they may show disagreement or rebel as they perceive it as merely a corporate tactic (Lawrence et al., 2023).

2. Community Relations in United States of America

USA is well-known as a generous community. In the year 2021, individuals, bequests (individual estates), foundations and corporations have given an estimated USD484.85 billion to US charities, churches and non-profit organizations. This was an increase of 4.0% in corporate giving as compared to USD466.23 billion in the year 2020. However, this growth in dollar did not keep pace with inflation. The story of charitable giving in the US was closely tied to the event of 2020 – the historic year that included a worldwide corona virus (COVID-19) pandemic, economic crisis and recovery, efforts to address racial justice and an unprecedented philanthropic response. Among the recipients of these corporate giving were religion, education, human services, foundations, public-society benefit organizations, health, arts, culture and humanities, international affairs and environmental and animal organizations ("Giving USA: Total US charitable giving remained strong in 2021 reaching $484.85 billion", 2022).

Corporations from all over the world responded generously to the communities impacted by the hurricanes that struck the Gulf Coast and the Caribbean in 2017. After Hurricane Harvey battered Houston, Texas and its surrounding areas, many companies donated cash through the Red Cross and other charity organizations, or matched employee contributions, 90 firms donated at least USD1 million. Others such as **Airbnb** creatively allowed hosts in nearby communities to offer free accommodations to those displaced by the storm; **Uber** donated rides and food and supply deliveries and **WeWork** offered free workspace (Lawrence et al., 2023).

In the aftermath of Hurricane Maria, **Tesla** sent batteries to Puerto Rico with employees to help attach those batteries to solar panels to generate electricity while the power grid was offline; **AT&T** sent its flying COW (Cell on Wings), a special drone to San Juan to provide connectivity and cell phone service while **DHL**'s disaster response team delivered relief supplies pouring from all over the world to the victims in the Caribbean islands (Lawrence et al., 2023).

3. Community Relations in Malaysia

The multi-ethnic compositions make up the social and political identities of Malaysia. Changes in lifestyle as a result of modernisation and industrialisation, increase awareness of individual rights and the realisation of collective power have brought about its development of community relations. Unfortunately, these developments focused on the urban societies, resulting into the marginalised community being overlooked, thus, causing the discrepancies in economic developments. These discrepancies triggered the active involvements of the more privileged and capable members in the community to aid and assist the underprivileged. Among the issues, the NGOs (non-governmental organizations) helped to provide equal access to education, physical and mental development for youth, humanitarian food aid service to the homeless and impoverished community, not to mention its recycling and waste management activities ("Community Development", 2021). Corporations such as Petronas, Maybank Foundation, Kuala Lumpur Convention Centre (KLCC) and RHB Banking Group also pledged back to the community via their CSR (Corporate Social Responsibility) and sustainability projects.

3.1. Petronas

Petronas, through its community outreach programmes, embarked on a Water For Life project, an initiative partnered with Malaysian Nature Society. Its aim is to provide clean water to rural areas that are affected by water disruption or unclean water. Their contributions involved installation of piping, filtration system and water tanks to enable the flow of clean water to the communities. Together with their employees, Petronas also participated into driving sustainability initiatives, environment and climate change projects, human rights, responsibility towards customers and workforce development ("Corporate Social Responsibility", n.d.).

3.2. Maybank Foundation

Working on humanising financial service, Maybank Group via Maybank Foundation embarked on its sustainability strategy involving a few pillars such as education, community empowerment, arts and culture, environmental diversity, healthy living and disaster relief efforts. For example, Maybank is committed to provide its humanitarian aid to disaster prone regions and support communities throughout the Philippines, Indonesia and Malaysia. Their employees have shown big compassion by volunteering their time and money when disasters strike. In 2020, Maybank contributed MYR300,000.00 to fight against COVID-19 pandemic. In addition, Maybank also donated USD10,000.00 to the City of Lebanon during the explosion involving large amount of ammonium nitrate stored in its port, causing 204 death and 6,500 injuries (Disaster Relief, 2023).

3.3. Kuala Lumpur Convention Centre (KLCC)

Known as the Malaysia's premier purpose-built venue, KLCC is not a stranger to travel and tourism industry. KLCC is committed to build a sustainable convention centre and events, led by its three main pillars – Environment, Energy and Community. Aiming towards carbon neutrality by Malaysia's aspiration 2050, KLCC adopted the AI-powered food waste management system, reverse vending machine and food composting system and roof-top hydroponic farm and herbs garden in 2022. In addition, the centre was built with environment in mind by maximising the use of natural light with minimal heat penetration, restrooms equipped with water-saving structures and the use of rainwater harvesting system. The 'war on single use plastics' and 'bring from home to recycle' are among the initiatives conducted to instil good recycling habits and awareness among co-workers, partners and the community (KLCC 5-Year SDG Roadmap, 2023).

3.4. RHB Banking Group

RHB Banking Group, through its Touch Hearts programmes, witnessed 14,000 of its employees volunteered to reach out and give back to the community through various humanitarian and environmental projects between 2016–2018. These included to nurture children and youth by providing resources and tools to develop their holistic potentials, hence changing the face of the community in the future. Working on four key pillars of Nurturing Future Generations, Environment, Health and Wellness and Arts and Culture, the Touch Hearts programmes raised more than MYR1.26 million in cash and in kind that benefitted more than 20,000 underprivileged and marginalised community members. In 2019, RHB received the Company of the Year Award (Financial Institution) at the prestigious CSR Malaysia Award ceremony (RHB drives environmental and social sustainability, 2019).

4. Conclusion

Corporations and its community are interdependent upon of each other in many ways such as job creation, public safety and services, and education. Community relations is a part of business strategies for a corporation to garner goodwill in the community it operates in. In many cases, it involves corporate philanthropy and/or strategic philanthropy which will benefit both the donors and the recipient (the community). Corporations in both developed and developing countries, for example in USA and Malaysia, have shown its extensive supports towards community development programmes by giving financial donations, promoting employee volunteerism, enduring non-profit partnership and many more. Moreover, community relations are not limited to the corporation's geographical area only and it is wider. It is based on the direct or indirect effects of corporation's actions in the community involvement towards the community itself. Effective community relations can develop strong ties between the corporations and its community as it is helping to make the corporation an integral part of the community. Besides, involvement in community programmes can be an effective platform for the corporations to increase brand awareness, to build trust, to establish reputation, to grow the business and most importantly, to pledge back to the society.

References

Community Development – 5 Malaysian NGOs Actively Involved in Communities. (2021, July 27). Retrieved May 25, 2023 from https://www.biji-biji.com/community-development-5-malaysian-ngos-actively-involved-in-communities/

Corporate Social Responsibility. (n.d.). Retrieved May 25, 2023 from https://www.mymesra.com.my/sustainability/corporate-social-responsibility

Disaster Relief. (2023). Retrieved May 25, 2023 from https://www.maybankfoundation.com/index.php/what-we-do/our-pillars/disaster-relief

Giving USA: Total US Charitable Giving Remained Strong in 2021 Reaching $484.85 Billion. (2022, June 21). Retrieved May 25, 2023 from https://philanthropy.iupui.edu/news-events/news-item/giving-usa:--total-u.s.-charitable-giving-remained-strong-in-2021,-reaching-$484.85-billion.html?id=392

KLCC 5-Year SDG Roadmap. (2023, March). Retrieved May 25, 2023 from https://www.klccconventioncentre.com/clients/asset_1D27A8C6-DE8C-4066-B3D8-0593D73C0267/contentms/img/Kuala-Lumpur-Convention-Centre-SDG-Plan.pdf

Lawrence, A., Weber, J., Hill, V. D., & Wasieleski, D. M. (2023). *Business and Society*. New York: McGraw-Hill Publishing.

RHB Drives Environmental and Social Sustainability. (2019, October 7). Retrieved May 19, 2023 from https://www.rhbgroup.com/files/others/highlights/RHB_press_release_touch_hearts.pdf

List of Contributors

A. Ayandibu
University of Zululand, South Africa

Alexandru Trifu
"Petre Andrei" University of Iași, Romania

Alicja Jajko-Siwek
Poznań University of Economics and Business, Poland

Andrew Enaifoghe
University of Zululand, South Africa

Constantinos Challoumis
National and Kapodistrian University of Athens (N.K.U.A.), Greece

Dora Naletina
University of Zagreb, Croatia

Elira Luli
Luarasi University, Tirana, Albania

Ersi-Iliana Savvopoulou
Ministry of Finance, Athens, Greece

Ghiță Simona Ioana
Institute of National Economy, Romanian Academy, Romania

Gogonea Rodica-Manuela
Bucharest University of Economic Studies, Romania

Hayati Yusof
Universiti Tunku Abdul Rahman (Perak Campus), Malaysia

Zulnurhaini Zolkaply
Universiti Tunku Abdul Rahman (Perak Campus), Malaysia

Hena Oak
University of Delhi, India

Ivana Štulec
University of Zagreb, Croatia

Kerstin Knees
Palacky' University Olomouc, Czech Republic

Konrad Gunesch
London Centre for Interdisciplinary Research, London, United Kingdom

M. Masuku
University of KwaZulu Natal, South Africa

Mia Dragica Milković
University of Zagreb, Croatia

Nejla Peka
Luarasi University, Tirana, Albania

Piotr Misztal
Jan Kochanowski University in Kielce, Poland

S. Zhou
University of Zululand, South Africa

Săseanu Andreea Simona
Bucharest University of Economic Studies, Romania

Somosi Sarolta
University of Szeged, Hungary

T. Chimucheka
University of Fort Hare, South Africa

Tanvir Alam Shahi Md.
University of Szeged, Hungary

Tarlan Ahmadov
Tallinn University of Technology, Tallinn, Estonia

Vasili Kulakov
Jan Kochanowski University in Kielce, Poland

Viktoria Bondegard
Tallinn University of Technology, Tallinn, Estonia

Wolfgang Gerstlberger
Tallinn University of Technology, Tallinn, Estonia

List of Figures and Graphs

List of Tables

www.ingramcontent.com/pod-product-compliance
Ingram Content Group UK Ltd.
Pitfield, Milton Keynes, MK11 3LW, UK
UKHW021921120926
8556IPUK00042BA/1095

9 783631 908426